CN00904003

THE COMPLETE ENCYCLOPEDIA OF

LOCOMOTIVES

THE COMPLETE ENCYCLOPEDIA OF

LOCOMOTIVES

MIRCO DE CET AND ALAN KENT

Text: Mirco De Cet and Alan Kent
Layout: Richard Saunders, Bacroom Design & Advertising, Birgmingham, England
Index: Marie Lorimer Indexing Services, Harrogate, England
The majority of pictures came from the Authors. Other contributors are mentioned in the acknowledgements.

Cover design: Amos Typographical Studio, Prague, The Czech Republic
Pre-press services: Amos Typographical Studio, Prague, The Czech Republic
Proofreading: Sarah Dunham, Jeffrey Rubinoff

ISBN 13: 978-90-366-1505-1
ISBN 10: 90-366-1505-4

Contents

The invention of steam to 1830

The late seventeenth and early eighteenth century was a period of great inventiveness and saw the emergence of steam as a source of power – a real breakthrough coming when steam power was finally made to work. Early developments took place in England, spearheaded by a military engineer and inventor named Thomas Savery, whose main aim

Thomas Savery, born at Shilston, Devonshire, entitled the pamphlet for his engine: A Description of an Engine to Raise Water by Fire.

was to produce an engine that would pump water from the deep mines of Cornwall – the deeper these mines went, the more problems there were with flooding. After making initial designs and plans, Savery built his machine and secured a patent for it in 1698. He then proceeded to print leaflets, which he distributed among the proprietors and managers of the mines, with a view to selling his idea to them. Some of these mines were filling up with so much water that work had to be stopped altogether – draining them was an extremely expensive commitment. One good example of this was a mine that employed 500 horses to remove the water using horse gins and buckets.

Thomas Newcomen, an English blacksmith, invented an atmospheric steam engine in 1705, which was an improved version of the Savery design. By 1712 he and his colleague John Calley had erected their steam engine at the top of a water-filled mine shaft, and used it to pump the water up and out of the mine.

Savery's steam engine was not used in the mines as expected; the mines were too deep and too much pressure was needed from the engine boiler.

The diagram depicted here explains the principle of the operations of the Newcomen atmospheric engine of 1712.

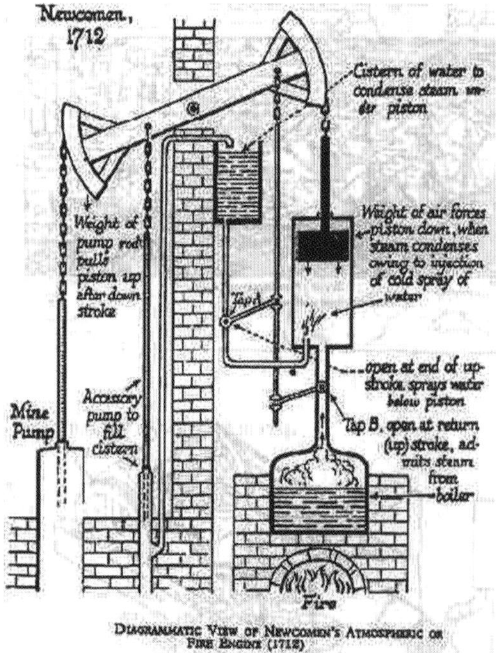

James Watt, whose steam engines would be used in such great numbers to increase productivity in so many different factories.

This is a model of the first fully developed watt rotative engine of 1788. It was a huge step forward from the previous Boulton & Watt engines.

James Watt was the son of a merchant. He was born in Greenock, Scotland, in 1736. At nineteen he was sent to Glasgow to learn the trade of a mathematical instrument-maker, establishing his own instrument-making business in 1757. It was during 1763 that he was sent a Newcomen steam engine for repair, and while re-assembling it, he realised he could make the engine run more efficiently. After working on the idea for a few months, he came up with a steam engine that cooled the used steam in a condenser, separate from the main cylinder. Following an unsuccessful venture with Scottish ironworks owner John Roebuck, Watt went to see Matthew Boulton, a successful businessman from Birmingham, who for the next eleven years produced the Watt steam-engine. These machines were mainly bought by colliery owners to pump water from their mines and they became very popular, being four times more powerful than the Newcomen engine. As ever, Watt continued to experiment and in 1781 he came up with a rotary-motion steam engine, which could be used to drive a number of different types of machinery. By 1800 there were over 500 Watt machines in Britain's mines and factories.

In 1550 the little German mining town of Leberthal, in the Alsace region, was using primitive wooden rails to move its wagons. These became known as wagonways and horses would be used to haul coal wagons over these wooden rails, making the movement of coal much easier than on the normal dirt tracks. These wagonways are generally classed as the beginning of the modern railway and were adopted by English collieries of the north in the seventeenth century. By 1776, these wooden rails were replaced by stronger types made from iron, which then led directly to the advent of the tramways, with horses still providing the pulling power. Like every new invention, refinement was constant and in 1789 the Englishman William Jessup designed the first wagons to use flanged wheels – a groove that gave the wheels better grip on the rails. It wasn't long before these two inventions – steam and wagonways – would come together and create the first successful locomotives.

It was in 1803 that Samuel Homfray decided to fund the development of a steam-powered vehicle to replace the team of horses that pulled his carts on the tramways. Richard Trevithick from Cornwall, England, had built the world's first practical steam locomotive, which ran at Coalbrookdale, Shropshire, in 1803 and he took up the challenge. His vehicle used a high-pressure engine and was tested in Wales on February 22 1804, between the ironworks of Pen-y-Darron, Merthyr Tydfil, to the

Seen here, an example of an early wagon used to transport coal from the mines of northern England. The rails would have been wooden, as shown.

These early wagons travelled on "wagonways." The shaped wheels would travel on the wooden rails – the primitive beginnings of the railway.

bottom of the Abercynnon valley – a distance of nine miles. The locomotive was loaded up with 10 tons of iron, 70 men and five extra wagons. It completed the journey in approximately two hours and became the first steam engine tramway locomotive. Trevithick continued to experiment and erected a circular railway track in Euston Square, London, England. This was an enclosed exhibition and rather than turning out to be a demonstration of "things to come," was treated more as a funfair attraction. He charged people one shilling – a fee that only few could afford – to ride his latest engine, called "Catch-Me-Who-Can," but the demonstration idea failed to capture the public imagination and was soon closed down.

It was the Middleton Colliery Railway in England that started using what was to become the world's first commercial steam locomotive, designed by Matthew Murray in 1812. This locomotive used two vertical cylinders and ran on cast iron rails. By now many of the collieries based in the north of England had engaged locomotive designers as their chief

Richard Trevithick worked with his father at Wheal Treasury mine and soon showed his aptitude for engineering. He later became engineer of the Ding Dong mine, Penzance.

The Stephenson family, with George seated, talking to Robert on his right. In the background is the Blucher locomotive and Killingworth high pit.

A painting by George Walker shows a miner with, in the background, the Matthew Murray steam locomotive at the Middleton Colliery, Leeds.

engineers. By 1820, men like Timothy Hackworth, George Stephenson and William Hedley had designed steam locomotives that were working in these collieries. The Hedley locomotive, named "Puffing Billy," was introduced in 1813 and was driven by a single crank on one side of the vehicle. Stephenson had designed an 0-4-0 configuration locomotive, powered by two cylinders, for the Killingworth colliery in 1815. All these developments were taking place on private railways owned by the collieries for the movement of coal and heavy equipment. With this, much design, manufacture and operating experience was gained and when the time came for the first steam railway to be built, all this knowledge became invaluable. The first railway was planned so that businessmen could transport their goods between the mines in the south of County Durham and the port of Stockton, on the River Tees. The man employed as chief engineer for the project was the young colliery engineer George Stephenson, who supervised the construction of the line and also found time to design the pioneer steam locomotive, Locomotion No. 1. It was this locomotive that hauled a 68-ton load along the Shildon to Stockton line in September of 1825, and although there were passenger carriages that day too, the line survived mostly with the transportation of goods, whilst people continued to be transported by carriages pulled by horses.

By 1820, Manchester was a main northern industrial town served by roads and canals from ports such as Liverpool, which was the entry point for important materials such as raw cotton, which was being shipped from the then new country of America. These roads and canals were now becoming inadequate for the volume of trade passing over them and something had to be done to improve that situation. So in 1822, two Liverpool businessmen set up a committee to construct a railway between the two towns. After much opposition from landowners, farmers, canal operators and the like, a Bill of Parliament was passed, permitting the building of the railway, in 1826. This was then given Royal approval shortly after, and

In 1812 William Hedley, was commissioned by Christopher Blackett, the owner of Wylam Colliery, to produce a steam locomotive. The result was Puffing Billy.

This is Locomotion, which George Stephenson took charge of on the day the Stockton to Darlington Railway opened, in September 1825, in front of a large crowd.

construction of the line started in the summer of that same year. Although quite a flat route, 63 bridges had to be built and probably the most impressive piece of civil engineering was the 60-foot high, 9-arch, Sankey viaduct. Unsure what type of power should be used to pull the trains – horse traction, stationary engines with rope haulage, steam locomotive or a combination of all three – the Liverpool & Manchester Railway (L&MR) company organized a competition, with the winner receiving £500 prize money. Four steam locomotives entered the competition, along with a horse-drawn machine and a manually powered machine. The competition took place in 1829, on a finished stretch of railway line at Rainhill. Each entrant had to haul three times its own weight over a length of 70 miles at a speed of at least 10 mph. The Rainhill Trials, as the competition became known, was open to the public and many came to see the new contraptions in action – crowds of 10,000 and 15,000 turning up to watch. The crowd's favourite locomotive was known as Novelty, built by London based John Braithwait and Swedish-born John Ericsson. Unfortunately its boiler was not up to the job and its components let the machine down. The final winner was Rocket, a machine built by George Robert Stephenson and one of several he had made in his quest to find the best machine for the railway. Its success was due to its revolutionary multi-tubular boiler, which was

Novelty was the crowd's favorite at the 1829 Rainhill Trials. It outperformed the Rocket and could have won if there hadn't been boiler problems.

William Allcard took on the design for the Sankey Viaduct, which was a nine-arch structure. Each arch has a 50 foot span, and rise from sandstone slabs quarried locally.

able to generate more steam. Stephenson was also able to test his prototypes at the Killingworth colliery lines before entering the competition, something his competitors were unable to do. During the trials Rocket completed the 70 miles in just over six hours, hauling 13 tons of train at an average speed of 13 mph and ran a top speed of 24 mph on the final run.

This is a replica of the Rocket, its piston and connecting rod can be seen clearly reaching to the front wheel to give it motion.

In 1830 a smoke box was added to Rocket and the chimney was shortened. Later the cylinders were reduced from 35 degrees to 8 degrees, for better stability.

Looking much smarter than the original Rocket, the replica does allow people to understand the kind of problems that were encountered at that time.

So the official opening of the world's first purpose-built passenger railway was between Manchester and Liverpool on September 15 1830. The age of the passenger steam locomotive had truly arrived.

By the third day the Rocket was the only locomotive left in the Rainhill competition. That day it covered 35 miles in 3 hours 12 minutes.

The Liverpool & Manchester railway was opened on 15th September, 1830 and the opening ceremony included a procession of eight locomotives.

The Prime Minister, the Duke of Wellington, and a large number of important people attended the opening ceremony. This is a ticket from the day.

Opening

OF

THE LIVERPOOL AND MANCHESTER

RAILWAY,

WEDNESDAY, 15TH SEPTEMBER, 1830.

CHAS. LAWRENCE, CHAIRMAN.

THE BEARER OF THIS TICKET IS ENTITLED TO SEAT No. 34.

NORTH STAR'S TRAIN.

YELLOW FLAG.

ENTD J. Read

United Kingdom – 1830 to present

Following the opening of the Stockton & Darlington Railway, there was great activity with the building of new locomotives and laying new tracks on new routes around the country. By 1830, nearly 100 new locomotives had been built, using both vertical and inclined cylinders. All this was soon to change though and whilst George Stephenson was busy designing and organising the new railway system, his son Robert set about creating new ideas for new locomotive designs.

It was in 1830 that he came up with the 2-2-0 Planet class locomotive, which would become the blueprint for all future locomotive layout.

Much practical experience had been gained at the Rainhill Trials, and although many improvements had already been made to Rocket, it still had a problem with pitching and rolling at high speeds. This was mainly caused by the position of the cylinders

Robert Stephenson, like many sons of famous people, made his name in his own right. A statue of him can be seen outside Euston Station in London, England.

This scene shows the crowds and the locomotive Locomotion, in the background, at the opening of the Stockton & Darlington Railway, opened on 27th September 1825.

on the outside of the vehicle. Further tests were carried out and in a short time this problem was further improved by fitting them at a more horizontal angle, therefore improving stability considerably. Robert Stephenson completed many more improvements, such as: fitting a dome on top of the boiler to keep the steam drier; fitting a larger smoke stack, which also acted as an efficient vacuum chamber, therefore improving combustion and steam-raising capabilities; and a new design firebox was fitted to later models. The most significant change though, was the relocation of the cylinders to the front of the vehicle, between the wheels.

All these new ideas and changes were incorporated into the new Planet class engine, which was introduced in 1830 and which became the world's first mainline locomotive type. These locomotives not only ran in Britain but were also exported to Europe and as far afield as North America. So it was that in

The Planet, an early steam locomotive built in 1830 by Robert Stephenson. This is a replica from the Liverpool and Manchester Museum of Science and Industry, England.

The original boiler size of the Planet was 11 inches by 16 inches. The boiler pressure was 50 pounds per square inch and the whole contraption weighed some 9.5 tons.

The Planet class locomotives were developed from the Rocket and were far superior. None of the original engines survived but this is an authentic replica.

less than three years, Robert Stephenson had transformed locomotive design from the rather ungainly colliery types of the Stockton & Darlington Railway, into the mainline Planet class, from which future designs would take their cue.

Others too were hard at work designing new engines. Timothy Hackworth, for example, had taken over responsibility for Stephenson's Locomotion engine, after its boiler had exploded and unfortunately killed a worker. Hackworth had improved its performance, but in 1827 had replaced it with a new locomotive, the Royal George. This engine was mounted on six wheels, the cylinders were in an inverted, vertical position on the outside of the boiler and the pistons and connecting rods drove the rear wheels. Hackworth had become manager of the Stockton & Darlington Railway and he too had decided to enter the Rainhill Trials, which took place during October 1829. Unfortunately after a promising start, Hackworth's Sans Pareil engine suffered a cracked cylinder. Despite its failure to win the competition the owners of the Liverpool & Manchester railway decided to purchase the engine, keeping it in service until it was sold in 1831. In 1833 Hackworth decided to go his own way and formed the Soho locomotive building company, at Shildon.

Another engineer who was building his own engines was Edward Bury, who was born in 1794. He established the Clarence Foundry in Liverpool and in 1830 started building locomotives for the Liverpool and Manchester Railway. His first locomotive was the Liverpool, which had a different

Translated, the name Sans Pareil means "Without Equal." Unfortunately at the Rainhill trials it did have equals. This is a magnificent replica with beautiful authentic carriages to match.

design layout to most of the other engines of the time. He used horizontal, inside cylinders, combined with a large tubular boiler, also positioned horizontally and rising to a dome well above the level of the boiler barrel. It also differed from others with its frame design, which was a bar type

The first locomotives built by the Leeds of England manufacturers, Todd, Kitson & Laird, were the Lion and Tiger. This replica Lion boiler measures 11 inches by 20 inches.

rather than the regular plate type. In 1833 Bury became the locomotive superintendent of the London & Birmingham Railway, where he tended to purchase most of the company's locomotives from his own firm of Bury, Curtis & Kennedy.

The Lion and Tiger freight engines were delivered to the newly formed Manchester to Liverpool Railway Company in 1838. Their design was based on the Patentee type.

In the meantime, Stephenson continued to improve the Planet type locomotive and was soon to present the new Patentee 2-2-2 type, of which the best known is the Lion. First manufactured in 1828, it became known as the Stourbridge Lion, after its builder painted a lion's face on the front. Obviously the name Stourbridge was the name of the town in England where it was built. The Stourbridge Lion was not only the first locomotive to be operated in the United States but was also one of the first locomotives to operate outside England.

As with many new ideas that are being developed by more than one person, things can go wrong. In the case of the railways, this became evident in the size of gauge the tracks should be set at. When George Stephenson was building the Stockton & Darlington Railway, it was he who had decided on the rail gauge

The driving wheel diameter of the Lion was five feet in size and the engine had a wheel configuration of 0-4-2. The boiler had a capacity of 411 gallons.

– the distance between one rail and the other. His decision that this measurement should be just over 4 feet, 8 inches seemed to have good reasoning behind it. Most chief engineers of the period followed the initial gauge used at the Killingworth Colliery, and so it seemed sensible to keep in line with that measurement. Unfortunately there were others, like Isambard Kingdom Brunel, who had different ideas. The only son of the French civil engineer Sir Marc Brunel, he was born in Portsmouth on April 9, 1806 and educated at Hove, near Brighton, and at the Henri Quatre in Paris. In March 1833, the 27-year-old Brunel was appointed chief engineer of the Great Western Railway, and it was his work on the line linking London to Bristol that established Brunel as one of the world's leading engineers. Impressive achievements on the route included the viaducts at Hanwell and Chippenham, the Maidenhead Bridge, the Box Tunnel and Bristol

Isambard Kingdom Brunel was a master of his generation. So many of his designs and buildings remain today as testament to his skill and genius.

Temple Meads station. When Brunel built the London to Bristol line in 1838, he decided to use what was to become known as the broad gauge, rather than the standard gauge being used by the others. The thinking behind Brunel's idea was that by using a wider gauge, he could use larger and faster locomotives. Brunel also pointed out that there was less likelihood of the trains leaving the rails on sharp bends when using the broad gauge. This did cause a problem though, as when the Great Western Railway finally opened in 1844, the line that operated between Bristol and Gloucester was confronted by a dilemma. When Brunel's broad gauge met Stephenson's standard gauge, they didn't match. So what happened was that the passengers would dismount from one train, change to the other gauge train, and continue their journey on that train. This was just one instance and became a huge inconvenience to the train traveller of the period. Something had to give, and in 1845 a Royal Commission looked into the railway gauge problem. Railway engineers were given some 6,500 questions to answer and it was then finally decided that the standard gauge, origi-

A view of the main platform area of Bristol Temple Meads station today, with a Virgin Express Pendalino type train awaiting departure from platform five.

This is Bristol Temple Meads Station in 2005. The main station has its entrance below the clock tower, but originally it was the buildings on the left that housed the main platforms.

nally used by Stephenson, was the one to be made standard throughout – the Gauge Act was passed by Parliament in 1846. The Great Western Railway kept its broad gauge until 1892, after which it too then change to the standard gauge. Other countries too encountered similar problems with different gauges. North America for example had differing gauges in the North and South, which was only rectified after the Civil War, when trade between the two halves of the country started to pick up again. It is also believed that Russia decided on a track size that was deliberately different to the one used by their neighbours, for fear of invasion by rail. It was a prominent American railroad engineer, George Washington Whistler, who as consultant, helped to build the first railway line in Russia – the Moscow to St Petersburg line. As the railroad expanded though, each country settled its differences and standardized their gauges.

Although finally rejected, Brunel decided he would use a larger gauge rail than most others of the time – this is the Great Western, which was designed for Brunel's broad gauge.

In the eighteenth century, Porthmadog and Blaenau Ffestiniog in Wales didn't exist: this part of the country was a remote mountain area. In 1798 W. A. Madocks acquired local land and carried out reclamation projects. This culminated in the building of the huge embankment, known as the Cob, across the estuary by Port Madoc, which is known today as Porthmadog. High up in the mountains around Blaenau Ffestiniog, slate deposits were being collected and laboriously taken by pack animal and farm carts over rough roads down to the River Dwyryd, where the slate was loaded into shallow-draft river boats, for transportation downstream. Here it was loaded onto sea-going sailing ships. On May 23, 1832 the Ffestiniog Railway was incorporated by Act of Parliament. The route, whose final mile crossed the Cob, enabled loaded slate trains to run down by gravity, while the horses that were used to haul the empty wagons back up the line

24 year old Isambard Kingdom Brunel won a second competition in 1830 to build a bridge across the Avon Gorge at Clifton.

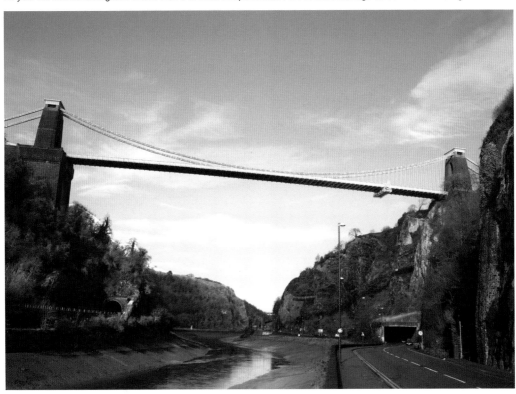

could feed and rest in "dandy" wagons. The 23.5 inch gauge, the same as that being used in the quarries, was wide enough to allow the horses to work efficiently when pulling the empty wagons, and narrow enough to enable the railway to negotiate the sharp curves made necessary by the mountainous terrain. As slate traffic increased, the horse and gravity system of operation came under pressure and thoughts turned to the steam engine. But in the 1840s steam locomotives on such a narrow gauge were thought impracticable and it was also illegal to carry passengers on new railways of less than the British standard gauge. These factors delayed the introduction of steam and it was only after Charles Easton Spooner took control of the railway in 1856 that he looked more closely into steam locomotive design and build. Tenders were sent out in 1862 and in 1863 contracts were signed with George England and Company, London, for four small locomotives. In July 1863 the Princess and Mountaineer engines were brought to Caernarfon by rail. They were then transported to Port Madoc by horse and cart, entering service in October of that year. In 1864 the Board of Trade gave the railway permission to run passenger trains, the first on a narrow gauge in Britain.

This 0-4-4-0 Double Fairlie, Earl of Merrioneth, was built by the Festiniog Railway Company at its own workshops at Boston Lodge - Started in 1972 and completed in 1979.

Merddin Emrys, built for the Festiniog Railway in 1879 to the design of George Percival Spooner and incorporating Fairlie's Patent articulated 0-4-4-0 locomotive design.

As passenger traffic increased, so did the requirement for better, more powerful engines. Robert Fairlie had designed a locomotive that could pull longer trains and so improved the capacity of the line. The new locomotive had to be able to get around the sharp curves and up steep gradients. The solution was a double-bogie engine, which looked like two locomotives back-to-back, but was in fact one long rigid boiler with central fireboxes and driving position. In this way the Ffestiniog Railway pioneered narrow gauge railways throughout the world. The railway introduced its first improved Fairlie engines, James Spooner, in 1872. Two more double engines were introduced, Merddin Emrys in 1879 and Livingston Thompson in 1886. It is worth noting that when the railway needed a new large locomotive in 1979, it again chose the Fairlie double-bogie design for their new Earl of Merioneth engine.

With more railways came longer distances and with longer distances came the quest for more power and speed. Designers were constantly striving to find ways of increasing power, and one of these ways was to use a longer boiler. The term "long boiler" is used when the firebox is positioned behind the rear axle, which also enabled fuel to be used more efficiently. Robert Stephenson introduced his long boilered engine in 1841. Long boiler locomotives could be produced in a number of forms and could cater for both passenger and goods transportation. Unfortunately with the sort of speeds now being attained, the passenger version started oscillating badly and causing discomfort to the passengers, besides being dangerous. So these engines were

The Kitson A No. 5, is an 0-6-0 pannier tank, built in 1883 by Kitson & Co. to the Stephenson "long boiler" design, for the Consett Iron and Steel Company.

A stokers view inside the cab of the Kitson A No.5 – The cylinder was 17 by 26 inches, the boiler had a diameter of four feet, with a working pressure of 140 psi.

mainly used for goods, with such lines as the North Eastern Railway, successor to the Stockton & Darlington line, using many of this type to haul goods on their line.

One of the other designers who was working with the idea of a large boiler was Thomas Russell Crampton. Crampton was an engineer, born in Broadstairs, Kent, in the south of England. A short part of his life was spent designing broad gauge engines, faster and superior to the standard gauge locomotives, to convince the Board of Trade and Members of Parliament that broad gauge was the way to go, even though he wasn't in total agreement with that thought. The main feature of the Crampton locomotive, patented in 1843, was the positioning of the driving axle behind the firebox. This allowed him to use large driving wheels, no matter the size or height of the boiler, whilst still keeping a low centre of gravity. Crampton left the Great Western Railway and began publicizing his new engine and it wasn't long before he was approached by the British managers of the Namur and Liege Railway in Belgium, who decided they would order two. Crampton locomotives were used by some British railways but were more popular in Europe, in par-

120 Cramptons were built between 1849 and 1860. Number 80 "Le Continent" was built for the CF Paris-Strasbourg line in 1852 and survives today in the Mulhouse Museum, France.

The key element of the Crampton design was the placing of the single driving axle behind the firebox, enabling large driving wheels to co-exist with a large low-placed boiler.

ticular France and Germany. In 1847 he developed the standard gauge Liverpool, which incorporated the basic Crampton design. It was capable of hauling 180 tons at 50 mph and became the most powerful engine of its time. During 1847 two further locomotives were built to Crampton's design, Courier and London, which were to run on the London and North Western Railway. At the same time two further engines, Liege and Namur, were built for a British-owned railway in Belgium. Amazingly, by 1878 all express trains on the Eastern Railway of France were Crampton-designed and six were Stephenson-built. Crampton designed engines were also supplied to Prussian Eastern Railways, around the early 1850s.

Many of the rich and famous who lived and worked in London, were keen to spend their weekends and holidays by the seaside, and one of the most popular places was Brighton, on the south coast of England. The introduction of a new railway line between the two destinations was bound to be a success. Over 3,500 men and 570 horses were used to build the railway line between London and Brighton, which was completed in September 1841. Included on this route was the amazing Ouse viaduct at Balcomb, Sussex – an incredible piece of art and amazing feat

Stirling 0-6-0 No.65 was built in 1896, at Ashford, England, as an "O" class locomotive. It went through a rebuild to class "O1" in 1908 and ran on until finally withdrawn in 1961.

of engineering. The first train entered Brighton Railway Station on September 21 of that same year with, initially, the rich and famous being transported to the coast, in the most comfortable first-class carriages. It didn't take long though for the company to realise they could increase the number of passengers by reducing their third-class fare. They did so in 1843 and in the following six months some 360,000 people travelled to Brighton by train. It was in 1847 that the London & Brighton Railway ordered a new locomotive from the E B Wilson Railway Foundry in Leeds. David Joy was the chief draughtsman who was given the task of designing what was to become their most famous locomotive class, the Jenny Lind, a 2-2-2 passenger engine. The Jenny Lind was very different from other locomotives of the period, having inside bearings for the driving wheels, and outside framing and bearings for the leading and trailing wheels. This locomotive was such a success that the company who made it, Wilson Railway Foundry, found themselves having to build one example every week for railways all over Britain.

The town of Doncaster became an important railway centre in 1853, when the Great Northern Railway Company opened its Locomotive Works – locally known as the "Plant Works" – there that year. For more than a century the Plant was a major employer in the town and the producer of some of the finest locomotives, of which the Flying Scotsman and the Mallard, designed by Sir Nigel Gresley, remain famous. In the town there is also an unusual monument to one of the Great Northern Railways locomotive superintendents, Patrick Stirling.

He became the superintendent of the GNR in 1866, replacing Archibald Sturrock, and it was Stirling who started the building of locomotives at Doncaster. The Plant produced 709 locomotives, of which the most famous were the Stirling 4-2-2 passenger engines.

The London, Brighton and South Coast Railway (LB&SCR) was allocated a new locomotive superintendent in 1870. William Stroudley succeeded John Chester Craven, a man who had created an exaggerated number of locomotive classes, believing in matching each locomotive to a specific line or route. By the end of the 1860s, during a time of recession, this policy was no longer a situation that

This is Knowle, the Terrier class loco, put into service on July 23, 1880. The Terriers were a very popular engine with both their drivers and the general public.

could be sustained. Due to this, when Craven resigned in November 1869, he left the railway system in some disarray. Standardization became the order of the day and this was an area in which Stroudley excelled. He began studying the best way to reduce stock and maximise commuter travel. Many people had moved away from London, but were still travelling back and forth to work. Stroudley took all the elements and requirements into consideration and came up with the D1 0-4-2T engine, which he allocated to general suburban travel. Unfortunately this was found to be inappropriate for the lighter South and East London lines, which required a lighter and more maneuverable loco, with matching coaches. In this way the pretty A1 engine was born, a robust and well made engine that became popular with both passengers and drivers. To many they became known as Terriers, although their drivers knew them better as Rooters. Later in life they moved out of London to more rural settings, finally ending their usefulness after some ninety years of service.

Joseph Beattie was another designer hard at work, designing his standard well tank steam locomotive in 1862. This worked on the London and South Western Railways, west London extension line. The locomotives performed so well that a total of 85 were built. They proved to be solid and reliable performers, working commuter and branch trains until the end of the nineteenth century. It was the tender version of the Beattie well tank that hauled the first passenger train from Swanage to Corfe Castle and Wareham, on Wednesday May 20, 1885.

Francis William Webb introduced his 2-2-2-0 locomotive class, the Teutonic, which was developed from the Dreadnought class and became the most successful and the largest of his 2-2-2-0, three-cylinder, compound engines. Using the same boiler, they had 7 foot 1 inch driving wheels, compared with 6 foot 3 inches on the Dreadnoughts. The axle boxes were lubricated by oil instead of grease, a feature that was introduced on that class, and all except the Jeanie Deans were named after ships of the White Star Line. The Jeanie Deans was one engine of the Teutonic class that was, for several years, the regular engine on "The Corridor," and was named after a Walter Scott heroine. "The Corridor" was the nickname given to the afternoon express that ran from Euston in London to Glasgow, Edinburgh and Aberdeen in Scotland.

Dugald Drummond was born in 1840 at Ardrossan, Scotland. He became an apprentice at Glasgow, before working under William Stroudley at the North British Railway, Cowlairs works, near Glasgow. The two moved to the Highland Railway, and then to the London Brighton & South Coast (LBSC) railway. In February 1875, Drummond moved from the LBSC to become the Locomotive Superintendent at Cowlairs. He remained there for several years before moving again, this time to become locomotive superintendent at the Caledonian Railway, which he left in 1890 for a peri-

Built between 1946 and 1953 at the British Railways Crewe Works, this is an Ivatt design with taper boiler. The wheel configuration is 2-6-0 and 128 were built in total.

Probably the most famous locomotive designer associated with the LNER, Sir Nigel Gresley served as its Chief Mechanical Engineer for most of its life.

od in private business. Drummond became locomotive superintendent of the LSWR in 1895 and the first new class he introduced was the M7 0-4-4T. Construction started in 1897 and continued up to 1911, by which time some 105 were built. Initially several of the class were given express passenger service duties between Exeter and Plymouth.

Of all Dugald Drummond's designs for the LSWR, it was his T9 express passenger class of 1899 that could probably be described as his most successful. They were popular with their crews and nicknamed "greyhounds" due to their excellent acceleration.

This probably has to be the most famous locomotive engine in the world. Today in 2006, the Flying Scotsman runs regular excursions from York in England.

LNER V2 number 4771, Green Arrow, speeding through the English countryside. This locomotive was designed by Gresley for heavy, fast, freight traffic in 1936.

Henry Alfred Ivatt was born in 1851 and educated at Liverpool College, England, before entering L&NWR's Crewe locomotive works as an apprentice. In 1877 he moved to the Great Southern & Western Railway (GS&WR) of Ireland, becoming locomotive engineer in 1886. He then returned to England, where he became the Chief Locomotive Superintendent of the Great Northern Railway in 1895. During this time there was a huge increase of rail traffic and a need for even more powerful engines. Ivatt's solution was bigger boilers with larger grate areas and the addition of superheating. With this he introduced his Atlantic 4-4-2 class in 1898, after building an experimental 4-4-2 in February 1897. Number 990 was the first Atlantic 4-4-2 locomotive built in Britain and quickly acquired the nickname of "Klondyke." Ivatt contributed to British locomotive design by being the first to introduce both the 4-4-2 Atlantic wheel

The unmistakable LNER A3 pacific 4472, the Flying Scotsman. Developed as a mainline express locomotive for the Great Northern Line Railway in 1923.

Seen here in all its glory, Flying Scotsman entertained many a railway fan - young and old - at the Crewe Works outing in 2005. A truly magical engine.

arrangement and the Walschaert valve-gear to Britain.

The first half of the twentieth century is classically known as the Golden Age of railways. The modestly designed engines of the late 1800s were to see a huge transformation as new ideas were presented, giving the engines more power and higher speeds. The railways were now a major part of everyday life,

The Gresley A1s were all upgraded to A3 specification between 1927 and 1947, except 4470 great Northern. All newly built A3s were left-hand drive.

with locomotives being used for moving freight and for transporting people all over the country, both for pleasure and work.

The early part of the new century saw the Ivatt designed Atlantic 4-4-2 type locomotive come into its own, maturing as one of the great locomotives of its period, having been introduced in the UK on the GNR in 1898.

William Paton Reid was apprenticed to the NBR works at Cowlairs in 1879 and appointed to the position of locomotive superintendent in 1903. He continued the practices of rebuilding and modernising pre-existing engines and introduced super-heating to the NBR. He is probably best known for his powerful D30 Scott and D34 Glen 4-4-0 classes. North British Railway (NBR) decided to build new and heavier rolling stock in 1905, needing locomotives more powerful than the existing 4-4-0s. Reid produced a two-cylinder simple expansion design, which was given the go-ahead, with fourteen then being ordered. These were given the classification of Class H, but unlike many other preceding NBR locomotives, these Class H Atlantics had outside cylinders. The first batch entered service in 1906 and there were initial concerns within the NBR regarding oscillation problems. They were all given Scottish names such as Aberdonian, Bonnie Dundee and the like.

No doubting which engine this is. The number has already gone into the history books and the name lives on – 4472 The Flying Scotsman.

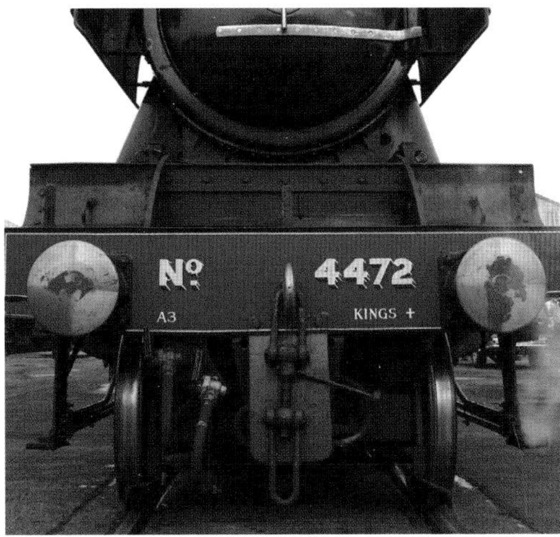

Probably the most famous locomotive designer associated with LNER was Nigel, later Sir, Gresley, who was with the firm for most of its life. During most of this time he was working as their chief mechanical engineer. Gresley was born in 1876, in Nethersale, Derbyshire and went to school at Marlborough College, before becoming an apprentice at Crewe Works. For design and drawing experience, he moved to the Lancashire and Yorkshire Railway (L&YR) in 1898, resigning in 1905 to become the superintendent of the Great Northern Railway's

(GNR) Carriage and Wagon Department. It was in 1911 that Gresley was made the chief mechanical engineer of the GNR and his early locomotives included a large-boilered, three-cylinder, 2-6-0 K3, introduced in 1920. The concept for the K3 2-6-0 began in August 1917 when Gresley was considering a new express goods engine for the GNR, based on his K2 2-6-0. Although very similar to the K1s and K2s, the K3s looked different due to their large diameter boilers and stout boiler mountings. Due to World War I, Gresley's express passenger design had to be shelved, although in 1920 he was able to return to his plans, which now included his conjugated valve gear system. In April 1922, No 1470 Great Northern became the first Gresley Pacific class A1 to enter service. Gresley had always intended the A1s to pull 600 ton trains, and in September 1922 he confirmed these capabilities by having No 1471 pull just such a test train. Just a year later, by which time GNR had become part of the London and North Eastern Railway (LNER), probably the most famous locomotive in the world was introduced – No 4472, better known as the Flying Scotsman. Displayed at the 1924 and 1925 British Empire Exhibition in its apple green LNER livery, it made an immediate impact on the general public and became an instant success. It was in 1934 that the Flying Scotsman, whilst pulling a dynamometer car, became the first steam locomotive to record an authenticated 100 mph.

When Richard Maunsell became the chief mechanical engineer of the newly formed Southern Railway, his first task was to assess the stock and update it. Prior to anything else though, there was an immediate need for more express passenger locomotives, and so it was that in the autumn of 1918 the LSWR works at Eastleigh produced the first three new express passenger 4-6-0 class engines, designed by Robert Urie. More were to follow but they weren't a great success, proving to be poor performers and unable to sustain high power outputs. At the same time Maunsell drew up plans for a new range of locomotives to his own designs. He proposed a range of "standard" locomotives to meet the future needs of the railway, with a large degree of commonality of engineering design and parts. He was set a tough challenge, because the future standard for main line express trains was to haul a load of 500 tons at a start-to-stop average speed of 55 mph, both on the South West section and on the demanding Eastern section. Maunsell started his development work and trials with the aim of producing what would be a "state of the art" locomotive. The prototype was built in 1926, numbered E850 and named after Lord Nelson, which eventually became the designation of the whole class, which were all named after famous British admirals. The class was highly regarded and proved to be very reliable in service.

31874, is a Maunsel designed, N Class, 2-6-0 locomotive, originally owned by Southern Railways. Built in 1925 it has two cylinders and uses Walscharets valve gear.

The Union of South Africa was built for the LNER in 1937 and has a 4-6-4 wheel arrangement. It gets its name from the then newly-formed Union of S. Africa.

By 1937 the 100th Gresley Pacific had been built by the LNER, and the railway honored her designer by giving it his name. The locomotive was saved from scrapping in 1966

The plaque speaks for itself. This was another incredible locomotive that caught the hearts of the nation. These were heady days for these wonderful machines.

No digital readouts here, just levers and gauges. Driving one of these trains took skill and dedication. This is the control panel of Mallard.

4468 "Mallard" is an LNER Class A4, 4-6-2 Pacific steam locomotive, designed by Sir Nigel Gresley. It was designed as an express locomotive and wind-tunnel tested.

Sir Nigel Gresley became one of Britain's most famous locomotive designers, and his famous line of Pacifics, which started life with the GNR A1, later upgraded to A3, peaked with the now well-respected A4 streamlined engines. It was one of these A4s, Mallard, that broke the world speed record for a steam locomotive in 1938, and it still stands today in 2005. The attempt was described as such:

The center big bearing was drowned in cylinder oil, and the return journey commenced. Grantham was passed at 24 mph. By Stoke signal box, the speed had reached 74.5 mph with full regulator and 40 per cent cut-off. At milepost 94, 116 mph was recorded along with the maximum drawbar of 1800 hp. 120 mph was achieved between milepost 92.75 and 89.75, and for a short distance of 306 yards, 125 mph was touched. There is some dispute over the top speed being 126 mph, but Gresley himself refused to acknowledge that speed.

Many of the A4 design ideas were also passed onto the V2 – one of Gresley's most successful locomotive types – and Mikado engines, later also produced by Gresley.

William Stanier was born in 1876, and became an apprentice with the Great Western Railway (GWR) at Swindon in 1892. Leaving in 1897, he returned to Swindon in 1912 to become works manager in 1920. In January 1932, Stanier became the London, Midland & Scottish (LMS) chief mechanical engineer and his first design was the Princess heavy Passenger Pacific. In 1937, the Coronation Class – later known as the Duchess Class – was produced and incorporated a number of improvements, including a larger superheater. Many people consider the Duchess Class as the finest British passenger locomotive ever built.

Whilst with the LMS, Stanier designed several other successful engines including the Black 5 mixed traffic 4-6-0 and 8F 2-8-0 freight engines, the latter being chosen by the War Department as their standard locomotive. All the "Big Four" companies constructed 8Fs for the War Department, including the LNER who built sixty 8Fs between June 1943 and September 1945; all carried the LMS marking.

Whilst all the heavyweight engines were transferring passengers and freight long distances up, down and across the country, the suburbs of Britain's big towns were being serviced mainly by smaller tank engines. These engines were more maneuverable, whilst still able to reach reasonably high speeds, but their greatest advantage was that they had no tender. This enabled them to pull carriages both backwards and forwards, therefore disposing of the tedious operation of having to turn them around. A whole selection of formats were designed, the 4-4-0 being one of the more popular early engines, later progressing to the 2-6-4 format before electrification took over. Shunters, so long the faithful old workhorses of the industry, would also soon feel the changeover to diesel power. Steam shunting-engines ended their duties in the

61039, or Steinbok as it was named, was a Thompson B1 4-6-0 Antelope class engine. Thompson became Chief Mechanical Engineer of the LNER in 1941.

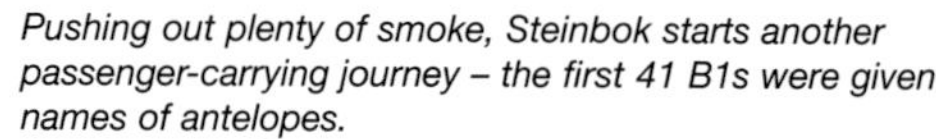
Pushing out plenty of smoke, Steinbok starts another passenger-carrying journey – the first 41 B1s were given names of antelopes.

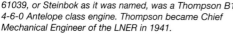

This is a Class 40 locomotive, introduced by LMS, in October of 1933 and designed by Sir William Steiner. Built at Crewe in England, it took the designation 42968.

The Princess Royal class of Pacific type 4-6-2 locomotives, of which the Duchess of Sutherland is one, was a result of a design introduced by William Steiner in 1932.

6201, Princess Elizabeth, is an LMS express passenger steam locomotive. These Pacifics had 4-6-2 wheel configuration and 13 were made between 1933 and 1935.

Just recently restored, this is steam locomotive 48151, an 8F 2-8-0 configured engine, seen at the Crewe works, England, opening day in 2005.

Plaque and wheels of the Leander, a 4-6-0 passenger locomotive which used to serve the Midland line to St. Pancras in London, England.

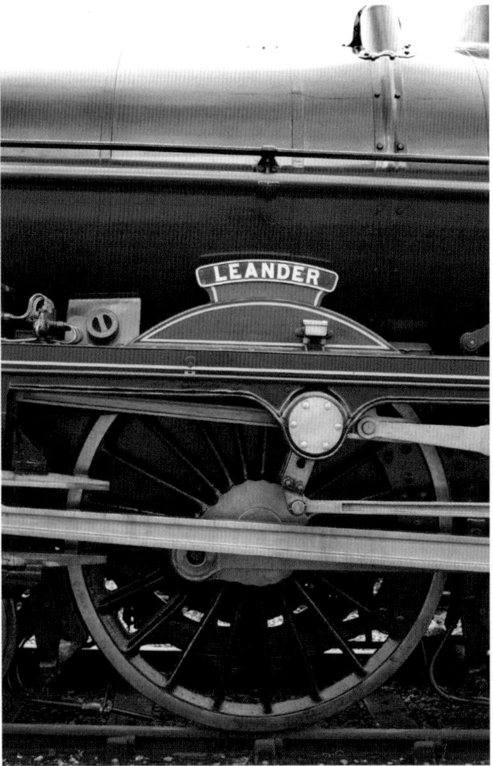

1950s, with only the National Coal Board using steam shunters at a few of their collieries up to the 1970s. It was now the time of the diesels to demonstrate their far superior, flexible shunting skills.

With the rail transport system in Great Britain having been developed during the nineteenth century, a grouping took place in 1923 after the Railways Act of 1921. The result of this was the creation of four large British railway companies, each dominating its own geographic area – Great Western Railway (GWR), the London, Midland and Scottish Railway (LMS), the London and North

The 4-6-0 Royal Scot was introduced in 1927 and was designed by Sir Henry Fowler. It used a parallel boiler and was rebuilt to Stanier design.

This is a B1 class engine, introduced in 1947 and designed by Edward Thompson. Thompson had taken over from Gresley after his death in 1941.

Eastern Railway (LNER) and the Southern Railway (SR). Under the post-war Labour government, Great Britain nationalised a number of important industries, including coal, steel, and transportation. British Railways (BR) came into existence on January 1 1948 with the merger of the Big Four, under the control of the railway executive of the British Transport Commission (BTC). The new system was split geographically into six regions, along the lines of the Big Four: Eastern Region (ER) - southern LNER lines; North Eastern Region (NER) – northern LNER lines in England;

Rolvenden is an austerity, standard war department, 0-6-0 saddle tank locomotive. These were made in anticipation of the invasion of the continent during the Second World War.

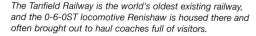

The Tanfield Railway is the world's oldest existing railway, and the 0-6-0ST locomotive Renishaw is housed there and often brought out to haul coaches full of visitors.

Stagshaw, now preserved at Tanfield Railway in England, is Hawthorn Leslie 3513. It was built in 1937 and worked for the National Coal Board up to 1972.

The drivers compartment of the locomotive Stagshaw. The loco was built on the frames of the experimental Hawthorn Leslie compressed steam loco.

This is Henry, a Hawthorn Leslie built 0-4-0 saddle tank, built in 1901. It was ordered for use by Websters Brick and Lime Works in Coventry England.

5637, based at East Somerset Railway at Shepton Mallet, is an 0-6-2 tank engine, built by the Great Western Railway in 1925.

London Midland Region (LMR) – LMS lines in England and Wales; Scottish Region – LMS and LNER lines in Scotland; Southern Region – SR lines; Western region (WR) – GWR lines. These regions would form the basis of the BR business structure until the 1980s and although they managed to retain a level of independence, there was some centralisation.

In 1955 a modernization plan was drawn up, which required the spending of £1.24 million over a period of 15 years. Services were to be made more attractive to passengers and freight operators with the electrification of principal routes, large-scale introduction of diesel and electric traction, with new coaching stock to replace steam locomotives and re-signalling and track renewal. Due to several factors that were overlooked, the plan failed and finances got worse. The plan was then reappraised in 1959, the new idea being to speed up modernisation and rationalisation. This led to mass orders for new diesel types, which were still in development and many of which proved later to be unsatisfactory. Amongst the better known and successful engines

This is Butler-Henderson, the only surviving passenger locomotive of the original Great Central Railway. Numbered 506, it was completed in 1919.

The builder's plate marks the loco as 1920, which goes to show that it was in fact finished prior to schedule. This 4-4-0 was classified as D11.

were the Deltics, used on the East Coast main line, the Brush Sulzer class 47s, used for high speed transportation of either passengers or goods. Others to be introduced were the class 40 English Electrics, used on the West Coast main line, with the Sulzer twelve-cylinder Peaks, happy to transport freight or people. These were just a few of the new engines being put into service.

It was in 1963 that BR chairman Dr Richard Beeching instigated his re-shaping of BR, which called for major rationalization of the system, with unprofitable rural routes being closed. The Beeching axe fell on most branch lines and some main lines, then the early 1960s also saw the "Great Locomotive Cull," with mass withdrawals of steam types, which were replaced by diesels.

During the early period of their tenure, BR inherited a number of locomotives from the Big Four, the vast majority of which were steam powered. BR also built 2537 steam locomotives during the period 1948 to 1960: 1538 were to pre-nationalization designs and 999 to its own standard designs. These locomotives would only have a short life as a decision was made to end the use of steam traction in 1968.

British Railways came into existence on January 1 1948 with the merger of the Big Four and controlled by the Railway Executive of the British Transport Commission.

Foremark Hall, number 7903, is a 4-6-0, modified Hall class locomotive, of which 71 were built between 1944 and 1949.

31602 diesel locomotive. The British Rail class 31 diesel locomotives, also known as British type 2, were built from 1957 to 1962.

Seen here is an English Co-Co Diesel electric Deltic prototype of the 1960s. It used two Napier deltic engines which produced 3,300 hp.

D123 came out of the Crewe, England works in November of 1961. It used a Sulzer 12LDA28B diesel engine and produced 2,500hp.

With the birth of BR came the new two-arrow logo and in 1973 locomotive classification was organized by the TOPS system – originally developed by the Southern Pacific Railroad.

The 1950s saw the advent of the diesel-multiple unit (DMU), which like the shunters, could run the stop-start type journeys more effectively and faster. These were introduced as part of the modernization plan and played a part in the demise of the steam-powered locomotives. These diesels generally ran as two, three or four car units and became known as the Heritage DMUs. A second generation of these units were introduced in the 1980s and were designated the Sprinter series. They were more advanced than their predecessors having better ride comfort and sliding doors. Less popular was the Pacer series, but the best of the bunch was the Class 158 express units, introduced in 1990 and used on medium and long-distance journeys.

As extensive electrification of lines was introduced in the 1950s, so came the electrical multiple units (EMUs). These were ideal for the busy suburban

A class 45, diesel powered locomotive, designed by British Railways in the 1960's. This one is stationed with the Royal Army Ordinance Corp.

Western Fusilier, a British Railways C-C Diesel-hydraulic class 52. This is number D1023, which was manufactured in 1963 in Swindon, England.

A British Standard Mogul, which were built at Darlington, England, during the 1950s. 78019 was completed in March of 1954 and initially based at Kirby Stephen.

A steam locomotive takes on water – not a sight seen too often these days but certainly shows the manpower needed to keep these locomotives going.

Seen here at Bristol Temple Meads station in 2005 is the latest Virgin Voyager, Diesel Multiple Unit (DMU) class 220. These are built by Bombardier Transportation.

England now has a whole array of different companies working their rail routes. This is a line-up seen near Birmingham station in the Midlands, England.

services and were used as four, eight or twelve coach units. These collected their power from overhead cables, rather like a tram, and were joined later by the third rail configured units, which picked up power from a third rail rather than an overhead connection. A combination of the electric and diesel units was also introduced, where the diesel motor would be used to generate electricity to drive the traction motors. These were known as diesel electric multiple units (DEMUs) and worked on the non-electrified sections of rail. As the technology progressed faster more sophisticated units began to appear, reaching speeds of 100 mph between major long-distance journeys throughout the country.

During the 1980s the whole railway system was sectorized into five areas – the passenger sectors were InterCity (express services), Network SouthEast

Seen at York station, northern England is this Great North Eastern Railway (GNER) train. These operate regular services between England and Scotland.

(London commuter services) and Regional Railways (regional services). These new sectors were then subdivided further, with new liveries being adopted. Under the Conservative government's Railways Act of 1993, BR was split up and privatised in November 1997 and passenger services in each sector were franchised out to private companies. Privatization had mixed results; passenger growth was stimulated but at an extraordinarily high cost to the taxpayer and passengers. By 2005 passenger-journey numbers had climbed back to the level last seen in the 1950s. As the new millennium established itself, a new desire for super-fast, more comfortable modern trains was establishing itself, to compete with the ever-growing number of airlines operating cheap flights.

Waterloo station in London, England is also the departure point for the Eurostar trains to Belgium and France. Seen here are a selection of commuter trains.

North American Railways

A long distance American locomotives winds its way through the mountainous countryside. The early pioneers had no idea what they were taking on.

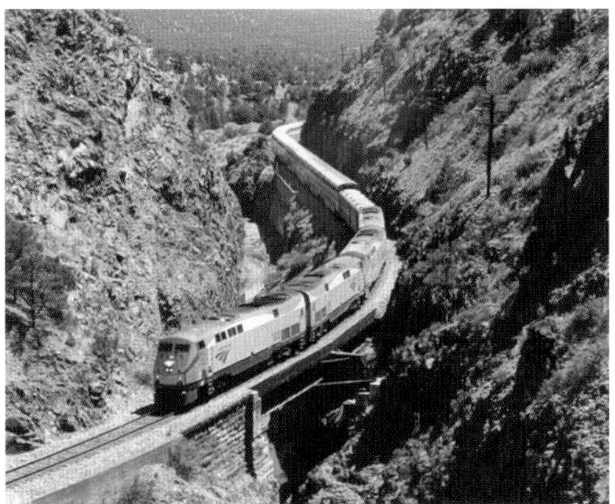

The pioneers who built the first railways in the United States had to overcome huge political, social, and topographical difficulties – situations that their British counterparts could never have imagined. What these brave pioneers, of this new and uncharted country achieved, is one of the most inspiring chapters in the history of America.

As settlements started to evolve, so did the transportation of people and goods, initially on the rivers, which were natural connecting routes – most of the landmass was covered in dense forests which contained dangerous animals and of course native Indians. But even the rivers had their drawbacks; most of them ran from the north to south and therefore anybody wanting to travel east to west, had to go overland. There were no trails as such until about 1796, when Ebenezer Zane hacked his way through the forests of south-eastern Ohio, and it was this that helped to open the way to the development of what was to become known as the turnpike roads. As more turnpikes opened up, it became obvious that due to the vast distances involved, neither road nor river were enough to meet the needs of the people, now scattered over vast areas of this huge landmass.

Networks of artificial waterways were designed and constructed, all dug by human muscle with pick and spade. Several thousand miles of canals were constructed in the United States, many of which even went over vast rivers on timber aqueducts, and others were dug over long distances and through dense forests. So many rivers were soon interlinked that it wasn't long before it was possible to travel from New York, on the East Coast, to New Orleans, on the west coast – a distance of over 2,700 miles – via these waterways.

It was as early as 1812 that John Stevens had convinced himself that the future development of his country depended not on water transport, but on

A sketch showing one part of the journey passengers had to endure on the Philadelphia to Pittsburg route, completed in 1832. Partly by boat and partly by rail!

steam railways. In 1812, construction of the Lake Erie canal was given the go-ahead and Stevens promptly proposed a cheaper and faster alternative in the form of a steam railway. This was seen as wild and impracticable and so the construction of the Erie canal went ahead. Another canal was due to be constructed also, from Philadelphia to Pittsburg; this ended up being part canal and part railway. The journey, which included crossing the Allegheny Mountains, was made by canal boat, travelling part of the way on the river and part on wheels. The system began with a single line laid between Philadelphia and Columbia - this section being one of the oldest railways on the American continent – and was completed in about 1832. The whole journey from Philadelphia to Pittsburg, a distance of about four hundred miles, could be completed between four days and a week.

It took six weeks for the Allegheny to travel between Liverpool in England and Philadelphia, docking in late August of 1831, with a cargo that was very unusual – one locomotive steam engine. Robert Stevens had bought this engine from the Robert Stephenson works and brought it back so that he could use it on his new railroad, which was still to be constructed. The engine had to be transported upriver to the town of Bordentown in New Jersey. Here it was unpacked with great care, reassembled and started. After he was happy that the engine worked, Stevens put the engine safely away and started to construct his new railroad. His route was between Camden and South Amboy, in New Jersey – the railroad would become known as the

This is the original John Bull locomotive, which was the first locomotive to be used for passenger traffic around 1893, in America.

Camden and Amboy Railroad and was one of the most successful early railroads in the U.S. Then in the spring of 1833, the John Bull, along with several other engines that Stevens had built, helped finish construction of the Camden and Amboy Railroad. It was after this that the engine had its cowcatcher added but not to defect any stray animals; it was included in a basic redesign of the engine that included an extra two wheels to help keep it on the tracks. The cowcatcher was more or less an afterthought.

The first meeting for the purpose of forming a railroad company in the United States was held in the city of Baltimore, on February 12, 1827. The construction started with the laying of a cornerstone on July 4, 1828 – carried out by Charles Carroll, of Carrollton, who was over ninety years old and the only survivor of the signatories of the Declaration of Independence – and the Baltimore and Ohio Railroad was completed in 1852. In August of 1830 the locomotive "Tom Thumb," designed by Peter Cooper, a New York inventor, made a successful thirteen-mile trip between Baltimore and Ellicott's Mills in Maryland. It pushed a small open car with eighteen passengers, covering the 13 miles in one and a quarter hours, non-stop. The return journey was covered in 57 minutes. Although successful in its trial, at times it still had to be assisted by horsepower – then again it was only intended as an experiment. Two further locomotives were tested but were incapable of carrying out the work required. It was not until July 1834 that an engine was found capable of hauling the cars, and therefore making it possible to do away with horses. It was during the year 1835 that the line reached Washington, and by 1842 it was extended to Cumberland.

A considerable number of other railways were chartered and many were constructed between 1820 and 1840. The Delaware and Hudson Canal and Railroad Company was one such, dated April 3, 1823. The Delaware, Lackawanna and Western Railroad, the Ithaca and Owego – chartered on January 28, 1828 but not opened until April 1, 1834. The Paterson and Hudson line was completed in 1834 and the Boston and Providence Railroad in 1835. With all these new lines and others that were being developed, came a demand for suitable locomotives.

The construction of the Baltimore & Ohio railroad commenced on July 4, 1828, with the laying of a cornerstone by Charles Carroll, a signatory of the Declaration of Independence.

On August 28, 1830, the Tom Thumb rolled along a track and alongside raced a horse. The engine lost a part, and also lost the race to the horse.

A depiction of the first steam railroad passenger excursion train in America. The John Bull ran from Albany to Schenectady, New York around 1830

This is a replica of the first steam locomotive built and tested in the United States. It was built by Peter Cooper for the Baltimore & Ohio Railroad in 1830.

John Stevens, now 75 years old, had constructed a locomotive with a multi-tubular boiler and was riding it around his circular track on his estate in Hoboken. This was classed as the first locomotive in America to be driven by steam on a track, but unfortunately it was unsuitable for commercial use. As a result of a visit by a commission of three American engineers to England, the Stourbridge Lion engine was imported. This was imported from England along with an engine made by Robert Stephenson, but it seems that the implementation of the Stephenson engine was delayed for unknown reasons. The Lion was used on the Delaware and Hudson Company coal road in 1829, but was unsuitably heavy for the tracks and therefore discarded. The "John Bull" locomotive, imported from the Stephenson factory in England, was used on the Pennsylvania Railroad from 1831.

It wasn't long before locomotives were also being constructed in the United States, the first being the "Best Friend of Charleston," constructed by the West Point Foundry of New York for the South

Many new lines soon opened up and more people started using the locomotives. This is a ticket from 1876 of the Baltimore and Potomac railroad.

BALTO. & POTOMAC
RAIL ROAD.
5 TRAINS TO PHILADELPHIA
WITHOUT CHANGE.
4 TRAINS TO NEW YORK
WITHOUT CHANGE.
ON AND AFTER JANUARY 1st, 1877, TRAINS WILL LEAVE AS FOLLOWS:
The Limited Express
AT 9.20 A. M.
The ONLY TRAIN from WASHINGTON composed exclusively of PULLMAN PARLOR CARS, RUNS OVER THE BALTIMORE & POTOMAC R. R. TO BALTIMORE, PHILADELPHIA & NEW YORK

2.05 A. M.
RICHMOND EXPRESS.
DAILY.
Arriving in West Philadelphia at 6.45 A. M., New York 9.45 A. M., Boston 6.11 P. M., via Springfield, 8.30 P. M. via N. Y. & N. E. R. R.
On this Train Sleeping Car is run Washington to Boston.

9.20 A. M.
LIMITED EXPRESS.
DAILY EXCEPT SUNDAY.
THE ONLY TRAIN FROM WASHINGTON COMPOSED ENTIRELY OF PULLMAN PARLOR CARS.
Only Train connecting with Steamers on Sound.
Arriving in West Philadelphia at 1.30 P. M., New York at 4.05 P. M., Boston 6.00 A. M., Boat, 6.15 A. M. Rail.
On this Train an Extra Seat Fare is charged of $1.75 to Philadelphia, $2.50 to New York and 25 cents to Baltimore.

1.30 P. M.
NEW YORK AND NEW ENGLAND EXPRESS.
DAILY EXCEPT SUNDAY.
Arriving in West Philadelphia at 6.50 P. M., Broad St. and Washington Ave. 6.50 P. M., New York at 10.05 P. M., New Haven 1.30 A. M., Boston 8.45 following A. M. via N. Y. & N. E. R. R.
On this Train Sleeping Car is run Washington to Boston.

5.30 P. M.
PHILADELPHIA EXPRESS.
DAILY.
Arriving in Philadelphia Corner Broad Street and Washington Avenue at 11.00 P. M.

9.20 P. M.
NEW YORK NIGHT EXPRESS.
DAILY.
Arriving in West Philadelphia at 3.10 A. M., New York 6.25 A. M. Boston 4.50 P. M. Sleeping Car is attached to this Train from Washington to Philadelphia, and persons securing Berths can remain in the Car until 7 o'clock, A. M. Also Sleeping Cars Washington to New York.

TICKETS, INFORMATION & BAGGAGE CHECKS
CAN BE PROCURED AT THE OFFICES OF THE COMPANY:
N. E. Corner 13th Street and Pennsylvania Avenue,
N. E. Corner 6th Street and Pennsylvania Avenue,
Baltimore & Potomac Depot, 6th St. and Pennsylvania Ave.

FRANK THOMSON, General Manager — ED. S. YOUNG, Ass't Gen'l Ticket Agent. — D. M. BOYD, Jr., Gen'l Passenger Agent.

Carolina Railway. This was put into service in 1830 and the company followed up with a second engine, but they proved too heavy for the light rails they ran on. Despite this progress people were still sceptical of the steam phenomenon and a backward step was made when stationary engines and long ropes were installed and used on many short-distance journeys. However, progress did not falter and soon locomotives became much improved, so much that by 1850 the United States had more mileage of track and locomotives than England and France put together.

In 1826, John Stevens demonstrated the feasibility of steam locomotion on a circular track, constructed on his estate in Hoboken, New Jersey.

This is a contemporary painting depicting the historic first run of the Stourbridge Lion at Honesdale, Pennsylvania, on August 8th 1829.

Although initially most of the locomotives on American rails came from England, new builders sprang up over the country, and soon America was building its own locomotives for not only its own lines but for export to other countries too.

Matthias Baldwin, who set up the Baldwin Locomotive Works, was born in Elizabethtown, New Jersey in 1795 and began his career as a printer, engraver and bookbinder. He was the first American to build steam locomotives of the same quality as those being made in Europe, and his company did much to establish the railroads of America. He built his first locomotive in 1831, which was based on a design shown at the Rainhill Trials in England. It was a small demonstration engine and was fuelled by coal rather than the usual wood. Baldwin's first railroad commission was in 1832, when his workshop was asked to re-assemble a British-built locomotive, the Delaware. With the knowledge he gained in reconstructing this locomotive, and his understanding of steam engines, he turned to producing his own locomotives. In 1832 he

Probably the best known and most important American builder of locomotives – the Baldwin works. This is a view inside the assembly shop.

Clearly belonging to locomotive number 20, shown here is the Baldwin Locomotive identification plate, fitted to the front of the engine.

Another Baldwin plate, with pipes running over the top and bottom. This again is the manufacturer's identification plate, showing also the date of 1906.

produced his first all-new locomotive, "Old Ironside," a type 2-2-0, which was tested in the November of that year. He was soon to follow this with a type 2-4-0, which was much more suitable for the American railroads. The Baldwin Locomotive Works were founded just after he introduced Old Ironside, and up to his death in 1866, they produced some 1,500 steam locomotives which were sold around the world.

Designed by John B. Jervis for the Mohawk & Hudson Railroad in 1832, the "Brother Jonathon" locomotive was the first engine in the world to have a four-wheel leading truck. He also designed the American No 1, the first 4-4-0, which was capable of regular speeds of 60 mph.

Planning and construction of railroads in the United States progressed rapidly but haphazardly, without direction or supervision from the states that granted charters to construct them. Before 1840 most surveys were made for short passenger lines, which proved to be financially unprofitable. Because steam-powered railroads had stiff competition from canal companies, many partially completed lines were abandoned. It was not until the Boston and Lowell Railroad diverted traffic from the Middlesex Canal that the success of the new mode of transportation was assured. The industrial and commercial depression and the panic of 1837 slowed railroad construction, but interest was revived with completion of the Western Railroad of Massachusetts in 1843. This line conclusively demonstrated the feasibility of transporting agricultural products and other commodities by rail for long distances at low cost.

The possibility of a railroad connecting the Atlantic and Pacific coasts was discussed in Congress even before the treaty with England, which settled the question of the Oregon boundary in 1846. Chief promoter of a transcontinental railroad was Asa Whitney, a New York merchant who was obsessed with the idea of a railroad to the Pacific. Whitney suggested the use of Irish and German immigrant labor, of which there were many at the time. Wages would be paid in the form of land, which would ensure there would be settlers along the route who could supply produce and start up settlements. Other routes across the country were also being reviewed and suggested and so Congress eventually decided to resolve the debate by appropriating money in 1853 for the Army Topographic Corps "to ascertain the most practicable and economical route for a railroad from the Mississippi River to the Pacific Ocean." With this, Secretary of War Jefferson Davis was directed to survey possible routes to the Pacific – four east to west routes, roughly following specific parallels, were to be surveyed. While sectional issues and disagreements were debated in the late 1850s, no decision was forthcoming from Congress on the Pacific railroad question. Theodore D. Judah, the engineer of the Sacramento Valley Railroad, became obsessed with the desire to build a transcontinental railroad and it was through his efforts and the support of Abraham Lincoln, who saw military benefits in the lines as well as the bonding of the Pacific Coast to the Union, that the Pacific Railroad finally became a reality. The Railroad Act of 1862 put government support behind the transcontinental railroad and helped create the Union Pacific Railroad, which subsequently joined with the Central Pacific at Promontory, Utah, on May 10, 1869, and signalled the linking of the continent.

By 1850 a typical freight train was made up of a dozen cars, each of about ten tons in capacity – the double truck, eight-wheel passenger coach had long since replaced the original stagecoach design. As for the locomotive, this would have been a wood-burn-

A contemporary illustration showing the completion and meeting of the Union and Central Pacific lines. The engineers are seen shaking hands.

A modern day re-enactment of the meeting of the Union and Central Pacific railroads at Promontory, Utah, on May 10, 1869.

During November 1868, Rogers Locomotive and Machine Works built Union Pacific 119 and seven months later it pulled Thomas Durant to Promontory Summit.

In September 1868, at Schenectady Locomotive Works, Jupiter was built for the Central Pacific Railroad, and it too would be at Promontory Summit.

ing American type – a swivelled, four-wheeled truck ahead of four drivers – beautifully painted with lots of brass fittings, a large headlight, a balloon chimney and a cow catcher at the front. The rather fragmented railways became a national network of 30,000 miles around 1860, with Iowa, Missouri, Arkansas, Texas, and California building their first lines during the 1850s. It is interesting to note that at this time the standard English gauge of four feet, eight and a half inches was used in the Northern and Western lines, whereas the Southern gauge was five foot in width. Chicago, later to become a huge railway hub, saw its first locomotive in 1848. It had a rail service to the East in 1853, and was served by eleven railroads with 100 daily trains in 1860.

The railroads played a major part in the Civil War. The Southern Confederate railway system suffered most from the conflict, as most of the battles took place in the South. The Northern armies took full advantage of the situation and locomotives were used for transportation of troops, animals and supplies. Repair teams were stationed strategically along the lines to keep them from being put out of action by the "Feds."

In 1868, Major Eli Janney, a Confederate veteran of the Civil War, devised the knuckle coupler. This was a semi-automatic device that locked up the cars, closing them together without the rail worker getting between them. This replaced the link and pin couple system, which was a major cause of injuries to railroad workers. The national rail network grew from 35,000 miles in 1865 to 93,000 miles in 1880, during which time more than 70,000 miles of line were built, with 164,000 miles in operation by 1890. During this time, speeds had increased as had the weight of the engines and what they could pull. Rails had to be more robust, bridges had to be strengthened and bigger turntables were designed to deal with the longer locomotives. Most important was the invention of the airbrake system in 1868, by George Westinghouse, which most locomotives went on to adopt – the hand brake was barely capable of stopping these long powerful monsters. 1886 saw the Baldwin Works produce what was the largest locomotive in the world, a type 2-10-0 Decapod. Although some would dispute this claim, the Decapod was certainly the heaviest engine in the Baldwin Exhibit at the Columbian Exposition. This locomotive was built

A typical American railroad scene of the period. This is a depiction of two lightning locomotives about to leave a railroad junction around 1874.

A wonderful depiction of a locomotive at full speed during the 1870s, passing a rapidly spreading prairie fire in the California area.

This picture was taken during the American Civil War and shows the ruins of a locomotive in the Petersburg railroad depot, Richmond, Virginia.

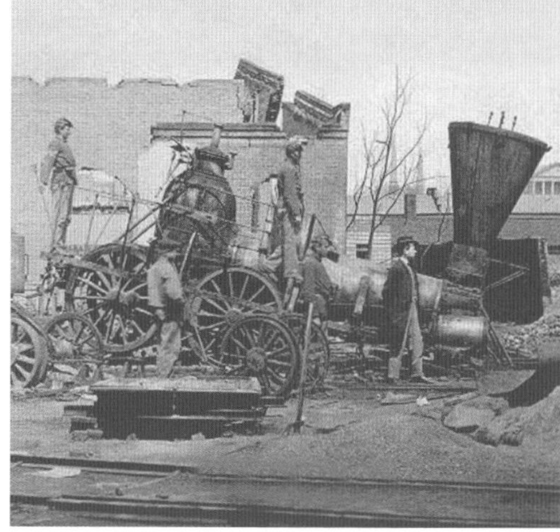

for the New York, Lake Erie & Western Railroad and had a Wootten firebox and a Vauclain type compound engine. On May 10, 1893, locomotive number 999 of the New York Central & Hudson River Railroad, hauled four heavy Wagner cars of the Empire State Express down a 0.2 degree gradient, at record-breaking speed. Although unverified, the conductor timed the speed at 112.5 mph over one mile, and at 102.8 mph over five miles. This 4-4-0 had 86-inch drivers for this run but was later fitted with normal 78-inch wheels. In this same year the first mainline electrification was established in Baltimore, Maryland. A rigid overhead conductor supplied 675 volts DC via a one-sided tilted pantograph to the 96-ton, four-axle, four-motor locomotives. These were very successful, hauling 1800 ton trains up the 0.8 degree gradient in the 1.25 mile Howard Street tunnel, where steam locomotives were not allowed to operate. In 1900 a railway driver by the name of Casey Jones went into folklore history. Having started regular runs on the Cannonball route – Chicago to New Orleans – on April 29, 1900, he agreed to take the southbound

Much propaganda was being touted around prior to the American Civil War. Even envelopes, like this one, were emblazoned with defiant messages.

journey in place of a driver who hadn't turned up. He left Memphis 95 minutes behind schedule but soon started to make that time up. When passing Vaughan, he crashed into two freight wagons that had been parked badly in the sidings, and although his fireman jumped from the train, Jones didn't and was killed. His climactic death led Wallace Saunders, an engine wiper and good friend, to write a song about him, which won the hearts of thousands of Americans.

After the panic of 1893, railroad construction declined and labor trouble accompanied the Depression, which contributed to a quarter of the lines going into receivership by 1894, although many were later reorganized. Standard time zones

A Baldwin locomotive steams its way through the night, vast areas were now being served by many different railway companies.

This photo was taken of locomotive number 999, hauling the Empire State Express, during its record breaking run on May 10, 1893.

A tribute to the brave engineer Casey Jones, this sell-out record was produced by the Southern California Music Company.

were adopted in 1883, and three years later the last of the five-foot gauge lines of the Southern states were changed to standard gauge. After the Civil War most locomotives burned coal instead of wood, and fuel oil was first tried in 1887. As engines became heavier and more powerful with extra drivers and a wider firebox, average train loads grew from one hundred tons in 1870 to five hundred or more tons by 1915. Labor productivity in freight services more than doubled between 1880 and 1916. Passenger travel became safer and more comfortable with the introduction of dining cars in 1868, steam heat in 1881, solid vestibule trains and electric lights in 1887, and all-steel coaches in 1904. The nation's rail freight grew from 10 billion ton-miles in 1865 to 366 billion ton-miles in 1916. In 1916 the nation's railways were carrying 77 percent of the intercity freight traffic and 98 percent of the intercity passenger business. But these were years

1930s Locomotive number 484, was part of a batch that were rebuilt to pull "time freight" trains, and took on the designation MCA.

The Virginian Railroad was formed when Deepwater and Tidewater Railroads came together. This locomotive was one of the Virginian Mikados.

Seen here pulling its compliment of coaches is the locomotive number 89, which is a Baldwin manufactured 2-6-0 engine.

of corruption, discrimination, and increased regulation.

Without doubt one of the most popular locomotives in America was the Mikado, which had a wheel arrangement of 2-8-2 and was first built by the Baldwin Works back in 1893. These had a three foot, six inch gauge and were built for Nihon Tetsudo – Japan Railways – which at the time was a private railway. The Lehigh Valley was also one of the early users of the 2-8-2, having purchased some 47 center-cab Wooten firebox-equipped versions, between 1902 and 1905. The locomotive became the principal freight engine of North America, where in excess of 10,000 versions were built up to 1945. That accounts for about one in every five locomotive on common carrier railroads being a Mikado – or as some called them after the attack on Pearl Harbor, the MacArthur.

Possibly the most successful type of articulated locomotive in America was the Mallet. These locomotives were first introduced on European railways in 1889 by M. Anatole Mallet, a noted French engineer. They were first built by the Baldwin Locomotive Works in 1904 for the American Railroad of Porto Rico, a meter gauge line, but it was two years later before they were employed to any extent on railways in the United States. The general features of the Mallet type consist of four cylinders, arranged on the compound system with the high-pressure cylinders driving the rear group of wheels, and the low-pressure cylinders the forward group. The front frames are hinged to the rear frames in such a way that when the engine enters a curve, the front group of wheels swings on a hinge-pin. The boiler is held in rigid alignment with the rear frames, and is supported on the front frames by sliding bearings. Flexible pipes convey the steam from the high to the low-pressure cylinders and from the latter to the smoke-box. Large locomotives of this type can be designed to negotiate the sharpest curves, generally encountered on trunk lines.

In 1917 America entered World War I and the railroads were completely unprepared for the vast amount of traffic that suddenly became necessary. There was a lack of locomotives, cars and proper maintenance. A disastrously severe winter caused

A 1923 Heisler Locomotive Works, two truck, two cylinder, geared, coal-burning, class 55-8-38, steam locomotive. Note one of the "V" configuration cylinder protruding from the side.

further havoc and so the President of the time, Woodrow Wilson, placed the railroads under federal control. It wasn't until the Transportation Act of 1920 that the system was returned to its owners. By now though the railways were coming under threat from interurbans – buses, trucks, private cars, airlines and pipelines. They were faced with stiff competition and it was going to get worse!

Pacific locomotives were the predominant steam passenger power in America in the twentieth century. Few railroads didn't feature 4-6-2 locomotives, although they were supplanted on many routes later on by larger 4-6-4 "Hudson," 4-8-2 "Mountain" or 4-8-4 "Northern" locomotives, as train weights increased. The Pacifics had a large firebox, used for burning poor lignite coal, and it was the New Zealand Railways chief mechanical engineer A W Beattie, who ordered the first true Pacific. Although there are some known examples of Pacifics prior to 1901, these were 4-6-0s that had been rebuilt and were not genuine Pacifics. Approximately 7,000 of these locomotives were produced for US and Canadian railroads, the largest user being the Pennsylvania Railroad, with 697, which included 425 class K4s, the largest single class of locomotive ever built in the United States.

The first commercially successful locomotive in America with an internal combustion engine, was built by General Electric in 1913 for the Dan Patch Line in Minnesota. Locomotive number 100 used two Model GM16 gas-electric, V8 engines, rated at 175 hp at 550 rpm each. It weighed 57 tons and rode on two, four-wheel trucks. Then in 1917 the first diesel-electric locomotive in the United States was produced, a prototype built by General Electric. Number 4 had one model GM50 air injection, two-stroke, V8, rated at 225 hp at 550 rpm, powering one of two trucks. It was never sold and served only as a laboratory model at the Erie Works. Just one year later the first diesel-electric locomotive to be built and sold commercially was Jay Street Connecting RR number 4. General Electric slightly revised its standard steeple cab straight electric locomotive car body, and installed a single GM50. Not a great success and after six months had to be returned to GE, where it was used as a laboratory test-bed. In 1925, the American Locomotive Company (ALCO), along with GE and Ingersol Rand, built their first diesel-electric loco, which was delivered under its own power to the Central Railroad of New Jersey, and given the designation CNJ 1000. At the end of its days it operated as a switcher in the Bronx until 1957. The first diesel-electric passenger locomotive built in North America was a two-unit 2-D-1-1-D-2 presented in 1928. A joint venture between Westinghouse, Canadian Locomotive Co., Baldwin and Commonwealth Steel Co., it was numbered Canadian National 9000. Each unit had a Scottish-

In July 1944, S3 4-8-4's numbered 260-269 were delivered from the American Locomotive Company – the last steam locomotives built for the Milwaukee Road.

The first 4-8-4 was built by the American locomotive Company in 1927. This is locomotive number 614 seen at Dalton, Illinois and still going strong.

Throwing out huge amounts of smoke is the Norfolk and Western 611 class J locomotive. Fourteen of these beautiful streamlined 4-8-4 Js were built.

A great view of this 1920s Canadian Pacific J-4-F class 4-6-2 Pacific, which was taken at Columbus, Wisconsin in 2004, during a Rail fan trip.

Locomotives are lined to fill up with coal, sand and water at the coaling station in the 40th street yard of the C & NW Railroad, Chicago, Illinois.

built Beardmore V12 engine, rated 1330hp at 800 rpm. A maximum safe top speed was declared at 63 mph.

The Union Pacific M-10000 was dedicated in February 1934. This Pullman-built, three-car, all-aluminium, articulated train, was the first streamliner in the United States. It was powered by a Winton V12, 600 hp, distillate engine, capable of 110 mph. On a 12,625 mile, coast-to-coast exhibition trip, almost 1.2 million people saw it at various stops. It went into service under the name of "City of Salina" on January 31, 1935.

This same year on April 18, the Burlington Zephyr – a Budd-built, three-car articulated train made from

This is the Ingersoll-Rand, 1925 Demonstrator 9681, which was later re-designated CNJ1000, and delivered to the Central Railway of New Jersey.

In 1929, Westinghouse and Canadian Locomotive Company teamed up to build CNR 9000, claimed as the first large diesel locomotive in North America.

stainless-steel, was dedicated. On May 26 it made a record-breaking, dawn to dusk run from Denver to Chicago – 1,016 miles – at an average speed of 77.6 mph and a top speed of 112.5 mph. It was the first diesel-electric streamliner in the US and used a Winton, inline, eight-cylinder, 600 hp, two-stroke engine. Again this year, construction of the first streamlined electric locomotives began. These were the Pennsy GG-ls, which pulled high-speed passenger trains between New York City and Washington DC. They developed 8500 hp and their production continued until 1943 – they were also used into the early 1980s by Amtrak. In 1935 EMC built the first self-contained diesel passenger locomotives in the US. The boxcar-like bodies housed two, Winton, V12, 900 hp engines, and were designed by Dick Dilworth and two draftsmen. Milwaukee Road was one of the first railroads with purpose-built streamlined steam locomotives, with their 4-4-2 Hiawathas. Many more colorful and uniquely designed streamlined steam locomotives were built in the following 15 years. Industrial designers like Raymond Loewy and Otto Kuhler worked their magic to transform these lumbering giants into wind-beating, good-looking locomotives. But even though these locomotives looked colorful and futuristic, the streamlining did little for the speed, and what effects there were, could only be noticed at very high speeds. Streamlining also had its negative side, in particular during maintenance. Often the additional bits added

The Union Pacific's M-10000 locomotive of 1934 was the railroad's first streamliner. It had an aluminium alloy hull, and a distillate engine power plant.

A Santa Fe Railroad freight train about to leave a snowy Corwith freight yard in Chicago, Illinois. From here it will make its way to the West Coast.

March 1943 and these locomotives are playing their part in the war, but even they have to refuel. They are shown taking on coal and sand at the Argentine yard, Santa Fe Railroad, Kansas City, Kansas.

View of the Super Chief being serviced at the Albuquerque, New Mexico depot, in March 1943. It is fitted with a headlight "blackout shield."

Streamlined locomotives were all the rage in the mid 1930s and well-known industrial designers were commissioned to give them a good look too.

At the time, these fabulous streamlined machines must have been quite startling – this is a Hiawatha for the Milwauke Road Railroad.

Shown here is a diesel Switch engine of the Southern Railway. This engine was built in the 1950s by EMD, Georgia, for the Southern and Florida Railroad.

Atchison, Topeka, and Santa Fe railroad conductor George E Burton and engineer J W Edwards comparing times before pulling out of Corwith for Chillicothe, Chicago, Illinois.

to make the engine look streamlined, got in the way of the maintenance work and often a locomotive would come away from the workshop with less streamlining than it went in with. Much of the streamlining was also removed during the war years when all kinds of metal and steel was requisitioned. These beautiful engines were made up to 1950, when the last streamlined steamers were constructed at the Norfolk & Western Roanoke Shops. On June 5 1960, Canadian Pacific Railway's 21-year-old Royal Hudson 2857, returned to Toronto from an excursion to Port McNicoll, Ontario. With this the streamlined steam train era came to a grinding halt.

World War II revived the railroads for a while, using nearly a third fewer locomotives, cars, and workers than in World War I; they provided freight and passenger services from 1942 to 1945. The wartime prosperity also enabled the railroads to retire US$2 billion of bonds, or nearly a fifth of their funded debt. Not only that but post-war America saw the introduction of many technical advances of which the diesel locomotive was probably the most important. These engines were not cheap but they more than made up for that in their low fuel and water consumption and modest maintenance costs. Their

Probably the best seats in the carriage. This is the lounge car of the Southwest Limited Amtrak train, travelling between Los Angeles and Chicago.

Passengers from the Southwest Limited, strolling by the Amtrak train at Albequerque, New Mexico, as it halts for refuelling, en-route to Chicago.

The Empire Builder, a Midwest long-distance Amtrak train, has been re-launched with several upgrades for the passenger's enjoyment.

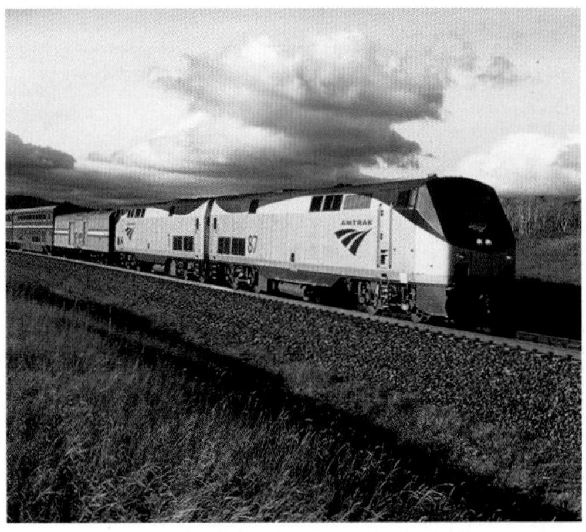

initial use was in 1941 for freight, but by 1957 they were providing 92 percent of all switching, passenger and freight services. Post-war, some passenger lines did manage to increase their turn-over, but generally the trend in both freight and passenger numbers took a downward turn. The 1960s, 1970s and 1980s saw an introduction of new technology. The use of welded rails, microwave communication, computers, mechanised track maintenance equipment, unit trains, and greater piggyback and container service, managed to slow the decline a little, but it was temporary and by 1987 railroads only provided 36 percent of intercity freight traffic and 3 per cent of passenger service.

America has invested heavily recently in upgrading its locomotive stock. This is the MP36 model, which is serving the Chicago area on their Metra service.

A new chapter in American railroad history began when the National Railroad Passenger Corporation, or Amtrak as it is better known, was created. It was to provide a modern, efficient, attractive service and would take over the nation's passenger railroads on May 1, 1971. Electro-Motive Diesel (EMD) had provided quality products and services to the railroad industry worldwide for more than 80 years; most notable was their E and F series locomotives during the 1950s. Later they supplied Amtrak with their SDP40F model, although it wasn't the most satisfactory locomotive for passengers. In the late 1970s came the F40PH, a turbocharged, 3000 hp locomotive, which was better received by Amtrak on their commuter lines. General Electric was another supplier of locomotives, with their P30CH, a huge six-axle, 3000 hp machine. During the 1970s, General Electric also introduced their E60 electric locomotives and more recently Amtrak have taken delivery of the new GE Dash-8 model, followed by the Genesis locomotives.

The Capital Limited locomotive, travels from Martinsburg, West Virginia, toward Cumberland, Maryland. It can encounter all sorts of weather.

Another Amtrak long-distance train, the Crescent, seen traveling through some stunning countryside. The passenger gets to rest while the train takes the strain.

The southbound Amtrak Empire Service locomotive, seen here traveling along the shore of the Hudson River in New York, passing Bannerman's Castle.

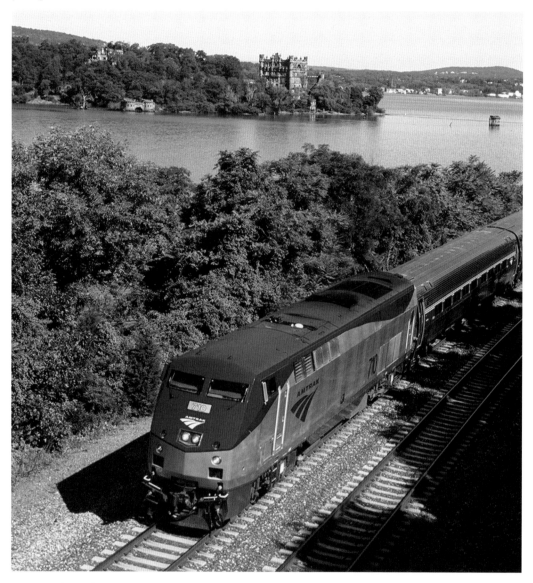

The new fleet of high-speed ground transportation is starting to capture the public's imagination and the Department of Transportation is currently testing new modes of propulsion, such as the linear induction motor, and a tracked air-cushioned vehicle capable of speeds up to 300 miles per hour. Passenger car interiors and exteriors are being redesigned to permit easier boarding and exit as well as great comfort, safety, and convenience of passengers. America is looking to the future and like Europe and parts of the Far East, it could rely much more on its clean rail system rather than the high polluting alternatives.

The new Acela high speed train is seen here on its journey through the Northeast corridor. These trains cover a lot of mileage in a very short time.

Dutch Railways

The Dutch railway system (Nederlandse Spoorwegen – NS) has been acknowledged as one of the best in Europe. This is thanks to the comprehensive scope of the system and the commitment to regular interval trains geared to meeting the needs of commuters and other passengers.

The availability of roads and the canal system in

A double-deck train is shown at speed with the locomotive - a class 1700- in the center of the train operating in push-pull mode.

Holland meant that the development of railways was perhaps less of an imperative than in other countries. In 1834 a plan was in place for a railway to be constructed from Amsterdam to the Ruhr in Germany but this did not come to fruition. However, other lines were eventually opened (largely using English and Belgian technology) and Dutch engineers had a major role in the overall development of the network. The first railway was opened in 1839 and ran from Amsterdam to Haarlem using a massive 2,000 mm gauge and British built locomotives. The line was re-laid to standard gauge in 1866.

A typical scene on a preserved railway with a steam tank locomotive easing through the Dutch countryside with a tourist's train.

The first railways were introduced by private companies but the State realized that there was a need for effective control to ensure the development of a coherent network and this was achieved in 1860. The national network was largely in place by 1900 and State control increased after World War I. The period between the wars saw a rationalisation of the network with the closure of some unprofitable lines and reductions in services. This culminated in 1938 with the total unification of the railways under public control. World War II had a severe and adverse impact on the railway. In particular, the system needed extensive renewal to repair war damage and to replace stock and equipment that had been removed by German forces. As a part of the process, in 1946 Dutch railway engineers visited the London and North Eastern Railway (LNER) in England to evaluate a locomotive developed for the Manchester to Sheffield line, construction of which had started before the war. It was agreed that the locomotive would work in Holland on trials which would help both railways with their respective developments. The locomotive, number 6000 (later British Railways 26000 of class EM1), successfully travelled 375 miles per day on passenger and freight services.

Subsequent years saw the renewal of the system and the construction of new lines. Today, Holland has a modern, integrated transport system which has the railway network at its heart. High speed lines have been introduced and modern trains operate, working

MBS is a museum line based at Haaksbergen. One of its steam tank locomotives shows off its colorful livery as it steams along the line.

Ex German 2-10-0 "Kriegslok," number 52 8139, is preserved at the VSM preservation site at Apeldoorn. This locomotive was built in 1944.

to a high frequency timetable. Over two-thirds of the network is electrified at 1500 v DC. Organizationally, NS is now a holding company with a series of individual operational units including those responsible for passenger services, international passenger services, stations and infrastructure. Freight is the responsibility of Railion Nederland – a part of the Railion Group in Europe which also includes Railion Germany and Railion Denmark.

There is an extensive range of steam locomotives preserved in Holland including a significant number from Germany. Most of the ex-NS locomotives are at the excellent National Railway Museum in Utrecht. This museum also holds a number of preserved electric and diesel locomotives. There are also several preservation sites throughout the country that run preserved locomotives and trains.

Two early steam locomotives need to be highlighted. "De Arend" (Eagle) and "Snelheid" (Speed) were 2-2-2 locomotives built by Stephenson in England for the 2000 mm railway from Amsterdam to Haarlem, opened in 1839.

The National Railway Museum has examples of other early locomotives from the nineteenth century plus others dating from the pre-World War II period and from the war years. One particularly interesting example is PO 3 class 4-6-0 number 3737 introduced in 1911 for express passenger work. Thirty-six of these locomotives were built by Beyer Peacock in England with a further eighty-four being built in Holland and Germany.

Of the German locomotives in Holland, steam class 52 Kriegslok is the most common but there are also

2-6-2 steam locomotive, number 23 071, is preserved at the VSM at Apeldoorn along with several Dutch and ex-German locomotives. This ex DB locomotive was built in 1956.

Class 1100 was based on SNCF class BB8100 and hauled passenger and freight trains. This class of electric locomotives has now been withdrawn. Number 1135 is pictured stored at Bleric in June 1996.

Class 1200, now withdrawn, was designed for freight train work but was also found on passenger services. Locomotive number 1202 waits to depart from Venlo, in May 1994.

Class 1200, number 1213, is stabled at Venlo awaiting its next train, in April 1994. Several examples of this class are now preserved.

examples of classes 23 and 01. Details of these classes are in the German section of this book. Other German classes also can be found at preservation sites in Holland plus others from Austria and Sweden.

NS has several classes of electric locomotives. Class 1001 was introduced in 1948 and comprised 10 locomotives for high speed passenger and freight work. The class was derived from Swiss Railways classes Ae4/6 and 8/14 and had a key role in restoring the NS services after World War II. These powerful and flexible locomotives had a maximum speed of 100 mph. Class 1100 has now been withdrawn but originally comprised 60 locomotives based on French Railway (SNCF) class BB 8100. Introduced in 1950, the class worked passenger and freight services for over 50 years and had a maximum speed of 85 mph. The class was rebuilt in the late 1970s and this included a radical change to the appearance of the locomotives by re-styling of the front-end to incorporate a "nose" similar to that carried by classes 1600 and 1700. Class 1200 is another post-war design but is particularly interesting because of the way in which the locomotives were designed and constructed. The striking design is typical American styling of the 1950s and some parts were supplied by the American locomotive builder, Baldwin. Other parts were supplied by Dutch companies with the final assembly taking place in Holland. The 25 locomotives were originally intended for freight services but were also used successfully on passenger services. Introduced in 1951, the locomotives have a maximum speed of 85 mph. Although the class has now

Class 1300 was introduced in 1952 and was based on SNCF class CC7100. Locomotive number 1313 heads through Venlo in March 1994.

Electric class 1600, number 1656, accelerates its passenger train out of Venlo station, in August 1993. This class was introduced in 1981.

Class 1700 are passenger train locomotives. Locomotive 1732 is about to leave Roosendaal with its double-deck train, in March 1994.

Class 2200 shunting and light freight diesel locomotive, number 2212, is stabled at Terneuzen, in June 1996. The class was introduced in 1955.

Ex NS class 2200 locomotive, number 2299, in original brown livery is preserved by VSM at Apeldoorn. This locomotive was built in 1958.

The front of class 2200, number 2299, showing its distinctive number plate, at the VSM preservation site at Apeldoorn.

been withdrawn from NS service, several have been acquired by ACTS, a private freight operator in Holland and others have been preserved. The 16 locomotives of class 1300 were introduced in 1952

Class 2400 worked for NS until the 1990s. Several were sold to SNCF and number 62470 is pictured in France, in March 2000.

and were essentially the same as class CC7100 in France. With a maximum speed of 85 mph, these locomotives are mainly used on heavy freight work but they also have limited use on passenger services. Class 1500 is also interesting in that they were locomotives acquired from British Railways in the early 1970s having been introduced in 1954 for express passenger work on the now closed 1500 v DC electrified line between Sheffield and Manchester (class EM2). The class was a development of LNER/ BR class EM1 electric, one example of which (26000) worked on trials in Holland in the late 1940s. Class 1500 was withdrawn from NS service in the 1980s but examples have been preserved in Holland and Britain. The class had a design maximum speed of over 87 mph. Class 1600 comprises 58 locomotives introduced in 1981 for freight work. The class is based on French class BB7200 and is identical in appearance to that class. The locomotives have a maximum speed of 100 mph. Just under half of the class have now been transferred to passenger work and have been redesignated as class 1800. Based on class 1600/1800, class 1700 is identical in appearance to that class. Introduced in 1990, the 81 locomotives have a maximum speed of 100 mph and are used on passenger services, including push-pull services using double-deck coaches. NS also has a number of main-line diesel classes. Class 2200 originally comprised 150 locomotives and was introduced in 1955. The locomotives have a maximum speed of 62 mph and are used on freight work. The majority are now withdrawn although several have been preserved. Twenty-five members of the class were sold

Class 6400 are now NS's standard shunting and light freight locomotives, introduced in 1988. In new red cargo livery, number 6512 is stabled at Zwolle, in September 1994.

The 120 locomotives of class 6400 are found throughout Holland on freight duty. Originally, the class's livery was the standard Dutch grey and yellow. Number 6440 is on freight duty at Roosendaal, in March 1994.

Class 200 are long serving small shunting locomotives used in stations, depots and freight yards. Some are fitted with a crane. Locomotive number 326 is stabled between duties at Terneuzen, in June 1996.

Small diesel shunter "Herculo" number 13 is preserved by VSM at Apeldoorn as part of its large collection of locomotives.

The builder's plate from locomotive number 13 "Herculo" showing that it was built by O and K of Amsterdam.

to Belgium Railways in 1995 to provide a fleet of locomotives for construction trains building new high-speed lines. They were designated as class 76. Class 2400 was introduced in 1954 and they were all withdrawn from NS service in the 1990s. These heavy shunting and short-trip freight locomotives had a maximum speed of 50 mph and several have been preserved. The power and versatility of these locomotives was such that French Railways acquired almost 50 of them for hauling trains associated with the construction of new TGV lines. In France, they are class BB62400. The 120 locomotives of class 6400 were introduced in 1988 and are used on shunting duties and freight work. They have a maximum speed of 75 mph. Some members of the class are equipped for working on freight duties into Belgium and Germany. Several members of the class were loaned to Norwegian Railways (NSB) for a short time in the 1990s. Class

For many years, British built class 600 was NS's standard shunting locomotive used throughout the system in freight yards and stations. Locomotive number 655 is stabled at Feijenoord, in June 1996.

200 are small shunting locomotives with a maximum speed of 37 mph, some of which are fitted with a telescopic crane. Introduced from 1934 to 1951, there were originally over 150 locomotives in the class but many have now been withdrawn. Known as "Siks" (goats), their versatility and popularity has resulted in a significant number being preserved. Class 500/600 was introduced in the early 1950s as locomotives for shunting in freight yards and stations. They have a maximum speed of 20 mph and the majority are now withdrawn or stored for possible future use. These locomotives were built by English Electric in Britain. Some class 600 locomotives were fitted with remote control equipment. Examples of the class are preserved in Holland and several have recently returned to England having been acquired by preservation railways. Class 700 are new diesel shunting locomotives introduced in 2003 for use in locomotive depots and carriage sidings. They are Vossloth type G400B and resemble Danish Railways (DSB) shunting class MK600. The 13 locomotives have an attractive two-tone green livery. There is a possibility that further examples of the class will be ordered.

Private railway companies are a feature of rail activity in Holland. The freight company ACTS uses ex-NS class 1200 locomotives, ex-British Rail class 58 locomotives, ex-Belgium Railways class 62 locomotives and new General Motor (GM) JT42CWR locomotives now widely used throughout Europe especially in Britain where they are designated as class 66. Shortlines, another freight company, uses the same GM type as do a number of other companies operating into Holland. Other locomotives in use are Vossloth 1200 types also widely in use throughout Europe – for example in Austria (class 2070) and Belgium (class 77).

DB tested three locomotives later acquired by German company HGK for work into Holland. Number 240 002 is pictured at Hamburg while with DB.

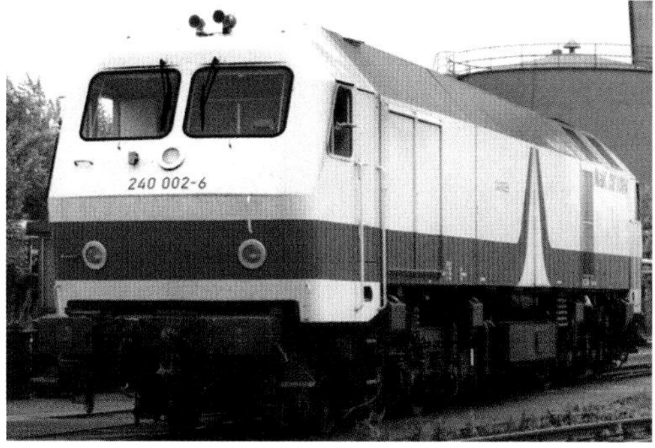

French Railways

The existing French railway system is extensive and uses a fascinating range of locomotives. The introduction of locomotives in France is inevitably linked to the way in which the railway system itself developed. In the early days, railways in France developed slowly because of the lack of a significant industrial base to support the financing of an extensive system. There was also a well-developed canal system that was quite capable of handling trade, and along with this a general reluctance on the part of government to encourage railways using private enterprise. This all changed in 1842 when a law was passed regarding railways. Even then, the government insisted that development would be a partnership between the state and private rail companies, with the state being responsible for planning and engineering and the companies financing track, stations and the trains. By 1870, the basic structure of the railway system was in place, although development continued until the end of the century. The system was used by a number of railway companies and based on several different regions of France – Nord, Ouest, Est, Midi, Paris – Orleans and Paris – Lyon. Each of these radiated from Paris, but the rigidity of the system made rail travel difficult between parts of France that were not linked up with Paris, which was seen as the hub of the system. By 1914 though, France had a well developed and extensive railway system totalling some 37,000 miles, using a mix of standard and narrow gauge

The plate from from the builder of locomotive number 6 L'Aigle, showing that it was built in 1846 by Stephenson at Newcastle upon Tyne, England.

Number 6 L'Aigle, a British built 2-2-2 steam locomotive, as preserved at the French National Railway Museum in Mulhouse. This locomotive worked on many routes, including Avignon to Marsailles.

The builder's plate from locomotive number 80, Le Continent, showing that it was built in 1852 for the Paris to Strasbourg line.

lines. However, perhaps because of the rigidity of the railway system, road transport experienced a significant growth in this period and many lines were closed, through lack of use, during the 1930s. The financial pressures on the railway companies were such that in 1938 the government nationalised the railway system and created the Societé Nationale des Chemin de Fer Français (SNCF), an organisation that controls French railways even to this very day.

The existing railway system in France comprises approximately 25,000 miles of track and is extensively used for both passenger and freight activity. There is also increasing involvement of regional government in the provision of passenger services. The major development since the late 1970s has been the introduction of the high speed TGV – Train Grande Vitesse – lines, between the principal cities in France, which have captured the imagination of the public and transformed rail travel in France. The French approach to high speed rail travel has undoubtedly influenced other railway systems in Europe and beyond. The other significant development has been the opening of the Channel Tunnel, between France and England, which has enabled high speed railway journeys to take place between London, Lille and Paris.

In considering French steam locomotives, the work of Andre Chapelon cannot be ignored. Between 1942 and 1946, he changed a poorly-performing 4-8-2 locomotive into a three-cylinder compound 4-8-4 locomotive, with spectacular results. The locomotive was able to pull heavy loads at high speed, and was very economical in its use of fuel and water. Its performance compared favourably with many larger steam locomotives in other countries, and it could out-perform electric locomotives in France. Some say that the locomotive was the greatest ever, but, unfortunately France was committed to electrification by this time and Chapelon's work did not progress to the extent of any further locomotives of that type.

Also worth a mention is the car manufacturer Ettore Bugatti. Around 1930, Bugatti was having some financial problems with the sales of his cars, due to the financial crisis of the previous year. It was now that he proposed a light "railcar," which would be driven by four similar engines as those of his famous luxury automobile – the Royale. The idea of the railcar was that of Bugatti himself, and he went on to patent many of the designs that he introduced on the train. Prior to this date, steam locomotives were the mainstay of the now numerous French routes but these were rather dirty, noisy and generally uncomfortable. The Bugatti railcars, as they were known, were built as single, double or even triple car units, using either two or four of the powerful 12.7 litre engines. The fastest and most comfortable of these trains was named the Presidential, which used four engines, produced 800 hp and reach a speed of 122 mph, achieved in 1934 – a new world rail speed record. These railcars could be used in a variety of combinations, depending on passenger numbers and routes taken and this made them highly successful. As well as being light, clean and comfortable, their chief asset was the high speeds they could attain, which enabled the railway companies to drastically reduce the travelling times of their long-distance routes. From 1933, and for the next five years, the Bugatti company built and maintained more than a 100 railcar units, which resulted in a huge expansion of the factory and helped to see the company through the difficult times being experienced.

French railways made an early investment in electrification, particularly in the early 1930s. The Midi Railway built a number of locomotives – class BB4200 and class BB4730. They were relatively

A Bugatti petrol-powered railcar, built in the 1930s. This was a departure for the Bugatti Company who were better known for their luxury cars.

In December 1993, vintage electric locomotives of classes BB4200 and 4700 await their next duty at their Paris depot.

small locos with a maximum speed of 47 and 56 mph respectively and worked off 1500 v DC. Many were still in regular use as shunting locomotives right up to the late 1990s.

Although ordered by the Midi Railway, the class BB300 locomotives were actually delivered after the creation of SNCF; these were also in use until the 1990s and worked off 1500 v DC. Their final use was as shunting locomotives. Another early heavy shunting locomotive is the class CC1100, which were introduced in the early 1940s. Again they operated off 1500 v DC and examples are still operational today. As electrification developed, there was a parallel development in locomotives. Class BB8100 locomotives were derived from the BB300, and were mainly used for freight work. Operating off 1500 v DC, they were introduced between 1947 and 1955 and their maximum speed is 65 mph. The class was in regular use until comparatively recently. Dutch railways had the same type of locomotive as class 1100.

For express passenger work, early locomotives introduced in the early 1950s were class 2D2 9100. This class relied on large driving wheels as found in steam locomotives, but experience elsewhere in Europe – notably Switzerland – showed the advantages of all the wheels of a locomotive being powered. As a result, SNCF ordered class CC 7000/7001, all of which were delivered by 1955. Operating off 1500 v DC, they were a spectacular success, and locomotive 7107 is the joint holder of the 1955 world speed record of 206 mph. This class of locomotives was in regular use until the late 1990s. Some examples of these locomotives were also in use in Holland – class 1300 and Spain – class 276.

In December 1995, electric locomotive BB319, built in the late 1930s and still in old green livery, pauses before entering Paris Austerlitz station to pick up empty coaching stock.

The joint record holder with 7107 was BB 9004, an experimental/prototype locomotive built in 1954, which was in service on passenger and, latterly, freight duty until 1976. Operating off 1500 v DC, the locomotive is now preserved in the French National

Class BB348, in orange and grey livery, was used for empty coaching stock duties at Dijon where it is pictured in August 1997.

Electric locomotive 8164 of class BB8100, introduced in 1947, is pictured at Nimes in August 1997 awaiting its next freight duty.

Railway Museum at Mulhouse, France. There are several other 1500 v DC locomotives that need to be included in the story of French electrification. Class BB9200 was introduced in 1957 and worked on both passenger and freight work until comparatively recently, as did Class 9400 introduced in 1959. Forty-two locomotives of this class were converted for push-pull passenger train work, and were renumbered in the 9600 series. Class BB9300 is an improved version of class 9200 and the locomotives are used on express passenger work. Introduced in 1967, the 40 locomotives in the class have a maximum speed of 100 mph. Class BB8500 was introduced in 1964 and still works on both passenger and freight duties. In 1969, class CC6500 made its debut as a powerful passenger and freight locomotive and

Introduced in the 1930s, center-cab electric locomotive CC1111 pauses before its next shunting duty at Toulouse freight yard, in August 1995. This class worked for over 50 years, before withdrawal.

Preserved vintage electric locomotive 2D2 9135 poses on the turntable at Paris Charolais in October 1991. Two of these early 1950s express passenger locomotives are preserved.

Electric locomotive CC7126 is pictured at Nimes in March 2000. Sister locomotive CC7107 is the joint holder of the 1955 speed record of 206 mph with BB9004.

Electric locomotive BB9004 is pictured at the French National Railway Museum in Mulhouse. Introduced in 1954, this locomotive is the joint holder of the 1955 speed record of 206 mph.

Electric locomotive 9336 of class BB9300, moves onto its next train at Tarbes, in November 2001. These express passenger locomotives were introduced in 1967 and are still in regular service.

Electric locomotive CC6574 is pictured at Nimes in March 2000. Originally express passenger locomotives, the class ended its days on freight duties.

finally, between 1976 and 1985, 240 class 7200 locomotives were introduced for mixed traffic use. Similar locomotives are used by the Morocco state railways – classes E1300 and E1350. In parallel with the 1500 v DC system, SNCF has also invested in an electrification system based on 25KV, which is mainly focused on the central and northern parts of France.

A line-up of 1950s BB12000 electric locomotives for freight work at Woippy freight yard near Metz, in November 1994.

The early locomotives were classes BB12000 and BB14000 for freight and BB13000 for passenger and freight. The first examples came into service in 1954 and each class worked until the 1990s, and in the case of the 12000s, into the 21st century. Similar locomotives to BB12000 are still at work in Luxembourg today – class 3600.

Classes BB16000 – passenger traffic – and BB16500 – passenger and freight – were each introduced in 1958 and are still working today. BB16500 numbered almost 300 locomotives. Class BB17000 was introduced in 1965 and is still used on suburban passenger trains in the Paris area.

Class BB15000 was introduced in 1971 and still work on the express services from Paris to the east of France. When you see an example of this class, it is easy to spot the pleasing and novel styling of the locomotive, developed by Paul Arzens. These features are also reflected in several other electric and diesel locomotive classes in France and elsewhere, such as Slovenia and Morocco.

BB17000 electric locomotive 8 17084 is pictured in Paris, in September 2005. The 8 before the number denotes a Paris passenger service locomotive.

To enable SNCF to provide through services, which took account of both the 1500 v DC and 25KV systems, a series of dual power locomotive classes was developed in the 1960s and 1970s. Classes BB25100, BB25150 and BB25200 were introduced in the late 1960s and are still in use today on both passenger and freight work. Class BB22200, totalling over 200 locomotives, was introduced between 1976 and 1986 and are used on both express passenger and freight work. Class BB20200 comprises 13 dual-voltage freight locomotives built in 1970. With a maximum speed of 87 mph, the class operates into Germany and Switzerland but are now

Electric locomotive BB15060 Creil is pictured at Metz in October 1992. This class works express passenger trains from Paris to Strasbourg.

BB electric locomotive 4 25109 is pictured at Woippy freight yard in July 2003. The No. 4 before the locomotive number denotes a freight locomotive.

Express passenger train locomotive CC40110 is pictured at Brussels Midi station in April 1996. This class has now been withdrawn.

Triple-voltage locomotive BB36039 is pictured at Dijon in March 2000. This class works freight trains into Belgium and Italy.

New BB electric locomotives for freight work, number 4 27010, is pictured at Miramas in June 2002.

being displaced by new class BB37000. Finally, to enable through passenger services to operate into Belgium, Netherlands and Germany, class CC40100 was introduced in the 1960s, with the capability of working under four different voltages. Belgium had similar locomotives – class 1800.

In 1988, SNCF began to modernise its electric locomotive fleet with the introduction of dual voltage "Sybic" class BB26000, for both passenger and freight work. Subsequently, the initial order was amended to enable a number of locomotives to be triple voltage for work into Belgium and Italy, as class BB36000.

The process of updating has continued by the recent introduction of classes BB27000 – dual voltage – and BB37000 – multi-voltage – for freight work. The major impact of the introduction of these locomotives and other new locomotive types currently on order, will be the withdrawal from service of a significant number of older locomotives.

Diesel locomotive number 62012 at Lens in October 1991. These American built locomotives are now withdrawn but several examples have been preserved.

Diesel locomotive BB63401 is pictured at Le Mans in August 1997. This is one of a large class of locomotives for shunting and short trip freight work.

In parallel with its use of electric locomotives, SNCF has an extensive range of diesel locomotives for shunting duties and for passenger and freight work over both electrified and non-electrified lines. The first class of note is the A1AA1A 62000 known as "Baldwins," because of the American constructor of these locomotives. Introduced immediately after World War Two, they provided a heavy shunting service in northern and eastern France. They lasted well into the 1990s and some examples have been preserved. The major diesel type found in all parts of France comprises classes BB63000, BB63400 and BB63500, which were introduced in the 1950s and 1960s. Many of the original 800 plus locomotives are still working and a number have been modified to provide more tractive effort – for example class BB64700. One class introduced in the late 1950s and worthy of mention is the CC65500. It was originally designed for freight work, but in recent years has been employed on construction trains, associated with the new TGV high speed lines. Another significant locomotive type is represented by classes BB66000 and BB66400, introduced in the 1960s for both passenger and freight duties, but now largely employed on freight work. A number of these locomotives have been modified for shunting duties. To reflect the demands of passenger and freight work on non-electrified lines, SNCF introduced class BB67000 in the early 1960s. A number of these locomotives were modified in the 1980s for work on construction trains on the new TGV lines, and in recent years the modified class has provided stand-by locomotives for use on emergency trains on TGV lines.

As a further development of class BB67000, Class BB67300 was introduced in 1967 for both passenger and freight work. Classes BB67400 and A1AA1A68000 were introduced in 1969 and 1963 respectively, initially for passenger work but later for mixed traffic. A small number of class A1AA1A68000 were re-engined to enhance their performance on freight work. Finally, SNCF intro-

BB diesel locomotive 4 69484 - originally 66484 - is pictured at Chalindrey in September 2005. The 9 in the number denotes a modified locomotive.

Diesel locomotive BB67549 waits at Cannes station in June 2002, prior to leaving with a local passenger service.

duced its most powerful diesel in 1967 – class CC72000. These locomotives perform well on high speed passenger services mainly in the north and east of France and are also used on freight duties.

To provide shunting services in stations, goods yards and in the large rolling stock workshops, SNCF has used a variety of locomotives over the years including classes Y2400, Y5100 – both built in the 1960s – and Y6200, Y 6300 and Y6400 – built in the early 1950s. All of these are now largely withdrawn from service, although some are still used as shunters in locomotive depots. The main classes now in use are Y7100 – introduced in 1958, Y7400 introduced between 1963 and 1972, with the most modern class Y8000, introduced between 1977 and 1990. In total, there are over 1200 of these locomotives in use.

France also has a number of interesting private railways and preservation lines. For example an 0-6-0 tank locomotive, number 36, is operated by the Transport Museum of the Sausseron Valley (MTVS). The locomotive was built in 1925.

Steam 0-6-0 tank locomotive number 36, operated by MTVS, is about to depart on a passenger service in September 2005.

Vintage 1950s shunting locomotive Y6213 is pictured at Dijon Locomotive Depot Open Day in June 1994.

Steam locomotive number 1 of the 1000 mm La Baie de Somme railway (CFBS) is a narrow gauge 2-6-0 130t Corpet-Louvet tank locomotive built in 1906. The Chemin de Fer de la Mure operates a 1000 mm electrified line and uses a variety of locomotives. Of particular interest are a small class of locomotives built by the Swiss company Secheron, in 1932, that have a dual voltage capacity and a maximum speed of 20 mph.

Shunting locomotive Y7138 at Marseilles in August 1995. This class was the first of SNCF's new shunting type, introduced in the late 1950s.

CC diesel class 1 72172 is pictured at Chalindrey in September 2005. The 1 before the number denotes a long distance passenger service locomotive.

German Railways

The German railway system is extensive and uses a significant number of diesel and electric locomotives. Recent years have seen the withdrawal from service of some of the older classes of locomotive and a large number of new electric locomotives have been introduced. It is likely that orders will be placed in the near future for new diesel locomotives to replace some of the existing diesel types. While the state system has focused on new locomotives and enhancing the service it provides, particularly using the ICE trains, a significant number of steam locomotives have been retained in museums, at preservation sites and displayed adjacent to various stations and at other sites throughout the country.

The British built Adler 2-2-2 locomotive was introduced in 1835 and hauled the first train in Germany on the Nurenberg to Furth Railway.

The first train ran in Germany in 1835 when the "Adler" locomotive completed a journey from Nurnberg to Furth. The locomotive was built by Robert Stephenson in Newcastle upon Tyne in England and in fact the driver was also English, having been employed specifically for the demonstration! The development of the railway system in subsequent years owes much to the various Lander (regions) who built their own systems and then collaborated to create a unified system.

There was an early indication of a commitment to the use of electric trains with the building of the world's first electric locomotive in Berlin in 1879 and the opening of the first long-distance electrified line in Germany – Bitterfeld to Dessau – in 1911. The first diesel-electric locomotive was introduced in 1912 and in 1933 the "Flying Hamburger" high-speed railcar began service.

The development of steam locomotives was not neglected and in 1936 locomotive 05 002 set a world record of 125.25 mph which was exceeded by the English locomotive "Mallard" in 1938 at a speed of 126 mph.

In structural terms, the Deutsche Reichsbahn Gesellschaft (DRG) was created in 1924, which became DR in 1937. In 1945 after the war a series of zones was created and operated by the allies until the creation of the German Federal and German Democratic Republics in 1949, in West and East Germany respectively. This political division was mirrored by the creation of DB – Deutsche Bundesbahn – and DR – Deutsche Reichsbahn – in 1952. The latter part of the twentieth century saw the further development of the system by the introduction of the first high-speed line in 1986. In terms of locomotive performance, electric locomotive 103 118 achieved 158 mph in 1973 and this was improved by electric locomotive 120 001 in 1984 by a recorded speed of 165.6 mph. In 1988 the prototype ICE achieved a new German high-speed record of 254.3 mph.

The "Flying Hamburger" high-speed railcars were introduced in 1933 for journeys between Berlin and Hamburg, followed later by other German cities.

In January 1994, DB and DR were combined to form Deutsche Bahn AG (DBAG) and this enabled the development of the national system to continue by the creation of an extensive system of new high-speed lines, the acquisition of new trains and the renewal of the locomotive fleet. Within this overall framework, the individual German regions have invested in railway provision and there are a large number of private railway companies providing passenger, freight and railway infrastructure services – sometimes using ex-DB locomotives!

A replica of the first locomotive to run in Germany, the "Adler," a 2-2-2, is at the Verkehrsmuseum in Nurenberg. This museum has a large number of locomotives and some very fine and rare examples. Unfortunately, the "Adler" replica – which itself was over 70 years old – and several other vintage steam and diesel locomotives were badly damaged or destroyed in a fire at the Nurnberg depot preservation store, in October 2005. In addition to the national collection, Germany has a large number of preserved locomotives some of which are still used on special trains and occasionally on DB scheduled services. There is also a thriving system of narrow gauge lines mainly in the old East. Preserved steam locomotives are found throughout Germany and the principal classes/types are well-represented. Perhaps the most notable of the early steam locomotives was the super-heated Prussian P8 class. Almost 4000 of these locomotives were built in the first quarter of the twentieth century, as passenger and freight locomotives. With a maximum speed of 62 mph, they were widely used throughout Europe and in Germany went under the designation of class 38.

Class 01 Pacific type was first introduced in 1925 and had a maximum speed of 80 mph. These were magnificent locomotives that were well able to maintain tight schedules, often travelling at more than a mile a minute. They were followed in 1940 by class 01.10 as a streamlined express locomotive with a maximum speed of 87 mph. Class 03 was introduced in the 1930s as a lighter version of class 01 and class 03.10 – a significantly lighter version of class 01.10 – was introduced in 1940.

Class 62 were a class of tank locomotives, introduced in 1928 for passenger services, and they were 4-6-2 locomotives with a maximum speed of 65 mph. The Class 41, introduced in 1938, were mixed traffic 2-8-2 locomotives, with a maximum speed of 56 mph, and class 44 were heavy freight 2-10-0 locomotives introduced in 1926 and built well into the 1940s. They had a maximum speed of 44 mph and over 1700 locomotives were built. One of the class was the last steam locomotive in DB service in 1977, although some DR locomotives ran into the 1980s. Over 3,000 class 50 2-10-0 locomotives were built between 1939 and 1948, as main and branch line locomotives with a maximum speed of

The builder's plate of 4-6-2 express steam locomotive 01.111 showing that it was built in 1934 by Schwartzkopff in Berlin.

In May 2002, preserved steam class 01 4-6-2 express locomotive number 01.164 is pictured at the German National Railway Museum in Nurenberg, alongside 2-8-2 passenger and freight locomotive number 41.1185.

4-6-2 tank passenger train locomotive number 62 015 is pictured at the Dresden Altstadt preservation depot, in April 1995. This type was introduced in 1928 and the locomotives were capable of achieving 62 mph.

50 mph. The major development of this locomotive was class 52 Kriegslok, of which over 6000 were built from the early 1940s. They were a basic, economically-built austerity locomotive and were widely used throughout Europe. They had a maximum speed of 50 mph. Class 23 was introduced in 1959 as a 2-6-2 locomotive with a maximum speed of 68 mph and were largely a means of modernising the fleets of both DB and DR. Early locomotive types

Preserved class 41 2-8-2 locomotive number 042 096 powers out of Braunschweig with a special train, in April 2004. This locomotive dates from 1938.

Ex SZD (USSR) locomotive TE 5933 is pictured at Lobau locomotive depot in April 1995. Originally, the locomotive was Kriegslok 52 5933.

2-6-2 locomotive 23 1019 poses at Cottbus in May 2003. Class 23 was built in 1959 as modern steam locomotives for DB and DR.

Class 17 4-6-0 locomotive number 1135 (actually 17 1055) waits for its next duty at the Dresden steam festival, in April 1995.

included class 55 that was introduced in 1905 as a 0-8-0 locomotive and the stylish class 17 was built in 1913 as a 4-6-0 locomotive . Class 57 was a 0-10-0 tank locomotive introduced in the early 1920s.

Finally, in terms of standard gauge locomotives, Class 18.2 is a streamlined Pacific locomotive that was created in 1961 from a 4-6-2 tank locomotive, and parts from a 2-10-2 locomotive. It is a magnificent machine. Its top speed of 100 mph makes it the fastest existing steam locomotive in the world.

Germany's narrow gauge lines comprise 1000 mm, 900 mm or 750 mm gauge systems, and use a fascinating range of steam and diesel locomotives. A number of the lines are now privatised but the locomotives have not lost their character. The 1000 mm system centres on the Harz Mountains and surrounding area. The steam class 99.5900 series comprises four Mallet steam locomotives, three of which were built in the late 1890s and one in 1918. They are 0-4-4-0 tank locomotives with a maximum speed of 20 mph. Steam locomotive 99.6001 is a 2-6-2 tank locomotive built in 1939 with a maximum speed of 30 mph. The steam class 99.7200 series are 2-10-2 tank locomotives mainly built from 1954 to 1956 – the original locomotive of the class was built in 1931. They have a maximum speed of 25 mph and are powerful, attractive locomotives. The 900 mm system is based around Bad Doberan in Northern Germany and is known as the "Molli." It mainly uses two steam locomotive of class 99.2300 series which are 2-8-2 tank locomotives, built in 1932, with a maximum speed of 30 mph. The 750 mm system uses a variety of steam locomotives on its routes in the eastern part of Germany. Class 99.1500 are Meyer type 0-4-4-0 tank locomotives built between 1899 and 1921. Locomotives 099.722 – 735 are 2-10-2 tank locomotives built from 1928–1933. Locomotives 099.736-757 have the same wheel arrangement and were built between 1952 and 1957. Finally, the two locomotives previously numbered 99.4632 and 4633 and now MH52 and 53 are 0-8-0 well-tanks, built in 1914 and 1925 for the Rugenschen

Locomotive 18 201 is pictured at Meiningen in June 1996. Built in 1961, this 4-6-2 locomotive is the world's fastest existing steam locomotive.

Kleinbahnen (RuKB). Each of these classes has a maximum speed of 20 mph. The system based on the island of Wangerooge off the North German coast, has several diesel locomotives numbered 399.101-104 built in the 1950s and two diesels built in 1999 and numbered 399.107 and 108. They are 1000 mm gauge locomotives with a maximum

Narrow gauge 0-4-4-0 tank locomotive number 99 5901 waits to take over its next service at Wernigerode, in April 2004.

Unique narrow gauge 2-6-2 tank locomotive number 99 6001 pauses at Wernigerode before moving to take its next train, in April 1998.

speed of 13 mph. There is also a class 99 0-6-0 tank locomotive preserved on the island which was built in 1929.

The large number of classes of electric locomotives reflects the size of the electrified system and the development by DB and DR of their own locomotive types. The creation of the unified DB AG resulted in a rationalization of the locomotive fleet and the withdrawal from service of a large number of locomotives – principally from the old DR classes.

The first practical electric locomotive in the world was built by Siemens in 1879. It carried passengers at the Berlin trade exhibition in that year on a narrow gauge track and is now preserved at the Deutsches Museum in Munich. A number of later

Powerful narrow gauge 2-10-2 tank locomotive number 99 7244 is stabled at Wenigerode, in April 1998. The class was introduced in 1954.

electric locomotives built in the 1920s and 1930s have also been preserved, some as working locomotives. In common with all but one class of German electric locomotives, they operate on the 15 kv 16 Hz overhead system. Class E04 was introduced in 1933 and class E18 was built in the mid-1930s, as express locomotives. They had a maximum speed of 93 mph and Austria had the same type of locomo-

The "Molli" system's narrow gauge 2-8-2 tank locomotive number 99 2323 accelerates up the gradient towards Bad Doberan station, in March 1999.

Narrow gauge 2-10-2 tank locomotive number 99 784 eases into Putbus station at the end of its journey from Gohren, in May 2001. This locomotive was built in 1953.

Narrow gauge 0-6-0 tank locomotive number 99 211 on Wangerooge Island off the North German coast, in May 2001.This locomotive dates from1929.

The first practical electric locomotive built by Siemens in 1879. It carried passengers at the Berlin Trade Exhibition and is now preserved.

tive as class 1018. Class E44 were mixed traffic locomotives with a maximum speed of 56 mph and were built throughout the 1930s. The E60s were designed for use as station pilot locomotives with a low maximum speed of 56 mph and were introduced in the early 1930s. Class E94 were initially built during the 1940s with further examples being built well into the 1950s. They had a maximum speed of 34 mph and were also in regular use in Austria as class 1020, until well into the 1990s – an example is shown in the Austrian section of this book. In terms of more modern locomotives, the principal DB express passenger locomotive until the turn of the century was class 103. They were introduced in 1969 and had a maximum speed of 124 mph. Following unification, these impressive locomotives were responsible for express services throughout Germany and a number of examples have now been preserved. Class 109 was introduced by DR in 1961, mainly as a passenger locomotive

Vintage electric locomotive number E04 01 at Dessau in November 2002. This is one of two preserved members of the class, introduced in 1933.

Pre-war electric locomotive number E18 08 waits to move off from its stabling point in Munich, in July 1996.

and lasted until the late 1990s. They had a maximum speed of 75 mph and a small number of locomotives have been acquired by private locomotive operators in Germany. DB class 110 was introduced in 1956 and 400 examples were built. Originally designed as a main-line locomotive with a maximum speed of 93 mph, the introduction of more modern classes of locomotive and unit trains has reduced their workload. However, many of the class are still in service. Class 113 is a small group of 110s geared for running at 100 mph. DB class 111, introduced in 1974, comprises over 200 locomotives and is a development of class 110. These locomotives are still providing excellent service on long-distance and push/pull passenger trains. Class 112 was introduced by DR in 1990 and comprises

Class 103 electrics were DBs express passenger locomotives for many years. Number 103 208 pauses at Bremen station in May 1993.

over 100 locomotives with a maximum speed of 100 mph. The locomotives are used on express passenger work throughout Germany with some locomotives reclassified as class 114 for use on local passenger services, including push/pull trains. Class 120 was the first of the most modern class of locomotives, introduced by DB in 1987 and with a maximum speed of 124 mph. It comprises 60 locomotives and they have been responsible for express passenger work for some years and can also be seen working freight trains. With the introduction of the most recent classes of locomotive, their role is now somewhat diminished. DB class 139/140 is a large class – over 900 locomotives – and is essentially a class 110 designed for freight work. With a maximum speed of 68 mph, the locomotives have been the mainstay of the system since their introduction between 1957 and 1973, but they are now being

Blue liveried electric express passenger train locomotive number 110 316 waits in the sun at Dortmund, in April 1994.

Electric locomotive number 110 423 is about to depart from Darmstadt station in April 2004 with a local stopping train service. This class was one of DBs standard passenger locomotives for many years.

Electric locomotive number 120 118 moves from its stabling point to pick up its next passenger train at Dortmund, in April 2004.

withdrawn from service in large numbers as new locomotive classes are introduced. DB class 141 are general-purpose locomotives that are used mainly on push/pull passenger services. Built between 1956 and 1969, with a maximum speed of 75 mph, the class of over 400 locomotives is now being withdrawn as more modern locomotives come into service. DR class 142 were designed as a freight version of class 109, and have all been withdrawn apart from a few exceptions currently in use by private railway companies. Introduced in the period 1962 to

Class 140 freight locomotive number 140 823 in old green livery, waits at Dortmund for its next duty, in April 1994.

In turquoise and blue livery, class 140 locomotive number 140 657 is stabled at Lehrte in May 1994 before its next freight duty.

Passenger locomotive number 141 387 waits at Emden station in June 2003, before leaving with a local service train.

Locomotive number 142 175 heads a line-up of members of the same class at Seddin, in May 1994. This class is now withdrawn.

1976, there were over 300 locomotives in the class, which had a top speed of 62 mph. All of the locomotives were fitted for push/pull passenger work but this could not prevent their displacement by more modern locomotives. DR class 143 has been a major success and now sees use throughout the railway system. Introduced between 1982 and 1990, the locomotives are all fitted with push/pull equipment for passenger work. There are almost 700 locomotives in the class which has a maximum

Freight locomotive number 150 146 poses in the sun at Osnabruck in May 1993. This type of locomotive is now largely withdrawn from service.

speed of 68 mph. DB classes 150 and the improved version – class 151 – are used for heavy freight work. Built between 1957 and 1973, class 150 has largely been withdrawn but class 151 – built 1973 to 1977 – is likely to have a useful life for some years to come. Class 150 has a maximum speed of 62 mph and class 151's maximum is 68 mph. Class 155 was introduced by DR between 1974 and 1984, as a heavy freight locomotive, with a maximum speed of 72 mph. Many of the original 270-plus locomotives

Green liveried freight class number 151 051 pauses before joining its train at Frankfurt, in February 1993. This class is still providing good service.

Passenger and freight locomotive number 180 017 waits in Dresden freight yard before its next duty, in May 1997. This type is also found in the Czech Republic as class 371/372.

are still in service and can be found all over Germany. DR class 171 is a small class of 15 locomotives used on the 25 kv, 50 Hz, Rubelandbahn system from Blankenburg to Konigshutte, in the former East Germany. Built in 1964, the class derived from classes 109 and 142 and has a maximum speed of 50 mph. These locomotives have now been placed in store pending a decision on the future of the line and what type of locomotives should be used. DR class 180 was introduced between 1987 and 1991 for passenger and freight working between Dresden and Prague, in the Czech Republic. The 20 locomotives each have a maximum speed of 68 mph and the Czech Republic has the same locomotives as class 371/372, and one of the DB locomotives has now been transferred to that country to augment its fleet. DB class 181 are dual voltage locomotives, for work into Luxembourg and France, and were introduced in two batches between 1967 and 1975. The 27 locomotives have a maximum speed of 100 mph. In 1996, the first of 145 class 101 locomotives came into service for express passenger work. With a maximum speed of 136 mph, they have displaced the traditional express locomotives such as classes 103 and 110. A number of the class 101s have distinctive liveries which advertise particular commercial companies or a message related to a particular issue. Also in 1996, class 145 was introduced largely as a freight locomotive but with a number of the

Dual-voltage locomotive number 181 202 waits to depart from Heidelburg station. These locomotives work across borders into France and Luxembourg.

80 locomotives in the class being equipped for 100 mph running on regional passenger trains. The normal maximum speed is 87 mph. In 2001, the first locomotives of 31 locomotives of class 146.0 were introduced for regional passenger work and are push/pull fitted. They have been followed by sub-classes 146.1 and 146.2, and all the locomotives have a maximum speed of 100 mph.

Class 152 was introduced in 1997 for freight work. The 171 locomotives have a maximum speed of 87 mph and are widely used throughout Germany. Class 182 comprises 25 locomotives for freight work which are identical to the Austrian class 1116. They have a maximum speed of 87 mph. The major investment in new locomotives has been class 185 for freight work. The 400 locomotives on order are still being delivered, with the first appearing in 2000. They have a maximum speed of 87 mph and are dual voltage machines, enabling them to work into a

Modern express passenger train locomotive number 101 145 waits to accelerate its train out of Halle station, in April 2004.

One of DB's new electric locomotives for freight work, number 152 070, waits at Nurnberg before taking over its next train, in August 2002.

Freight locomotive number 182 018 waits at Muhldorf in May 2002 before its next duty. This type is also found in Austria as class 1116.

Classic main line diesel locomotive number 220 071 is preserved at the Speyer Museum where it is preserved, in May 2002.

In immaculate condition, diesel locomotive number 204 671 poses in the sun at Saalfeld prior to its next duty, in September 2005.

Heavy shunting diesel locomotive number 298 156 is stabled at Engelsdorf, in April 2004. The yellow fitting on the front is an automatic coupler.

Diesel locomotive number 212 173 is stabled at Frankfurt before resuming shunting duties, in April 2000. This class is now largely withdrawn.

Diesel locomotive for passenger and freight work, number 215 134, prepares to move to its train at Ehrang, in October 1992.

number of other countries. Class 189, introduced in 2002, comprises 100 four-voltage freight locomotives, derived from class 152. They have a maximum speed of 87 mph and are designed to work into a number of other countries, for example Benelux, Poland and Italy.

In common with electric locomotives, German diesel classes have been rationalized since unification primarily because of the impact of new unit trains. Again, the former DR classes have been par-

A line-up of now withdrawn class 216 diesel freight locomotives, headed by number 216 119, at Duisberg in August 1993.

ticularly affected. DB class V200 were express passenger hydraulic locomotives with a maximum speed of 87 mph. Introduced in 1953, they gave excellent service until their withdrawal from service in the 1980s. Several examples have been preserved in Germany with ex-German locomotives operated until comparatively recently in Switzerland and in Greece. The former DR classes 201, 202 and 204 which totalled almost 900 locomotives are now largely withdrawn from service. They were built

Diesel locomotive number 217 020 is stabled at Nurenberg, in July 1996. This class preceded class 218 which is identical in appearance.

Romanian built passenger train locomotive number 229 120 waits at Berlin Pankow for its next duty, in May 1994.

Preserved diesel locomotive number 120 338 poses at Dresden Altstadt in May 1995. This type is found in a number of former eastern bloc countries.

Main line freight and passenger train locomotive number 228 683 is stabled at Lobau, in May 1995. This class has been withdrawn.

between 1964 and 1978 with the class designation being based on engine type. They were mixed traffic locomotives with a maximum speed of 62 mph. A small number of class 201 locomotives were converted for use on the narrow gauge Harz system and were designated class 199 – their maximum speed being reduced to 31 mph. Several class 201s were adapted in the late 1970s to become class 298 heavy shunting locomotives, with a maximum speed of 37 mph. This class was augmented by class 293 which was derived from class 201 and which subsequently became class 298.3, following re-building in 1981. DB classes 211, 212, 213 and 214 totalled over 700 locomotives and were passenger and freight locomotives with a maximum speed of 62 mph. Class 211 was built between 1958 and 1963 with class 212 introduced in 1962, as a higher powered version. Class 213 comprises a small number of locomotives rebuilt from class 212 locomotives to cope with steep gradients. Class 214 are a small class of rebuilt 212s for hauling emergency trains for high-speed lines. Although class 211 locomotives have been withdrawn from service as have the majority of class 212, a number of each class has been acquired by railway construction companies and see wide use throughout Europe, including Britain.

DB classes 215 and 216 were introduced in 1968 and 1964 respectively as passenger and freight locomotives with a maximum speed of 87 mph (215) and 75 mph (216). Virtually all of the 216s have been withdrawn from service as have a number of 215s. Over 60 class 215s have been reassigned to freight only duties and have been redesignated as class 225. Class 217 was introduced by DB in 1965 as a small class of locomotives with train heating and a maximum speed of 75 mph. They are used as passenger and freight locomotives. Following success with this class, DB introduced class 218 which comprised over 400 locomotives for passenger and freight work. They are the most powerful diesel class with a maximum speed of 87 mph. Although a small number of locomotives have been withdrawn, it is likely that the class will be in use for some years to come. DR class 219 are impressive-looking locomotives introduced in 1976 with a maximum speed of 75 mph. Twenty locomotives were rebuilt into a higher powered class 229 which could attain a speed of 87 mph. Neither of the classes has been a success and they have largely been withdrawn from service. Class 220 was introduced in 1966 as heavy duty locomotives with a maximum speed of 62 mph. These Soviet built locomotives are found throughout the old Eastern Bloc countries as class M62 in a number of countries, class 781 in Czech Republic

A pair of class 232s numbers 232 288 and 232 588 in old and new livery are stabled at Cottbus, in April 1995.

Main line diesel freight locomotive number 232 534 waits for its next duty in the yard at Lehrte, in April 2004.

and Slovakia and ST44 in Poland. All of the German locomotives have now been withdrawn from service. DR class 228 was a large class of locomotives introduced in the early sixties mainly for passenger work. They had a maximum speed of 75 mph and the class had a series of sub-classes as new engines were fitted. They have now all been withdrawn although some examples have been preserved. DR classes 230, 231, 232 and 234 comprise nearly 1000 locomotives built in the Soviet Union. Introduced in the 1970s with a maximum speed ranging from 62 mph – class 231– to 87 mph – class 234 – all of classes 230 and 231 have been withdrawn from service. Class 232 can still be found on both passenger and freight trains and class 234 mainly on passenger trains. DB class 290 comprises over 400 locomotives used as heavy duty shunting locomotives and for working freight trains for relatively short distances. They have a maximum speed of 50 mph. Built between 1964 and 1974, a large number of the class has been fitted for remote control and has been re-designated as class 294. It is likely that some locomotives will receive new engines and will be designated class 296 with a maximum speed of 62 mph. The remaining diesel

Heavy shunting locomotive number 290 056 in old turquoise and blue livery, is stabled at Bremen, in May 1993.

Vintage ex DR small diesel shunting locomotive number 310 589 pauses at Meiningen in June 1996. This class was introduced in the early 1930s.

A former DR diesel shunting locomotive number 311 632 is stabled at Meiningen in June 1996. This class is now withdrawn.

One of DRs large class of diesel shunting locomotives, number 346 807, on duty at Wismar, in July 1994. The total of this type was over 900 locomotives but most are now withdrawn.

classes can be defined as small shunting locomotives. The largest classes of locomotives are DR class 310 and DB class 322/323/324. Known as Kofs, these small locomotives were built in their hundreds from the 1930s through to the late 1950s and early 1960s. They had very low maximum speeds of 20 mph – class 310 – and 28 mph – 323 – and were used for light shunting work in locomotive/carriage depots, railway works and stations. Although both classes have been withdrawn, a

Broad gauge diesel shunting locomotive number 347 975, at the train ferry terminal at Mukran, in May 2001.

Diesel shunting locomotive number 360 176 is stabled at Trier, in November 1994. This type is now DBs principal small shunting locomotive.

Germany's Siemens Company has a fleet of electric locomotives for hire to private railway companies and to state railways. Hungary (MAV) has two locomotives and they are shown at Ferencvaros, in October 2005.

number remain in use as depot shunting locomotives and in preservation. DR classes 311 and 312 were introduced in 1959 and 1967 respectively. Class 311 was a small shunting locomotive with a maximum speed of 21 mph. Class 312 was a more powerful development of class 311 with a higher maximum speed of up to 34 mph, and was used for light duties in stations, freight yards and locomotive depots. All of class 311 have been withdrawn but a few 312s remain. Classes 332, 333 and 335 were introduced by DB in 1959 – 332 – and 1967 – 333/335– as shunting locomotives with a maximum speed of 28 mph. Over 300 of class 332 were produced and a few still remain in service. Over 250 of class 333/335 were produced and many are still in service. Class 335 is a class 333 with remote control fitted. Classes 344, 345, 346 and 347 were introduced by DR in 1959 and the combined total of locomotives was over 900. They are general purpose shunting locomotives with a maximum speed of 37 mph. Class 347 are broad gauge locomotives for shunting work in the train ferry terminal at Mukran in Northern Germany. Although some locomotives are still in service, their numbers have been decimated because DB AG has favored other locomotive types. Classes 360, 361, 364 and 365 are the old DB equivalent of the DR classes mentioned in the previous paragraph. Introduced in the 1950s, the combined total was over 1,000 locomotives and many remain in service on station, locomotive/carriage depot and freight yard shunting duties. They have a maximum speed of 37 mph. Classes 364 and 365 are fitted with remote control and were previously classes 360 and 361 respectively. In the last few years, a number of locomotives have been fitted with more modern engines and have been re-designated as classes 362, originally 364, and 363, originally 365.

Finally, in Germany there has been a dramatic growth of private companies providing passenger and freight services and using the national railway network. The companies use a mixture of ex-DB locomotives, ex-industrial locomotives and newly built locomotives to provide their services.

Class 185 electric locomotives are used by a number of private railway companies in Germany. Rail4Chem's locomotive number 185-CL 007 displays its attractive livery at Nordhausen, in April 2004.

EVB is a private railway company that owns a number of ex-DB locomotives. Class 232 number 622 01 is stabled at Bremervorde, in May 2003. This was previously numbered 232 103.

Austrian Railways (OBB)

Austria has an interesting railway system, which has to provide services in mountainous areas and through narrow, winding valleys. In addition to the extensive standard gauge lines, there are several narrow gauge systems, some of which use steam locomotives. OBB has invested heavily in new electric and diesel locomotives in the last few years to update its fleet and to enable through services into adjacent countries to be provided. Austria also has a series of independent companies providing both freight and passenger services.

To celebrate 50 years of Bundesheer, new OBB class 1116 Taurus, locomotive, number 1116 246, has been given a special livery. This is one of 282 locomotives in this class.

Although the first horse-drawn railway service began in 1832, the first steam locomotive hauled train ran in 1837. Shortly afterwards, in 1839, the locomotive "Bucephalus" achieved the first official speed record of 39 mph and in 1840, Austria produced its first home-built locomotive "Patria."

One of OBB's new class 1016 locomotives prepares to depart with a container train. This locomotive is one of a class of 50 locomotives introduced in 2000.

In 1855 the first express service was introduced between Vienna and Ljublijana and in 1873 the first rack railway was introduced – the Kahlenberg Railway. 1880 saw the first electric railway at a trade exhibition in Vienna and the first public electric railway, between Modling and Hinterbruhl, was introduced in 1883. In 1911, the electrified Mariazell railway opened and is still operational today using vintage electric locomotives.

To enable railway services to operate through mountainous regions, a number of major tunnel construction projects were undertaken. The Arlberg tunnel – 33,800 feet – was constructed in the 1880s and opened up services west of Innsbruck. The Karawanken tunnel – 26,167 feet – and the Tauern tunnel – 28,050 feet – were constructed in the early 1900s and opened up services to the south of Austria, Slovenia and Italy.

Organizationally, there has been a number of significant changes since the creation of the state railways in 1841. In 1884 the Imperial and Royal State Railways were founded and the Railway Ministry was created in 1896. The state administration for traffic (DOStB) was created in 1918 and quickly became the OStB in 1919. The Osterreichische Bundesbahnen (OBB) came into existence in 1921 but was taken over by the DR in 1938. After the war, OBB was re-established in 1945. The last twenty years have seen significant developments. The huge Kledering marshalling yard near Vienna was opened in 1986. With 75 mi of track and a capability of dealing with over 6,000 wagons a day, the yard is one of the largest in Europe. In 1988, the first passenger train ran at 93 mph, and OBB has continued to make progress with the recent introduction of many new

Pictured at Vienna in July 1996, 52.4984 was originally a German "Kriegslok," then became a Yugoslavian railways class 33 before joining OBB's Nostalgia Fleet.

Veteran 4-6-2 tank locomotive, number 77.250, was built in 1927. It is now preserved and is shown at Vienna in August 1994. The locomotive is currently undergoing a restoration program.

electric locomotives. OBB has the capability of providing efficient freight and express passenger services throughout Austria and into other neighbouring countries. It also acquired a significant number of new freight and passenger diesel locomotives and is continuing to invest heavily in high-speed lines.

Austria has a fascinating range of locomotives within both the OBB system and independent companies. Narrow gauge steam and diesel locomotives can be found on a number of independent lines and OBB has established a "nostalgia" fleet of steam, electric and diesel locomotives. A large number of all types of locomotive have been preserved at museum sites or on plinths at stations. OBB has a fine pedigree of standard gauge steam locomotives and many classes are represented in the nostalgia fleet and in preservation generally. The class 52 Kriegslok is a relic of the last war and several examples have been retained in Austria and in other countries. Details of the locomotives can be found in the German section of this book.

Class 33 were 4-8-0 locomotives introduced in 1923 and class 77 were 4-6-2 tank locomotives introduced in 1927. Other tank locomotives were classes 93 and 95 built in the 1920s. They were 2-8-2 and 2-10-2 locomotives respectively. Narrow gauge steam locomotives in Austria are an interesting mix of design. Class 399 was introduced in 1906 for the 760 mm lines and the locomotives are capable of 25 mph. Class 999 was introduced in 1893 and are 0-4-2 tank locomotives operating on the rack railway 1000 mm gauge. This class was augmented in the 1990s by a further batch of brand new steam locomotives! The Achenseebahn has 3 similar locomotives introduced in 1899 and that railway has also recently acquired a newly built locomotive of the same type. The Zillertalbahn based in Jenbach operates a 760 mm system, and an ex-Yugoslavian class 83 0-8-2 locomotive is used. Built in 1909, it has a maximum speed of 22 mph. There are several interesting diesel

The Achenseebahn, based in Jenbach, has several interesting locomotives including 0-4-0 tank rack locomotive number 1 which was built in 1899.

This Zillertalbahn 0-8-2 tank locomotive was previously Yugoslavian Railway number 83.076. Number 4 pauses before its next duty at Jenbach in September 2002.

classes used by OBB. Class 2020.01 was a diesel hydraulic locomotive introduced in 1959 as a prototype. Fifty of this type were produced and were sold to Bulgarian railways where they became class 04. The prototype, which had a maximum speed of 120 kph, was withdrawn in 1980. Class 2045 were the first main-line diesel-locomotives and had a maximum speed of 50 mph. They were introduced in 1952.

The earliest electric locomotives still in service are narrow gauge class 1099, which date from 1909.

Prototype diesel locomotive, number 2020.01, is displayed at Vienna, in August 1994. This type was sold to Bulgarian railways as class 04.

Narrow gauge vintage electric locomotive, number 1099.006, prepares to leave Mariazell with an afternoon train to St Polten, in September 1994.

They were built for the 760 mm gauge St Polten – Mariazell line and have a maximum speed of 30 mph. Although these locomotives were given new bodies some 40 years ago, they still retain their character and hopefully they will last for some years to come. Class 1010 are standard gauge electric locomotives now withdrawn from service – although several have been preserved including some examples in the operational nostalgia fleet. They were introduced in 1955 for passenger and freight work and had a maximum speed of 80 mph.

Now a member of OBB's Nostalgia Fleet, electric locomotive number 1010.010 is stabled at Vienna, in April 2004.

Preserved electric locomotive number 1018.05 leaves its depot building in Linz, in August 1994. Several examples of this class have been preserved.

Massive electric locomotive number 1020.47 poses at Vienna Florisdorf in April 1998. The class was introduced in 1940 in Germany as class E94.

Class 1110 were introduced in 1956 and are also now withdrawn. Some examples have been retained as nostalgia locomotives and in general preservation. Their original use was as passenger and freight locomotives, particularly in the more mountainous areas, and they had a maximum speed of 68 mph. A number of the class had rheostatic braking for specific use as banking locomotives on the steep gradients associated with the mountain routes. One example of class 1018 has been retained in the nostalgia fleet and a number of other examples have been preserved in museums or on museum lines. Introduced in 1939 for express passenger work, these locomotives had a maximum speed of 80 mph. This locomotive type is also found in Germany as class E18. Class 1020, introduced in 1940, lasted well into the 1990s and a number have been preserved. The locomotives were originally class E94 in Germany but trans-

1950s electric locomotive, number 1041.024 is stabled at Attnang-Puchheim in July 1996. The class was used on passenger and freight trains but has now been withdrawn. Several examples have been preserved.

Electric locomotive number 1142.558, a member of a class of over 250 locomotives, awaits its next duty at Vienna, in April 2004.

ferred to OBB after the war. They were passenger and freight locomotives with a maximum speed of 56 mph and their distinctive shape and length made them look particularly impressive. Class 1040 was introduced in 1950 and were passenger and freight locomotives with a maximum speed of 50 mph. They have all been withdrawn, although a number have been preserved including two in the nostalgia fleet. Classes 1041 and 1141 were introduced in 1952 and 1955 respectively as passenger and freight locomotives with a maximum speed of 50 mph for 1041 and 68 mph for 1141. A number survive in preservation. Class 1042 was introduced in 1963, and comprises over 250 locomotives. They can be found all over Austria on passenger and freight work, although some locomotives have now been withdrawn as newer locomotives are introduced on their routes. The maximum speed of the class is 80 mph, although a significant number of locomotives fitted with improved braking capacity have a maximum speed of 93 mph. Some locomotives received different bodies as they were modernised in the 1990s. Another sizable class – over 200 locomotives – is class 1044, which provide passenger and freight services throughout Austria. They have a maximum speed of 100 mph and were introduced in 1974. Their work takes examples into Germany on both express passenger and freight work on a daily basis. The ten locomotives of class 1043 are the same as Swedish railways class R2 locomotives, and worked on passenger and freight duties in the south of Austria around Villach. Introduced in 1971 with a maximum speed of 84 mph, they have now been withdrawn in Austria. However, several locomotives have been sold to independent railways in Sweden. In its new guise, an example is shown in the Swedish section of this book. Classes 1046 and 1146 were passenger locomotives that have now been withdrawn. Class 1046 was introduced in 1956 as motorised luggage vehicles and saw regular service until the turn of the century. In 1987, two locomotives were converted to class 1146 with a dual voltage capacity to enable them to work into Hungary. Each class had a maximum speed of 78 mph. Class 1822 was a small

Class 1044 comprises passenger and freight locomotives. Number 1044.056 waits in the sun at Linz for its next duty, in August 1994.

Dual-voltage locomotive, number 1822.005, is stabled at Innsbruck, in September 2002. This class is likely to have a limited future with OBB.

A pair of class 1014 locomotives, numbers 1014.003 and 1114.017, stable at Vienna, in August 1994 within a few months of their delivery.

class, introduced in 1991 as dual-voltage locomotives, with a maximum speed of 87 mph. Their success appears to have been limited since they do not have a long term future with OBB.

In 1993, OBB introduced class 1014/1114, which have a dual voltage capacity to enable the locomotives to work beyond the Austrian borders, notably into Hungary. The locomotives have a maximum speed of 106 mph and are used on express passenger work. This class of 20 locomotives was the first successful new technology class in Austria but, to an extent, their role has now been taken over by recently introduced locomotives.

The first of a class of 282 locomotives, number 1116.001 heads a freight through Gyor in Hungary, in October 2005.

"Taurus" Classes 1016 and 1116 are the recently introduced classes of electric locomotive for freight and passenger work. Introduced in 2000, Class 1016 are 50 single voltage locomotives with a maximum speed of 143 mph. Class 1116 is the dual-voltage version with the same maximum speed and consists of 282 locomotives. Both classes can be found throughout Austria and in Germany. Class 1116 also work into Hungary. OBB has now introduced a tri-voltage version as class 1216, designed to work into a number of other countries, including Italy.

OBB also has a number of classes of electric shunting/short trip working locomotives. The vintage classes included class 1045, introduced in 1927 with a maximum speed of 37 mph. The class is now withdrawn although examples can still be seen. Class 1245 was used on a variety of freight duties and has

Preserved vintage electric locomotive, number 1045.12, at Attnang-Pushheim in July 1996. The class was introduced in the mid-1920s.

Vintage electric shunting locomotive, number 1062.010, at Vienna in April 1998. This class has been withdrawn, although two examples have been preserved.

Narrow gauge diesel locomotive, number 2095.012, waits at St Polten Alpen for its next job. The class was introduced in 1958 and examples are found on most of OBB's narrow gauge lines.

A rather forlorn-looking narrow gauge diesel locomotive, number 2092.002, is stabled in the snow near Zell am See in March 2003. This class was introduced in the early 1940s.

Locomotive number 2043.069 at Villach, in April 2003. This class was one of OBB's standard diesels before the arrival of class 2016.

also been withdrawn, although several have been preserved. Introduced in 1934, these locomotives had a maximum speed of 50 mph. Class 1062 was found in the freight yards around Vienna and was introduced in 1955. They have all been withdrawn but preserved examples remain. They had a low maximum speed of 30 mph. Class 1063 was the first modern shunting locomotive and was introduced in 1982. Over half of the 50 locomotives are dual-voltage and the class has a maximum speed of 62 mph which enables short trip working to take place. Class 1163 are single-voltage center-cab locomotives, introduced in 1994. The 20 locomotives have a maximum speed of 62 mph which makes them ideally suited to a variety of freight duties. Class 1064 was introduced in 1984 as heavy duty shunting locomotives for use in the Kledering marshalling yard in Vienna. The 10 locomotives have a maximum speed of 50 mph. OBB has several classes of narrow gauge diesel locomotives. Class 2095 is the most powerful class and consists of 15 locomotives introduced in 1958 for 760 mm lines. The class is used on passenger and freight work and has a maximum speed of 37 mph. Class 2092 is used on 760 mm lines on light duties. Introduced in 1943, the locomotives have a maximum speed of 16 mph. Class 2190 originally comprised 3 locomotives introduced in 1934 for use on the 760 mm system. They were used on shunting duties and had a maximum speed of 28 mph. The surviving locomotive worked until the turn of the century and is now preserved.

Ex DB class 211 diesels were acquired by OBB and became class 2048. Number 2048.029 pauses between duties at Vienna Nord, in July 1996.

Class 2050 locomotive number 2050.02 sports its original green livery at Vienna, in April 2004. Several locomotives of this class have been preserved.

OBB has several classes of main-line, standard gauge diesel locomotives. Class 2043 was introduced in 1964 and is used on both passenger and freight work. There were originally over 80 locomotives which have a maximum speed of 68 mph. Some locomotives have been withdrawn as the latest diesel classes are introduced. Class 2143 was introduced in 1965 and is used on passenger and freight work. The 77 locomotives have a maximum speed of 62 mph.

Class 2048 were originally DB class 211 which were purchased by OBB in 1991 and fitted with new engines. They had a maximum speed of 68 mph and were used on freight duties. The class has now been withdrawn but several locomotives have been acquired by independent railways in Austria and Germany. Class 2050 were heavy freight locomotives introduced in 1958. The 18 locomotives had a

Immaculate diesel locomotive, number 2016.059, moves onto its stabling point between duties at Vienna, in September 2005. This is one of 100 new locomotives introduced in 2002 for passenger and freight services.

New freight and shunting locomotive number 2070.014 prepares to leave for its next duty at Vienna in September 2005. This class has replaced many of OBB's traditional shunting and light freight locomotives.

Shunting locomotive, number 2067.010, waits for its next train at Villach in April 2003. This class is being displaced by class 2070.

maximum speed of 62 mph and although they have been withdrawn as new locomotive classes come into service, several have been preserved. Class 2016 consists of 100 locomotives introduced in 2002. They are powerful passenger and freight locomotives with a maximum speed of 87 mph. The class is the diesel version of electric class 1016/1116. Class 2070 are freight locomotives introduced in 2001 with a maximum speed of 62 mph. This type of locomotive is part of a large family of Vossloth/MAK manufactured locomotives increasingly found in a number of independent and state railway systems throughout Europe.

OBB also has several classes of diesel shunting locomotives. Class 2060 are light locomotives introduced in 1954 with a maximum speed of 60 kph. Many locomotives have been withdrawn although several have been preserved. Class 2062 was introduced in 1959 and most locomotives have been withdrawn. The class was used on general shunting work and had a maximum speed of 37 mph. Class 2067 was introduced in 1959 and the majority of the 100-plus locomotives are still in service on shunting and light freight work. The class has a maximum speed of 40 mph. The future use of these locomotives will be affected by the introduction of class 2070. Class 2068 was the first new class of locomotive introduced in 1989 for shunting and short trip work. They are powerful locomotives with a maximum speed of 62 mph and there are 60 locomotives in the class. Class 150 are small depot/workshop shunting locomotives built in the early 1940s in Germany and acquired by OBB. The locomotives are the same as DB class 323.

Finally, Austria has a number of independent railways which use electric and diesel locomotives, some of which were acquired from OBB. Two examples are diesel locomotives used by the Zillertalbahn based in Jenbach. Another example are the Wiener Lokalbahn's three new electric locomotives, which are the same as an OBB class 1116. The locomotive is leased from Siemens and is one of a large fleet of "Dispoloks" which are widely used by a number of countries and private railway companies.

Modern shunting locomotive, number 2068.005, waits in the sun at Vienna, in September 2005. This class was introduced in 1989.

One of Wiener Lokalbahnen's new electric locomotives on hire from Siemens, number ES 64 U2 022, accelerates its freight through Passau, in September 2005.

Hungarian Railways

Hungary has a comprehensive railway system that includes a number of narrow gauge lines. There is an interesting mix of diesel and electric locomotives and there has been a major commitment to preserving historic and other locomotives throughout the country, but in particular in the major transport museums.

The first true railway in Hungary opened in 1846 when a line was introduced between Pest and Vac. Unfortunately, in terms of railway development, the 1848 to 1849 revolution of independence against Austria intervened, and there was little progress until 1867, when an agreement between Austria and Hungary resolved their differences and created a stable situation. From that time, railway expansion was rapid, primarily using independent companies, and in 1868 MAV – Royal Hungarian State Railways – was created. The ethos of the government was a nationwide railway system to help with economic development and in subsequent years many of the private companies were nationalised. In 1891, MAV took over the Hungarian lines of the Austro-Hungarian state railway, which left only three independent companies. One of these, the Gyor/Sopron/Ebenfurthi Railway (GySEV), is still in existence and operating services in the north of the country.

Following World War I, Hungary lost a significant proportion of its territory and its railway network reduced from almost 12,400 miles to less than 5,600 miles. This provided an opportunity to modernise services and the process continued until after World War II, when Hungary became a satellite of the Soviet Union, at which time the Royal part of MAV's title was dropped. The 1950s saw the beginning of extensive electrification of main lines and the acquisition of new electric and diesel locomotives. Steam traction ceased in the mid-1980s. Today, MAV's network has been reduced to just under 5,000 miles of railway and over one-third of the lines are electrified. Prior to 1960, new electrified lines operated on the 16 KV but, subsequent to that date, all new electrified lines were 25 KV. There was also a plan in place to convert all of the MAV 16 KV electrified system to 25 KV and this had been achieved by 1972. This change did not affect the electric locomotives in use at that time since they had the capacity to operate on a dual voltage basis using a manual switching system. In recent years MAV has acquired new unit type trains and has invested in a small number of new dual voltage electric locomotives. MAV has extended the life of certain classes of diesel locomotives by undertaking major rebuilding programs to modernize the fleet and achieve more efficient performance. In parallel with this process, MAV has invested in new freight terminals and has built facilities for operating roll-on, roll-off trains to enable road wagons to be carried across borders – notably into Austria. These developments should help MAV to continue to make progress. The other development that is likely to influence the future provision of railway services in Hungary is the open access policy, under which companies with a license to operate in the EU can have access to the Hungarian network. This may be seen as a threat to the concept of a solely state-owned and state-run system, but it could also provide opportunities for expanding rail services and for increased collaboration with independent companies and other countries.

A magnificent display of steam locomotives of various classes at Fusti Preservation Museum in Budapest. This museum has a comprehensive collection of steam, diesel and electric locomotives plus other historical railway items.

Budapest Local Railway 0-6-0 tank locomotive number 28, built in 1902, at the Szentendre Urban Transport Museum, Budapest in September 2004.

Although steam haulage is no longer available on scheduled services, steam specials still operate, and Hungary is committed to the preservation of old locomotives, many of which are designated as National Monuments. The Fusti Preservation Museum in Budapest is a magnificent railway facility with a large number of preserved steam, electric

Built in Hungary in 1951, 4-6-4 locomotive number 303.002 is preserved at the Fusti Museum, in September 2004.

and diesel locomotives. It is complemented by the collections of other museums and the locomotives set on plinths in various railway locations throughout the country. Built in 1902, the 0-6-0 tank locomotive number 28 had a maximum speed of 28 mph. It is preserved as a part of the excellent Urban Transit Collection at Szentendre, Budapest. Built in 1901, the 0-6-0 locomotive class 370 had a maxi-

MAV Nostalgia Locomotive 411.118 at the Fusti Museum in Budapest in September 2004. This 2-8-0 locomotive was built in 1944.

Veteran electric locomotive V41.523 is displayed at the Fusti Museum, Budapest in September 2004. This

mum speed of 31 mph and were used on freight work. Steam class 303 were 4-6-4 locomotives and were built in the early 1950s. Class 375 was a large class of 2-6-2 tank locomotives introduced in 1907 with a maximum speed of 37 mph. The final locomotive of over 500 examples was completed in 1959, which illustrates the success of the design. Class 424 was another large class (over 350 locomotives), which was introduced in 1924. The last locomotive was completed in 1958. The class was particularly successful and 140 further examples were sold to various countries including Czechoslovakia and the Soviet Union. The 4-8-0 locomotives had a maximum speed of 56 mph. Class 411 comprised over 500 locomotives built in the early 1940s. They were 2-8-0 locomotives with

Electric locomotive number V42 527, built in 1966, is pictured at the Fusti Museum in September 2004. Other examples of this type are used throughout Hungary as carriage heating units.

a maximum speed of 50 mph and were acquired by MAV after the war as war surplus locomotives. They were built in the USA.

By comparison with the range of operational diesel locomotives, there are relatively few classes of electric locomotives. Class 41 was introduced in 1962 with a dual-voltage capacity. The locomotives had a maximum speed of 50 mph and were used on shunting and light work. They have all been withdrawn although one example has been preserved. Class V42 was introduced in 1966 and totalled 42 locomotives. The maximum speed was 50 mph. All have

Electric shunting locomotive, number V46 016, waits to move onto its next train at Dombovar, in September 2004. This locomotive was built in 1991.

Veteran electric locomotive V55 004, dating from the 1950s, is shown preserved at the Fusti Museum, in September 2004.

Electric locomotive V43 1224 hurries through Ferencvaros station in Budapest with a train of road wagons, in September 2004.

Passenger and freight electric locomotive V63 143 awaits its next duty with another member of the class at Ferencvaros, in October 2005.

Modern electric locomotive 1047 002 pauses before moving into Linz station in Austria to pick up its next train back into Hungary, in September 2005.

now been withdrawn – one has been preserved and the majority of the rest of the class are used as train heating locomotives at various locations throughout Hungary. Class V46 locomotives are similar in appearance to the V42s and were introduced in 1983. The 60 locomotives have a maximum speed of 50 mph and are used on shunting and light freight work. Vintage class V55 was introduced in 1954 and 10 locomotives were built. They were MAV's first post-war electric locomotives with a maximum speed of 62 mph, but have all been withdrawn, although one has been preserved. Class V43 originally comprised 379 locomotives and is MAV's standard passenger and freight locomotive. Built between 1963 and 1982, the locomotives have a maximum speed of 80 mph. A number of locomotives have been modernised to enable them to work push-pull trains.

For many years, class V63 was the premier electric class and originally consisted of 56 locomotives. The vast majority are still in service on passenger and freight work. Built in the 1980s, the class was later sub-divided to modify certain locomotives for higher speed running. The normal maximum speed is 87 mph and the modified locomotives have a higher maximum of 100 mph. The latest electric locomotive is class 1047, which is the same as OBB class 1116. The 10 locomotives mainly operate express passenger services and their dual-voltage capacity enables them to operate into other countries. There is a possibility that more of these locomotives will be acquired as older locomotives are withdrawn.

MAV's diesel classes range from small shunting locomotives to large and powerful main line locomotives. A particular feature of MAV's approach has been the modernization and up-grading of existing locomotives to increase performance and extend their working life.

1950s built diesel shunting locomotive, number M28 1006, poses in the sun at Ferenvaros, in September 2004.

Diesel shunting locomotive number M31 2019 waits its next duty at Szeged, in October 2005. Originally totalling over 50 locomotives, number 2019 is one of the few remaining members of this type.

Class M28.1 is a small class of 24 locomotives used for light shunting work. The locomotives were introduced in 1956 and have a maximum speed of 31 kph. Class M28.2 was developed from the original class and are marginally larger locomotives with a higher maximum speed of up to 30 mph. The 10 locomotives of the class were introduced in 1959. Class M31 shunting locomotives were introduced in 1958 and the majority of the original 50-plus locomotives are now withdrawn. Class M32 comprised 50-plus locomotives for shunting and general light work and was introduced in 1972. Each of these classes had a maximum speed of 37 mph. Class M40 was introduced in 1966 as passenger and freight locomotives, some of which were fitted with train heating boilers. The original 80 locomotives have been affected by withdrawals and less than half remain in service. The class has a relatively high maximum speed of 62 mph.

M41 is a large class of over 100 locomotives used for passenger work. Introduced in 1973, the class has a maximum speed of 62 mph. Class MDmot is something of a curiosity. The 42 locomotives were introduced in 1970 and are basically a railcar with a capacity to carry parcels. However, they are capable of a maximum speed of 62 mph and are in charge of passenger services in a number of areas, notably on branch lines.

Between them, classes M43 and M47 originally totalled over 200 locomotives. The classes differ marginally externally but mechanically are virtually the same. Introduced in 1974 for shunting duties and branch line work, class M43 has a maximum speed of 37 mph and M47 a maximum of 44 mph. A significant number of M47s have been modernized and have received new engines over the last few years to improve performance. Class M44 was originally a large class of over 200 locomotives and was introduced in 1954. The class is used for light freight and shunting work and has a maximum speed of 50 mph. This type of locomotive has been successfully exported to a number of other countries. A significant number of locomotives have received new engines in recent years, as a means of extending the working lives of the locomotives and improving efficiency of operation.

Main-line class M61 is part of a large family of classic locomotives found in a number of countries

Newly refurbished class M32 type number 043 at Cegled, in October 2005. This locomotive appears to be ready for use by a private railway contractor, as indicated by its number.

including Belgium, Luxembourg, Denmark and Norway. They are powered by General Motor engines and are affectionately known as "Nohabs" after their Swedish builder. Introduced in 1963 with a maximum speed of 65 mph, the MAV fleet comprised 20 locomotives and, although most have been withdrawn, a number remain with MAV or in preservation. Class M62 was introduced in 1965 and originally comprised almost 300 locomotives. The type is found in many countries including the Czech Republic and the Baltic states, which is not surprising given that the Russian manufacturer built over 7,000 examples. The class is used on freight and some passenger work and has a maximum speed of 62 mph. MAV has fitted a number of locomotives with new, more efficient engines and a small number have been converted for use on broad gauge work on lines in the northeast of Hungary that link with Ukraine.

An interesting feature of railways in Hungary is the extensive range of narrow gauge lines, including one in Budapest that is run by children. These lines use a

Diesel locomotive number M41 2208 waits to head out of Szombathely station with a special train, in October 2004.

High-speed diesel locomotive number MDmot 3008 pauses before backing onto its passenger train at Pecs, in September 2004.

Diesel shunting locomotive number M47 1301 is ready for its next duty at Pecs, in September 2004. Many locomotives of this class have been re-built with new, more efficient engines.

variety of locomotives with the principal diesel type for 760 mm lines being class Mk48 introduced in 1960. This class has a maximum speed of 30 mph. Class C50 is a small type of diesel introduced in 1958 with a maximum speed of 20 mph for use on 760 mm lines.

Finally, mention needs to be made of the long standing GySEV railway's locomotives. This independent company is jointly owned by Hungary – 60 percent – and Austria – 33 percent – plus a small interest held by Hamburger Hafen. It has a number of pre-

Veteran diesel shunting locomotive number M44 209 has retained its old green livery as it rests at Bekescsaba, in October 2005.

Classic diesel Nohab number M61 001 is preserved at the Fusti Museum where it is pictured in September 2004.

served steam locomotives and a fleet of diesel locomotives, which includes examples of MAV classes M40 and M44. There are also two classes of electric locomotive – class V43, which are the same as MAV class V43, and class 1047.5, which are the same as MAV class 1047. The distinctive GySEV livery adds to the appearance of the locomotives. GySEV also operates narrow gauge steam locomotives and has preserved several others. Class 394 were 0-6-0 tank locomotives introduced in 1915 for 760 mm lines. Examples of the class were still being built into the late 1940s. Two examples remain in preservation. Class 492 were 0-6-0 tank locomotives introduced in 1909 and also built into the late 1940s. Designed for the 760 mm lines, one operational example has been retained for use by the museum railway at Nagycenk.

Narrow gauge diesel locomotive type C50, number GV 5713, waits to depart from Balatonfenyves station, in October 2005

Broad gauge diesel locomotive number M62 508 moves onto its next train at Zahony on the Hungarian Ukraine border, in October 2005.

GySEV electric locomotive, 1047 503, awaits its next duty at Ferencvaros, in September 2004. The attractive GySEV livery enhances the appearance of the locomotive.

Older GySEV locomotive number V43 320 prepares to move to its next duty, in October 2005. This locomotive type works both passenger and freight services and is the same as MAV class V43.

Canadian Railways

The first railroad charter in Canada was incorporated on February 25, 1832, with a commitment to build a line from Dorchester – today known as St. Jean – to a point on the St. Lawrence River near Laprarie. On July 21, 1836 the Champlain and St. Lawrence Railroad opened; this was the first Canadian public railroad and the inaugural train was pulled by the locomotive the Dorchester. In 1857 this line became part of the Montreal and Champlain Railroad which was leased to the Grand Trunk in 1864, and which now forms part of the Canadian National System. In September of 1839 the Albion Mines Railway had its official opening and used the Timothy Hackworth Steam locomotives Samson, Hercules and John Biddle, which were imported from England. July of 1847 saw the incorporation, by the Legislature of the Province of Canada, of La Compagnie du Chemin à Rails du Saint-Laurent et du Village d'Industrie, to build a line from Lanoraie, on the Saint Lawrence downstream from Montreal, to Village d'Industrie, a distance of 12 miles. Village d'Industrie was later renamed Joliette after its founder Barthelemy Joliette. This railway originally had wooden rails surmounted by iron straps. It was taken over by the Quebec, Montreal, Ottawa and Occidental Railway in 1878 and acquired by CP in 1884. On July 31, 1851, the five foot, six-inch broad gauge, was adopted as the standard gauge for Ontario and Quebec, and was used until about 1870. After this there was a gradual change to the standard four foot, eight and a half inch gauge. On May 16, 1853, the first train in Ontario ran between Toronto and Aurora on the Ontario Simcoe and Huron Railroad Union Company line. The name was changed to Northern Railway of Canada on August 16, 1858 and it became part of the Northern and Northwestern Railway on June 6 1879. Today it is part of Canadian National. The first train was driven by W T Hackett, who also took the first locomotive into Kansas City. On July 15, 1853, the Grand Trunk Railway was formed by the amalgamation of six companies, and as time progressed a vast number of new lines started to open up, giving greater mobility for people and goods all over the Canadian landmass.

An amazing view of a steam locomotive of the Canadian Southern Railway, passing what seems to be Niagara falls on the American/Canadian border.

September 10, 1860 saw the then Prince of Wales – later to become King Edward VII – travel between Toronto and Collingwood, Ontario, and return. The special train of two coaches and open observation car was hauled by Northern Railway 4-4-0 locomotive, the Cumberland. July 12, 1871 saw North America's first public narrow gauge railway – the Toronto and Nipissing – open for traffic between Toronto and Uxbridge. On June 1, 1875, a ceremony was held to commemorate the turning of the first sod on the Canadian Pacific Railway, on the left bank of the Kamistiquia River, in the townsite of Fort William, about four miles from the river's mouth. On

A contemporary picture showing the Great Western Railway 4-4-0 locomotive number 8 Dakin, alongside which are the railway employees.

Another period view, this one of the Wabash Railroad Company, coal burning, steam locomotive number 69. the driver and stoker can just be seen in the cab.

October 9, 1877, the locomotive Countess of Dufferin arrived at St Boniface on a barge towed by the steamer Selkirk. It was brought in by the contractor Joseph Whitehead to work on the Selkirk – Emerson line and was the first locomotive in Manitoba and on the Prairies. January 31, 1880, an Ice Railway was opened between Longueuil and Montreal by the Quebec, Montreal, Ottawa and Occidental Railway. A railway track was erected on large timbers laid on the ice of the St. Lawrence River. During the summer months the QMO&O used a car ferry but an ice railway was laid each winter until 1883. November 8, 1885, the CP special train arrived in Port Moody at Pacific Tidewater, the first railway train ever to travel across Canada from sea to sea. June 3 1889, the first CP train arrived in Saint John, NB from Montreal, marking the completion of the Canadian Pacific Railway as a coast to coast railway. On September 19, 1891, the single-track St. Clair tunnel, under the St. Clair River, was opened by the Grand Trunk Railway. The construction of the tunnel – which connects Sarnia with Port Huron – had commenced in 1888. For September 24, 1897, a new double-track steel arch bridge was completed by the Niagara Falls Suspension Bridge Company and the Niagara Falls International Bridge Company. The upper floor of the new structure was leased to the Grand Trunk Railway. July 3, 1904 saw the first run of the Ocean Limited passenger train, between Montreal and Halifax, N S – this was the longest running train in Canada, having operated continuously over the same 840 mile route. On May 17, 1908, electric operation started through the St Clair Tunnel, between Sarnia and Port Huron, which ultimately ended the steam operations that had asphyxiated several crew members. On June 22, 1909, Canadian Pacific completed the viaduct on the Crows Nest Pass Line at Lethbridge. This was 5327 feet long and had a maximum height of 314 feet above Oldman River – the highest railway bridge in Canada. The bridge was opened to traffic on November 3, 1909, although it had been used by construction trains before this. On May 2, 1917, the Drayton-Acworth report was produced, outlining its findings by two out of three members of a Royal

Seen here is Canadian National Railways steam locomotive number 3254, a 2-8-2 Mikado type, built by the Canadian Locomotive Company, Kingston Works in 1917.

Visitors wander around the depot at the National Park Service's Steamtown, where there is a collection of rare steam trains to be viewed and ridden.

Commission which was set up in 1916. Sir Henry L Drayton was Chairman of the Board of Railway Commissioners for Canada, while William Ackworth came from London. The third member was Alfred H. Smith, President of the New York Central Railway. The report recommended that the government take over the Grand Trunk, the Grand Trunk Pacific and the Canadian Northern companies and operate them as one system together with the Intercolonial and the National Transcontinental Railway. The recommendations were accepted by the government. On October 17, 1917, the first train ran across the Quebec Bridge, over the St. Lawrence River, which was constructed by the Dominion government for use by the National Transcontinental Railway. This bridge was notorious in that it fell down twice during construction. On January 19, 1923 the Grand Trunk Railway was amalgamated into the Canadian National System, by order in council P.C. 114, and by 1923 the system included the Canadian Government Railways – including the Intercolonial, the Prince Edward Island and the National Transcontinental Railways; the Hudson Bay Railway; the Canadian Northern and its subsidiaries; the Grand Trunk Pacific; and the Grand Trunk - including the Grand Trunk Western and the

Steaming up is Canadian National Railroad locomotive 7470, which is preserved at the Conway Scenic Railroad. This engine has an 0-6-0 wheel arrangement.

Grand Trunk New England lines. Between November 1, and November 4, 1925, Canadian National diesel electric car Number 15280 made a run from Montreal to Vancouver in a total elapsed time of 72 hours, with an actual running time of 67 hours 7 minutes, which set world records for endurance, economy and sustained speed. August 26, 1929 saw Canadian National Railways place in service – hauling the second section of the "International Limited" between Montreal and Toronto – the first road diesel electric passenger locomotive. This locomotive, number 9000, consisted of two units, weighing a total of 335 tons.

On April 21, 1933, the London, Midland and Scottish Railway (UK) 4-6-0 steam locomotive Royal Scot arrives in Montreal with eight passenger cars en route to the Century of Progress Exhibition in Chicago. The train then ran via the Toronto, Hamilton and Buffalo Railway through US cities to Chicago. After the exhibition, it left Chicago on October 11 and ran via the US to Vancouver, Winnipeg, Minneapolis and Detroit.

The train ran via CP on the outward trip and in western Canada, and on CN on the return leg in Ontario. It returned to the UK from Montreal on November 24. In September 1936, a new lightweight streamlined passenger train attained an officially recorded speed of 112 mph on the Canadian Pacific, Winchester Subdivision, near St. Telesphore, Quebec, with 4-4-4 locomotive number 3003. In December 1937, Canadian Pacific took delivery of its first diesel electric locomotive, a switching unit numbered 7000. In May of 1939, the Royal Tour of Canada commenced with the arrival of King George VI and Queen Elizabeth at Wolfe's Cove, Quebec on the Empress of Canada. The 12-car train in royal blue and aluminium left Quebec City on May 18. CP used 4-6-4 locomotives 2850 and 2851 for the royal and pilot trains respectively, except for the Ottawa to Brighton, Ontario section, which was over CN track. 2850 hauled the royal train without change right through to Vancouver, a total distance of 3224 miles. Royal crowns were affixed to the running boards of both locomotives and these were eventually fitted to the entire class – 2820 through to 2864 – which, following approval from their majesties came to be known as Royal Hudsons. In 1949 Canadian Pacific accepted its last new steam locomotive, a class Tl-c 2-10-4 number 5935, from Montreal Locomotive Works. It also acquired its first road diesel-electric locomotives, numbered 8400 through to 8404, for conversion of motive power on the Montreal-Newport-Wells River line. On February 16, 1951, Canadian National began

Used for the Royal tour by King George VI and Queen Elizabeth in 1939, this is a Royal Hudson, semi-streamlined 4-6-4 Hudson steam locomotive.

Preserved in the Canada Science and Technical Museum, is this Canadian National Railways locomotive number 6400, painted in the CN steam era olive green.

Seen here in Canadian Pacific Rail colours and as number 1820, this diesel locomotive was delivered in 1953 from EMD. It is possible this locomotive was once used for cold weather testing.

Constructed by the Montreal locomotive Works in 1969 as a road switcher type, this is model 636, an iron ore transportation locomotive.

Canadian Pacific 5584, and SD40 model built by GMD as A4338 in 1983, passing by Milwaukee in Wisconsin, USA. This freight train shuttles between Canada and the USA.

There are several types of grain hoppers. This one is an articulated type, the most popular of the ones used by Canadian National. Generally used for wheat transportation.

testing a Budd model RDC-1, self-propelled diesel rail car, between Montreal and Ottawa. Then in 1953, Budd-built rail diesel cars (RDC) were introduced on several Canadian runs. These were called "Railiners" by CN and "Dayliners" by CP. Services on Canadian Pacific were introduced November 9

Locomotive 6444, built in 1958, belonging to Via Rail, used for freight and passenger work and is powered by an Alco 1800 hp engine. In service up to the early 1990s.

1955 and on April 25, Canadian Pacific inaugurated its new stainless steel, scenic-domed, transcontinental passenger train "The Canadian," between Montreal/Toronto and Vancouver. On August 9 1958, Canada's longest running named train "Moccasin," ceased running between Montreal and Brockville. Although unofficial, it had been used almost since the train service went into operation on November 19, 1855. Then on April 25, 1960, locomotive number 6043 made the last scheduled run of

This photograph has caught the tail end of a turbo train during 1974, which is en-route to Toronto. These trains entered service during 1968 in Canada and the USA.

A group of diesel locomotives, led by number 560, are seen at a Toronto stacking yard. These double-decker carriages are great for viewing the scenery.

Locomotive number 7498, a General electricB36-7 engine now working on the Rocky Mountain Tours agenda, an ideal engine for this work.

a steam locomotive on Canadian National, between The Pas and Winnipeg. November 6, 1960 saw the last steam locomotive to operate officially on Canadian Pacific, which pulled a special train to St Lin from Montreal – locomotive class Al-e number 29, 4-4-0 built in 1887. On July 17, 1962, following tests on the Ocean, Canadian National's transcontinental train, the Super Continental, appeared for the first time in the new black and white colour scheme, with orange-red locomotive fronts. This ultimately replaced the traditional olive green, gold and black design. November 16, 1967 saw Canadian Pacific start tests on Canada's first remote-controlled, mid-train diesel locomotives, in regular freight service, using a new Robot radio-command system. On April 21, 1970, Canadian Pacific unveiled Canada's first double-deck passenger train, comprising nine air-conditioned cars built by Canadian Vickers Limited, at a cost of $2.8 million. The cars went into operation on April 27, on the Montreal Lakeshore suburban service. On January 3, 1986, the Skytrain commenced operation between Vancouver,

Locomotive number 2039, part of the Cape Breton & Central Nova Scotia Railway, which used to be a secondary line owned by Canadian National Railway.

There is nothing quite like the Agawa canyon during the Autumn or Spring. As the leaves turn their rustic colours a locomotive makes its journey between the trees.

Bright reds and deep greens surround the passenger train, which is making its way through the dense autumn colours of the Agawa canyon.

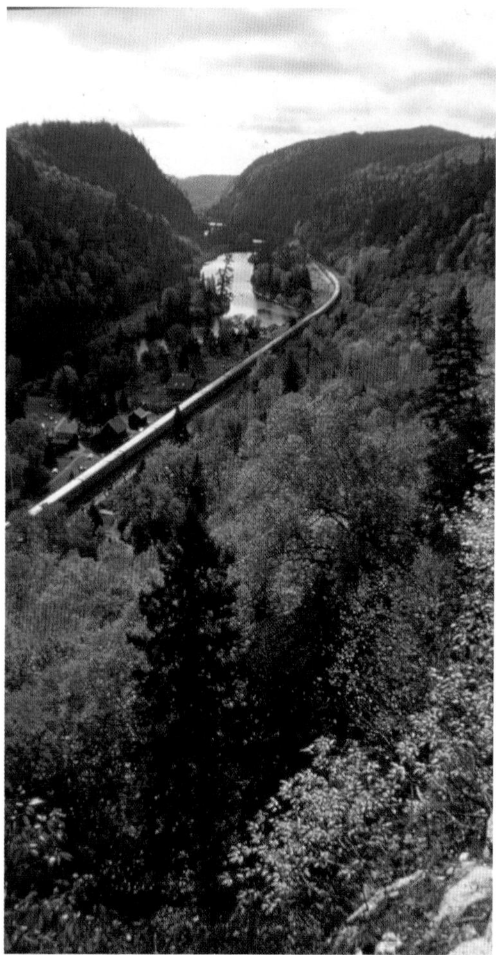

Waterfront and New Westminster, BC. December 12, 1988, the first revenue train ran through the CP Rail, 9.1 mile, Mount MacDonald Tunnel – the longest rail tunnel in the Americas. On October 26 1995, the CN commuter line between Montreal Central station and Deux Montagnes was reopened with modernised equipment. The new electric multiple unit trains, operating at 25 kv AC, replace aging equipment, some of which went back to the opening of the line in 1918. On September 12, 1996, Rocky Mountain Railtours ran the longest passenger train in Canadian history, when three GP40 locomotives hauled 34 cars from Vancouver to Kamloops. December 12, 2001, VIA Rail Canada retired the last of its 6900 series LRC locomotives, as a result of the delivery of 700 series General Electric Genesis locomotives. On October 31, 2002, BC Rail ended 88 years of passenger service with the last run of the Cariboo Prospector between Prince George and North Vancouver. The next day, two 20-seat "rail shuttle vehicles" started service to isolated communities between Lillooet and D'Arcy, BC.

The Canadian is the ultimate Canada train trip between Toronto, Jasper and Vancouver. Look out for the wildlife, it can often get in the way of the locomotive!

Meandering through the Rockies, take the train from Jasper to Prince Rupert on the Pacific and enjoy the scenery on this two day exotic journey.

The trains that pull you through this wonderful snow covered Canadian landscape have observation carriages, giving a better panoramic view of the landscape.

Russian/CIS Railways

In 1836 the Cherepanovs constructed a railway from a place known as the Vyiskii Factory to the nearest copper mine, a distance of about two miles.

At 12:30, on the afternoon of October 13, 1837, the station bell rang out twice and the Provorny steam engine gave a long squeal from its whistle. The first train in Russia began its journey along the St. Petersburg-Tsarskoe Selo public railroad. The early trains used on this line were all Patentee 2-2-2, produced in England by Timothy Hackworth, Robert Stephenson and Tayleur and Company. It is thought though that this might not have been the first steam engine railroad in Russia, as back in 1834 a talented craftsman – serf Efim Cherepanov, along with his son, built a railroad at Nizhny Tagil metallurgical works in the Ural, for which he also built two steam engines to run on the line.

Prior to this a manifesto was pronounced by the Tsar, pointing out that the development of agriculture and industry, the ever-growing population and the turnover reached by domestic and foreign trade, had already outgrown the old-style transportation system. A new group was organised, which took control of the construction and operation of all transport systems, and an Institute – Augustine Betankur, a well-known Spanish scientist, engineer and builder, organized the Institute and became its first Director – prepared the engineers who would

This is a replica of the locomotive that Efim Cherepanov and his son built for their railroad at the Nizhny Tagil metallurgical works in the Ural.

develop the future systems. Many famous names were amongst the railway engineers and scientists attending the Institute, and it was they who strove to increase the mileage of the Russian railways of the period.

This is the Leningrad terminal at Moscow station, a beautiful piece of architecture, designed by K A Ton, who was a promiment architect of the period.

February 1, 1842 was a memorable day. After reports from P P Mel'nikov and N O Kraft, Emperor Nicholas 1 signed a royal edict, giving permission for the St. Petersburg to Moscow railroad to be built. By August 1, construction had begun with two teams – one going north and one going south – managed by Mel'nikov and Kraft . The routes were designed with profitability and passenger requirements in mind, and were built with a track gauge of five feet, which later would become standard on the Russian rail-

K A Ton not only designed railway terminals, he is better known for his churches. This though is the Moscow terminal at St. Petersburg, another masterpiece.

road. Some 190 bridges had to be built along the route and the architect K A Ton designed two large railway terminal buildings in Moscow and St. Petersburg, which are still there today. On November 1, 1851, a train left St. Petersburg on what was the longest railroad, and reached Moscow 21, hours 45 minutes later, arriving at nine the next morning. The main locomotive builder of the time was the Alexander works, based in St. Petersburg and it was they who supplied the engines that hauled the carriages along the route. Passenger volumes grew rapidly and by 1852 the railroad was carrying 719 thousand passengers and 164 thousand tons of freight – by now a fast train could do the 400 mile journey in about twelve hours.

There was a rapid spread of new lines and Russia found it could no longer cope with the vast supply of engines needed, and so many were brought in from England, France, Germany and Austria.

In 1887 three expeditions were sent out to find the best route for a proposed Trans-Siberian railway and in 1891 the Siberian railway construction committee was formed. In February of the same year, it was decided that the Great Siberian route construction could be started from two directions – Vladivostok and Chelyabinsk. On May 19, 1891, at ten o'clock in the morning, a ceremony saw the laying of the first stone in place and a silver plate was placed in the railway station to commemorate the event. In this way the Trans-Siberian railway construction began for real. The most dreadful conditions were encountered by the workers as the majority of the track had to be built through low, or non-populated areas, with thick forests, fast running Siberian rivers, lakes and swamps, with much of it being in permafrost areas. Direct railway connection between Chelyabinsk and the Pacific coast was established only in October 1916, after putting into operation the Amurskaya line and the bridge across the Amur River. As far as administration was concerned, the Trans-Siberian railway was divided into four sections – Sibirskaya, Zabaykalskaya, Amurskaya, and Ussuriyskaya. Passenger numbers grew rapidly and where 1897 saw 609,000 passen-

An old steam locomotive number L-0029 hooked up to some old style carriages departs from Rostov-na-Donu, Capital of the Rostov oblast region.

Looking as smart and powerful as ever, this steam locomotive, Su250-64 was spotted at Rostov-Bereg station, in the Rostov region of Russia.

Squashed between to larger exhibits, also seen at the Rostov museum at the Gnilovskaya station in the Rostov region, is this strange Mz/2 gas shunter.

gers transported, by 1912, 3.2 million people were using it. It took 12 years to build and is 4,700 mi long – extending from the Ural Mountains to the Sea of Japan. 1895 saw the first of a batch of 29 0-6-6-0 Mallet articulated, compound tender-engines put into service, on the narrower gauge Vologda to Archangel railway. By 1900 the Russian railway network totalled some 280,000 mi and more was being added. Although the next few years passenger and freight numbers increased rapidly, this was interrupted when World War I started. There was much destruction during the war and in particular to railway networks and to the trains themselves. Between the Civil War and World War I, more than 60 percent of the railway network, 90 percent of locomotives and 80 percent of carriages were destroyed. It wasn't until 1928 that the system recovered to the point of where it was in 1913 – once again passenger and freight numbers increased. During World War II – or as it is often known, the Great Patriotic War – the railways were hit again, but this time still managed to transport equipment and supplies to the troops on the front lines. In 1946 the People's Commissariat of Communications, which ran the railway system, was renamed the Ministry of Communications of

In beautiful condition is this TEP10-163 diesel locomotive, which was spotted at the Varshavsky terminal museum in St. Petersburg.

An Electric AC powered train, number ER9-12, pulling out of Gorky-Moskovsky station. This locomotive is a local suburban train belonging to the Gorkovskaya Railway

Electric locomotive VL61- 012 can be seen at the Rostov railway museum, in the Rostov region. Rostov is a major railway junction and one of Russia's oldest cities.

the USSR, and in 1954 it obtained independence from the Ministry of Transport, being reorganised in 1992 as the Transstroy concern. In 1956 the Ministry of Communications declared that steam construction was to cease and so an electrification programme was put in place. Line mileage increased in the 1960s and with it traffic volume grew too, until just over 51 percent of the traffic was being transported by electric locomotives and 47 percent by diesel locomotives. Although a large chunk of the industrial lines continued to use steam power locomotives, where cheap fuel was not available, TO-4, TO-6A and TO7 diesel engines were used. Freight traffic commanded a larger volume of transportation than all the rest of the world put together and the post-World War II L Class 2-10-0 locomotive became a successful workhorse at this time. The Bryansk Engineering Works (BZK), was one of the largest train manufacturers in Russia and is credited with some very important engines. During World War II the factory was completely destroyed but the government gave them a big contract after the war and in 1945 the works built the first locomotive of the post-war era. The M1-1 was a small narrow-gauge locomotive. Then a year later the plant started to build steam mainline locomotives, like the legendary P series, designed by Lebedyansky. Although it was classed as one of the best steam locomotives in history, the end of the steam era was nearing rapidly. The P series locomo-

Locomotives ChME3-3469 and ChME3-3465, two diesel shunters are pulling a coal train at Inta-I station, in the Komi republic, Russia.

In 1960 the engineers at BMZ, Russias biggest locomotive manufacturer, designed the huge 1200 hp, diesel-electric locomotive TEM-2, which acquired all the TEM1 upgrades.

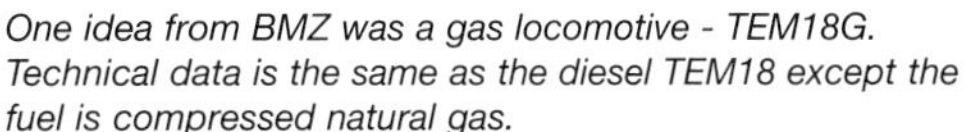

One idea from BMZ was a gas locomotive - TEM18G. Technical data is the same as the diesel TEM18 except the fuel is compressed natural gas.

tives were changed to L series, but differed little – some of these engines were still in service in the mid-1970s. In 1958 BMZ moved to more modern stock and built its first 1000 hp diesel locomotive – TEM 1, which was the first shunting diesel-locomotive, made in series, in Russia. In 1960 the engineers of BMZ designed the larger 1200 hp diesel-electric locomotive TEM-2, which became the most popular

Seen here is TEM2-6623 diesel shunter, at the Inta loco shed in the Komi republic. The TEM loco was made by BMZ and became one of the most commonly used engines in Russia.

A local suburban electric train, at Saratov station, which is part of the Privolzhskaya Railway system. The majority of Russian trains are now electric powered.

shunting locomotive in Russia. Although in private hands, BMZ continues to build diesel-electric engines today.

With the formation, in 1991, of the new Commonwealth of Independent States (CIS) after the collapse of the USSR, the railways were divided amongst the member countries, which caused some confusion at first. The CIS inherited some 93,000 miles of the five foot lines, and 1,500 miles of the narrow gauge line. The CIS is made up of the following states – Armenia, Azerbaijan, Belarus, Georgia, Kazakhstan, Kyrgyzstan, Moldova, Russia, Tajikistan, Ukraine, and Uzbekistan. Turkmenistan discontinued permanent membership as of August 26, 2005 and is now an associate member. Since its formation, the CIS have signed a large number of documents concerning integration and cooperation on matters of economics, defence and foreign policy. Many of the CIS members have been left with, or already had, some pretty poor railway equipment and stock.

In 2005, the Demikhovsky Engineering Plant manufactures AC and DC trains for suburban and inter-region transit systems, like this ED4M locomotive.

A high speed electric DC train ER200 of the Moskovskaya Railway, nears a snowy Malino platform - Moscow Oblast - on the Saint Petersburg-Moscow line.

Russian Railways take you beyond the legendary journeys between Moscow and St. Petersburg and to the Far East. Russia's colossal railway network was privatized in 2003 and RZhd was designated with overseeing the country's 16 regional operators. Direct train services are offered to dozens of European and Asian gateways.

The Armenian railway infrastructure is old and out of date, and rail transport has been slow and unreliable. Between 1989 and 1999 the Armenian railways lost about 93 percent of its traffic volume. However after recent changes in tariff structure, disposal of obsolete assets and staff reduction, the financial performance of the railway has shown improvement. Armenian railways (ARD) were restructured in 1998, when they were divided in to three state closed joint stock companies – Rail freight, rail rolling stock and rail infrastructures. Further restructuring is required but this is a healthy start.

Azerbaijan has 1,318 miles of rail lines, excluding several small industrial lines. Most lines are broad gauge, and the principal routes are electrified. Some improvements to the network have been made in the last few years, with EU funding, but the government estimates that 435 miles, or about one-third, of the rail system is in such poor condition that reconstruction is necessary and speed restrictions have been imposed. The network and the trains are operated by Azerbaijan State Railway (ADDY – Azerbaycan Doövlet Demir Yolu). Some investment has been made in trains recently with the consequent improvement in the quality of services.

The Belarus railway structure seems well-organized and uses up-to-date equipment. The operational

Locomotive number VL80S-1060, an electric engine, passes through Gorky-Sortirovochny station, which is in the Nizhni Novgorod region of Russia, during 2005.

Seen approaching the outskirts of the Gorky-Moskovsky station, in the Nizhni Novgorod region, this is locomotive number ChS4T-304, an electric engine.

This locomotive was seen at the main Baku railway terminal, Azerbaijan, numbered DR1P-403 DMU, it is the official train of the ADDY - Azerbaijan State Railways management.

length of the Belarusian railways consists of 3,400 mi of track. They have integrated their system with the major European counterparts and the majority of their transport is freight.

This is Khachmas station in Azerbaijan. People wait for the local commuter train to take them to their destinations. Safety is not at the top of their list it seems!

As Georgia brings its railway system into the 21st century, a lot of hard work is needed to lay new lines. These people are building two-rail tracks on the Marelisi-Dzirula stage.

During Soviet times the Georgian Railroad played an important transportation role for the Caucasus. Unfortunately today the general condition of the railway network is poor. In 2000, the European Bank for Reconstruction and Development opened a credit line of US$20 million for the rehabilitation and maintenance of the Georgian Railway network. There are future plans to begin the construction of a new international railway line for Tbilisi to Karsi (Turkey), which will greatly help the economic revival of the southern regions of Georgia, as well as promote economic links between Turkey and Georgia and the whole region.

A vital transport corridor in Kazakhstan will be upgraded through a US$ 65 million (EUR 61.3 million) loan from the European Bank for Reconstruction and Development (EBRD) to Kazakhstan Temir Zholy (KTZ), the state-owned railway. Guaranteed by the Republic of Kazakhstan,

This picture shows an old steam locomotive, which is stationary on the Bakyriani branch of the then Georgia Railway system.

the loan will support ongoing restructuring of the railway and greater commercialisation.

Kyrgyzstan is another remnant of the once great Soviet Railways, but today's spartan services are dedicated solely to providing connections in and out of Bishkek, the country's capital and principal city. Beyond a handful of locals, international services connect to a number of CIS destinations, most notably Moscow.

Like so many of the others, Moldova Railways needs to be brought up to date with its rail system, although the international mainline that crosses Moldova links the capital Chisinau with other cities in Russia, Ukraine, Romania, Bulgaria and Belarus. Ungheni, Tiraspol and Balti are among domestic destinations.

Domestic transport of passengers in Tajikistan comprises only 13 percent of rail services. However, passenger use of rail services grew between 1992 and 1998. Passenger movement on railways peaked in 1995 at almost 135 million passengers per km, which is probably accounted for by troop movement – much of it Russian – during strife between government and United Tajik Opposition (UTO) forces. As for goods, rail carries about 90 percent of total external cargo shipments.

In November 2000, SYSTRA contracted with EBRD

Plans to bring the Georgian railway system up-to-date include building new locomotives and carriages. Progress can be seen here at the wagon-building plant.

Moldova too has applied for loans to upgrade its old railway system. Here a man signals the on-coming train and makes sure there is nobody about to cross the line.

An early Soviet made steam tank engine, which has been restored and left on a plinth for visitors to enjoy at a museum in Uzbekistan.

Another Soviet-made steam train on display in Uzbekistan, who are to be assisted with a loan from the European Bank for Reconstruction to upgrade their ageing railway system.

and UZ (Ukrainian Railways) to assist and support the Ukrainian Railways in implementing its investment programme and restructuring. The investment programme covers track renewal and maintenance, in particular on the main railway line between Kyiv and Lviv.

Uzbekistan's railways will be modernised and restructured with a $40 million loan from the European Bank for Reconstruction and Development (EBRD) to the national railway company, Uzbekistan Temir Yollari (UTY). Guaranteed by the Uzbek government, the loan will contribute to the modernisation of UTY's locomotive fleet by funding the purchase of new 8-10 electric freight locomotives. These will enhance energy efficiency, increase equipment reliability and lower maintenance costs. And so in 2005 these newly independent states strive to bring their ageing railways up to date, enabling them to compete in a highly volatile railway market.

Czech and Slovakian Railways

Although they are now two quite distinct Republics, the railways of the two countries need to be linked because their development was a part of the history of the old country of Czechoslovakia.

One of the electric trains introduced by CD in 1998 for fast passenger train work. The unit type trains consist of double-deck coaches.

Following the creation of the two new Republics, new railway organizations were established and the railway locomotives of the former Czechoslovakia were allocated to those organisations according to need. This has resulted in each country having a largely identical range of locomotive types – although several specialist classes were wholly allocated specifically to one country.

The Czech and Slovakian Republics each has an extensive railway system which runs through spectacular scenery, particularly in Slovakia. The locomotive fleets consist of electric and diesel locomotives some of which are relatively old. The

Pilzen is probably the oldest and best known company in the Czech Republic. This is one of their locomotives, now an attraction for visitors.

locomotives are often very attractive as a result of the wide range of liveries in which they are painted. Each country has retained a range of steam locomotives – some in museums, some on plinths at various sites and others as active locomotives used on special trains. Many are designated as national monuments. The majority of lines are standard gauge although some narrow gauge lines exist and Slovakia has a broad gauge line which links with the Ukraine.

Although a series of horse-drawn railways opened in the late 1820s and early 1830s, the first steam loco-

A typical scene at a rural station with a veteran railcar waiting to depart. The railcars are used extensively by CD and ZSR.

motive run in Czech was in 1838 when the locomotive "Moravia" operated a train into Brno. This was followed in 1839 by the first train from Vienna to Brno, on the line of the Northern Railway, and a service into Prague started in 1848.

In Slovakia, the South Eastern Railway introduced the first steam railway into Bratislava from Devinska Nova Ves in 1848, and services from Budapest to Zvolen in Slovakia were introduced by the Hungarian Northern Railway in 1871.

The intervening years had seen a significant number of new lines and this expansion continued throughout the 1870s. The 1880s saw the transfer of several lines to the state and in 1918, when the Czechoslovakian republic was created, CSD took over all the state railway system. The further expansion of the railways was formalized in law in 1920 and this gave a particular emphasis to new lines in Slovakia. In 1939, the railways were controlled within a German Protectorate, which lasted until after the war, when CSD regained control. In organizational terms, the next major change took place after the Czech and Slovakian Republics were created. In January 1993, CSD was discontinued. It was succeeded by CD in the Czech and ZSR in the Slovakian Repuplics. Since that time, developments have continued including the construction of high-speed lines and high-speed tilting trains. There have also been organizational changes in both countries to create individual operational units within the overall railway structural framework.

In parallel with these organizational changes over the years, locomotive development continued. 1920 saw the completion of the first steam locomotive built by Skoda (434.1100) and that company has subsequently built numerous steam and electric locomotives for the state system. In 1964 steam locomotive 498.106 achieved a CSD speed record of 101 mph during tests. The last steam locomotive for CSD was built by Skoda in 1958 and steam operation ceased on scheduled services in the early 1980s.

Electrification was a feature of development work from the early 1900s and a number of electric lines opened in subsequent years. The first line to be electrified was from Tabor to Bechyne, which opened in 1903 using 700 v DC power. In 1924 1500 v DC was adopted as the standard power system for CSD, and this lasted until 1946 when the 3000 v DC system was chosen. In 1959, it was decided to electrify the Plzen to Ceske Budejovice line to 25 KV. As a consequence, both CD and ZSR operate 3000 volts dc or 25 KV single voltage locomotives, and a number of dual voltage locomotive classes. CD currently has 5,900 mi of railway of which just over 30 percent is electrified with 1,060 mi at 3000 v DC and 770 mi at 25 KV. Narrow gauge track – 750 and 760 mm – totals almost 60 mi. ZSR has over 2,200 mi of railway of which 43 percent is electrified with 470 mi at 3000 v DC and 510 mi at 25 KV. Narrow gauge – 1520 mm, 1000 mm and 750 mm – totals just over 60 mi. It is perhaps surprising that over 80 percent of the CD network is single track and ZSR has 72 percent single track.

Both CD and ZSR are major freight carriers. CD carries over 59 billion tons/mile of freight annually of which over half comprises coal, lignite and steel. ZSR carries over 35 billion tons/mile of which over half is iron ore. Some of the traditional state railway freight cargoes are now being taken over by private railway companies and this is likely to have financial and other implications for CD and ZSR in the future. Another of the major challenges facing both CD and ZSR in the future is likely to be the eventual renewal of its electric locomotive fleet but this should not detract from the progress already made. Other unknown factors are the impact of the "open access" policy and the demands and opportunities presented by increased collaboration with other countries and cross-border working.

Although the majority of locomotives detailed were ordered by CSD, their allocation to either CD or ZSR has been included in the text to illustrate the scope of their use and their current ownership. Both CD and ZSR have preserved a sizeable range of steam locomotives. Some are located in museums, many are set on plinths at stations and other railway locations and a number are held at locomotive depots for use on special train services.

Class 310.0 were introduced by CD in 1899 as 0-6-0 tank locomotives, with a maximum speed of 25 mph. 138 examples were built and the last working member of the class ceased to operate in 1968. Several of the class have been preserved. Class 310.4 was used by ZSR and originally totalled 53 locomotives, although a total of over 530 locomotives of this successful class were built and were used in a number of countries. The class was introduced in 1885 and ZSR withdrew its last locomotive of the class in 1957. Several locomotives have been preserved. These 0-6-0 tank locomotives had a maximum speed of 28 mph. Class 331 were 2-6-2

ZSR 2-6-2 tank locomotive, number 331 037, at Bratislava in August 2000. These Hungarian built locomotives were first introduced in 1915.

4-8-2 locomotive, number 475 179, at Decin, in June 1996. This Skoda built class was introduced in the early 1940s and was used in the Czech Republic on express train work.

tank locomotives built in Budapest in 1915/16 and taken over by CSD in 1918. A further batch was taken over after World War II. The locomotives were used on a variety of duties in Slovakia. Class 354.7 is particularly interesting as 380 locomotives were produced following their introduction in 1909. Of this total, 152 locomotives were acquired by the then CSD and were gradually rebuilt to improve their performance. These 2-6-2 passenger locomotives had a maximum speed of 50 mph and the last example was withdrawn from service in 1970. CD and ZSR class 433 comprised 60 locomotives used for passenger train and freight work. These 2-8-2 tank locomotives were introduced in the 1940s and had a maximum speed of 37 mph. The last operational locomotive was withdrawn in 1980 and several examples have been preserved. Class 464.2 comprised two 4-8-4 tank locomotives built in 1956 for CD and were among the last steam locomotives built by Skoda. These powerful 56 mph maximum speed locomotives were used on passenger trains on mountain lines and were withdrawn in 1975. One member of the class has been preserved. Class 475.1 were 4-8-2 locomotives built in the 1940s by Skoda. These magnificent machines for express work were the predecessors of class 476, which included a number of features based on Andrés

Powerful 2-10-0 freight locomotive, number 556 0510, is stabled outside the depot at the excellent Luzna Museum where it is preserved, in September 2000.

Chapelon's work in France. These locomotives were less successful and were subsequently rebuilt. Classes 476.1 and 477 totalled 60 locomotives used by CD on suburban passenger train work. These 4-8-4 locomotives were built in the 1950s and had a maximum speed of 62 mph. The last member of the class was withdrawn from service in 1979 but two examples have been preserved. Class 498.0 and 498.1 were superb 4-8-2 express passenger locomotives. Class 498.0 were built in the mid-1940s and the updated version of the class – 498.1 – was introduced in the mid-1950s. The updated version incorporated many features based on Chapelon's work in France. One member of this class holds the CSD maximum speed record for a steam locomotive of 100 mph. Class 534 was a pre-war 2-10-0 design mainly built by Skoda. Over 200 examples were built up to 1947 and the class was sufficiently successful to last until the end of steam services. The class had a maximum speed of 37 mph. Class 555 were former German "Kriegslok" acquired by the then-CSD after the World War II. Details of this type of locomotive are given in the German section of this book. Although the last operational CD locomotive ceased work in 1973, several locomotives were sold to other countries and lasted until the 1990s. Class 556 were powerful 2-10-0 freight locomotives and Skoda built 510 examples until 1958. A member of the class operated the last scheduled steam service in 1981. The locomotives were able to haul massive trains at a relatively high speed of 50 mph. There are several classes of narrow gauge steam locomotives, some of which were used by CD and ZSR and others used by small railways serving forest work and industry. Class U36 was designed for use on 760 mm forest railways. These 0-6-0 tank locomotives were introduced in the late 1940s and have a maximum speed of 13 mph. Class U37 originally comprised 15 locomotives and was designed for use on 760 mm lines. Introduced in the 1890s, these 0-6-2 tank locomotives had a maximum speed of 22 mph. Class U46 are 760 mm gauge 0-8-0 tank locomotives built for the Romanian forest railways. Two examples have been acquired by private narrow gauge operators in the Czech Republic for use on former CD lines in the Osoblaha and Jindrichuv Hradec areas respectively. Built in the 1950s, the locomotives have a maximum speed of 19 mph.

Early electric locomotives included class 423 built in 1927 and used on shunting and general freight work. This small class of locomotives had a maximum speed of 31 mph and they were withdrawn from service in the mid-1970s. One example has been preserved. Class 436 was built in 1928 and comprised 4 locomotives with a maximum speed of 37 mph. They were used in the Prague area until their withdrawal in the 1970s. One example has been preserved. Class 100 was built in 1957 and consisted of 4 locomotives. The class had a maximum speed of 31 mph and were used on passenger train services. The last example was withdrawn in 2004. Electric locomotives of class 110 were built in the early 1970s and are used as shunting locomotives on both the CD and ZSR 3000 volts dc systems. Over 50

CD electric locomotive, number 100 001, has been preserved and is stabled at Tabor, in September 2002. The class was introduced in 1957.

CD center-cab electric shunting locomotive, number 110 020, moves off from its stabling point at Ceska Trebova, in August 2000.

ZSR electric shunting locomotive, number 110 042, waits in the afternoon sun before moving onto its next train at Zilina, in September 2003.

Fresh from a major overhaul, an immaculate electric shunting locomotive, number 111 006, moves slowly through Prague station, in April 2005.

Vintage electric locomotive, number 121 060, accelerates out of ZSR's Zilina freight yard with a train of empty wagons, in September 2003.

In June 1996, newly painted CD electric locomotive, number 122 055, moves to its stabling point at Usti nad Labem.

examples were built by Skoda and the class has a maximum speed of 50 mph. Class 111 are CD locomotives used on shunting and light duty work. Introduced in 1981, the 35 3000 volts DC locomotives have a maximum speed of 50 mph and were also built by Skoda. Class 113 is a small class of 1500 volts DC locomotives for CD developed from class 110 and introduced in 1973. They are used on shunting duties and light work. Class 121 are used by both CD and ZSR mainly on freight work and were introduced by Skoda in 1960. They are 3000 volts DC locomotives with a maximum speed of 56 mph. Classes 122 and 123 are developments of class 121 and were introduced in 1967 and 1971 respectively largely for freight work on CD lines. They also have a maximum speed of 56 mph. One of the class 123 locomotives became class 124.6 and is used at the Cerhenice test track. This locomotive achieved 136 mph at the test track in 1972 and in 1973 achieved 139 mph in Russia, which is the highest speed ever achieved by a Skoda locomotive. ZSR class 125 are broad gauge 3000 volts DC locomotives for use on freight lines linking with the

Powerful ZSR double locomotive, numbers 125 807 and 808, has just taken over a freight on the Slovakian/Ukraine border, in July 2004.

Ukraine. The 44 members of the class were developed by Skoda from class 123 and were introduced in 1976. They normally operate in pairs to create a double locomotive and have a maximum speed of 56 mph. The line from the Ukraine carries an estimated 10 million tonnes of iron ore into Slovakia – all hauled by these locomotives. At certain steeply graded sections of the line, the 125s act as banking locomotives to the locomotives heading the train. Class 130 are CD locomotives introduced in 1977 for freight work. They were developed from classes 123

ZSR double locomotive, numbers 131 076 and 075, speeds through picturesque Margencany with a train of empty freight wagons, in September 2003.

and 125 and have a maximum speed of 62 mph. This type of locomotive is also used in industry. ZSR class 131 are 3000 v DC freight locomotives introduced by Skoda in 1980. In effect, the class comprises 100 single locomotives that normally operate in pairs to create a powerful double locomotive with

Veteran electric locomotive, number 140 085, is stabled at Olomouc in September 2003. This class is used by CD and ZSR.

a maximum speed of 100 kph. Introduced in 1953, class 140 are CD and ZSR 3000 v DC locomotives originally used for express passenger trains, freight and other passenger work. They had a maximum speed of 75 mph but their use is now limited and many examples have been withdrawn. However, some examples remain in preservation in both CD and ZSR, designated as historic locomotives. Class 141 was introduced in 1959 as a development of class 140 for CD as express passenger and freight train locomotives with a maximum speed of 75 mph. They are now largely withdrawn. Other countries acquired locomotives developed from class 141, notably Poland – class EP05 – and the former Soviet Union – class ChS3. CD class 150 are 3000 v DC 87 mph express passenger locomotives introduced by Skoda in 1978. Class 151 are modified class 150

CD express passenger locomotive, number 151 006, waits to leave Prague main station with an afternoon train, in April 2005.

locomotives with a maximum speed of 100 mph. Classes 162 and 163 were introduced by Skoda in the late 1980s and are used by CD and ZSR on fast passenger and freight work on the 3000 v DC systems. Class 162 has a maximum speed of 87 mph and class 163 is limited to 75 mph. A number of 162s have been converted to class 163 by a change of bogies. CD class 181 is a large class – 150 locomotives – of 3000 v DC locomotives introduced by

ZSR electric locomotive, number 163 123, waits in the sun before moving to its next duty at Cadca, in September 2003.

CD electric locomotive, number 181 074, is stabled at Ceska Trebova in August 2000. This class was introduced in 1961 for freight work.

CD electric locomotive, number 182 118 begins to move out of the freight yard at Valasske Mezirici, in August 2000.

A locomotive on "banking" duties, ZSR electric locomotive number 183 002, waits to attach itself to the next train at Strba, in July 2004.

Skoda in 1961 for heavy freight work, with a maximum speed of 56 mph. Class 182 is a development of class 181, was introduced in 1963 and is used by CD and ZSR on freight duties. Class 183 is used by ZSR on freight work. Built by Skoda in 1971 for the 3000 v DC system, the locomotives have a maximum speed of 56 mph. Some are also used as bank-

ZSR center cab electric shunting locomotive, number 210 032, rests between duties at Kuty, in September 2003. This class is also used by CD.

ing locomotives on steep gradients. The existence of 25 KV lines has created a need for a range of locomotives able to operate on that system. CD and ZSR each have center-cab class 210 locomotives introduced in 1973 by Skoda and developed from class 110. They are used for shunting and light passenger and freight work and have a maximum speed of 50 mph. CD class 230 was introduced in 1966 by Skoda and the locomotives have a maximum speed of 68 mph. They are mainly used on freight work. Similar locomotives are in use on Bulgarian Railways as class 42. The appearance of these locomotives is par-

CD center-cab electric shunting locomotive, number 210 073, in an attractive blue livery waits at Brno, in July 2004.

Immaculate CD electric locomotive, number 230 028, displays its "art deco" cab at Tabor, in April 2005. Introduced in 1966, the type is also used by Bulgarian Railways as class 42.

ticularly distinctive because of the "art deco" design of their cabs. With the same impressive cabs as class 230, class 240 is used by CD and ZSR and was introduced by Skoda in 1968 for passenger train work. The class has a maximum speed of 75 mph. Three examples have been modified to run as dual-voltage locomotives for cross-border work into Austria and are now class 340. CD class 242 is a development of class 240 and was introduced in 1975. With a maximum speed of 75 mph, the locomotives are used on both passenger and freight work. CD and ZSR class 263 is a small class of mainly passenger train locomotives, introduced in 1985 by Skoda. They have a maximum speed of 75 mph. To enable through train working on all systems, a series of Skoda dual-voltage locomotive types has been acquired by CD and ZSR. ZSR class 350 are impressive express passenger locomotives introduced in 1974 with a maximum speed of 100 mph. They are derived from CD class 150/151 and have a similar body style. Classes 362 and 363 are operated by CD and ZSR. Introduced in 1981, the 362s are express passenger locomotives with a maximum speed of 87

ZSR electric locomotive, number 240 111, in pristine condition, pauses at Bratislava before leaving with an afternoon train, in October 2001.

CD electric locomotive, number 242 203, waits for its next duty at Cheb, in July 2004. This class was introduced in 1975.

In supurb condition and sporting an attractive livery, ZSR electric locomotive, number 263 003, leaves its stabling point at Kuty, in September 2003.

ZSR express passenger electric locomotive, number 350 004, is immaculate as it stands in the sun at Bratislava, in August 2000.

CD electric locomotive, number 363 082, is about to depart from Prague's main station in October 2004. This class is also used by ZSR.

CD electric class 371/372 locomotives work passenger and freight services into Germany. Locomotive number 372 014 is at Decin, in September 2003.

mph. Class 363 are the same locomotive but have different gearing to enable them to operate both passenger and freight services. 363s have a maximum speed of 75 mph. Introduced in 1986, CD class 371/372 are essentially the same locomotives and are designed for fast passenger and freight work. Class 371 was created by modifying and re-gearing certain 372 locomotives to give a higher maximum speed of 100 mph. Class 372 locomotives are limited to 75 mph. This class is the same as DB class 180 and, in 2003, CD acquired one of the DB locomotives to compensate for one of CD's locomotives being damaged in Germany.

CD and ZSR have large fleets of diesel locomotives, some of which are visually very attractive in terms of both their design and their liveries. A feature of both CD and ZSR is that a number of locomotives in particular classes are specifically numbered outside the normal number range to reflect specialist use or specialist ownership within the overall state system. Other locomotives, owned by industry or by independent railway companies, can often be found on CD and ZSR lines. Both CD and ZSR have rebuilt a number of locomotives from various classes to produce a more modern and efficient locomotive. Class 700 are small shunting locomotives used by CD. Over 150 were built following the introduction of the class in 1957 and a further batch of over 450 locomotives was built for industry or for specialist use within CD. The class is now largely withdrawn from CD although several have been rebuilt to new shunting class 799. The locomotives have a maximum speed of 25 mph. Class 701 was introduced in the late 1970s for CD and ZSR. They are essentially class 700 locomotives with a different engine and over 270 were built for industry in addition to those for the state systems. Class 702 was also derived

Small ZSR diesel shunting locomotive, number 701 004, is stabled between duties at Zilina, in September 2003. This class was introduced in the 1970s and is also used by CD.

from class 700. Introduced in 1967, mainly for CD, 100 examples were built with a further 200-plus being built for industry Again, these classes have been affected by withdrawals and a number have become class 799. Class 703 are shunting locomotives, introduced in 1977 for CD. They are normally used for shunting work in locomotive depots and have a maximum speed of 25 mph. Classes 799 (CD) and 199 (ZSR) are small shunting locomotives used in locomotive depots. Introduced in 1992, each class is a major rebuild of locomotives from classes 700, 701 and 702. The class has a very low maximum speed of 6 mph. It is clear that the experience of converting these locomotives and the success of the design has enabled further conversions to take place creating class 797 used by industry and for specialist rail activities. Introduced in 1988, CD class 704 have a more modern appearance than classes 700 to 703. The class comprises 20 shunting locomotives with a relatively high maximum speed of 37 mph.

Class 708 comprises 13 locomotives that were built in 1995 for CD with a maximum speed of 50 mph. They are used for shunting, light freight and branch-

In an attractive green livery, ZSR shunting locomotive, number T211 0551 is stabled at Zvolen, in September 2003.

line passenger train work. Class 705.9 are narrow gauge (750 and 760 mm gauge) locomotives built in the 1950s for CD. They work on lines in Southern Bohemia that were privatized in 1998. Most of the locomotives have a maximum speed of 31 mph. Class 710 is a class of shunting locomotives used by CD and ZSR. Built between 1961 and 1965, the locomotives have a maximum speed of 37 mph.

One of ZSR's small diesel shunting locomotives, number 701 005, waits at Zvolen for its next duty, in September 2003.

Locomotive, number 799 009, waits for its next duty at Louny, in April 2000. This class is used by CD as depot shunting locomotives.

CD's relatively modern light shunting locomotive, number 704 001, prepares to shunt a coach at Brno, in September 2003.

Diesel class 708 are modern shunting locomotives, introduced in 1995 for CD. Locomotive number 708 011 is at Kralupy nad Vltavou in April 2004.

Narrow gauge diesel passenger and freight locomotive number 705 915, displays its attractive blue livery at Jindrichov Hradec, in July 2004.

Class 710 locomotives are used by CD and ZSR for shunting. ZSR, number 710 003, waits at Spisska Nova Ves, in July 2004.

Light freight and shunting locomotive number 720 053 is stabled at Rakovnik in April 2005. Most of CD's examples of this class have now been withdrawn. The class is also used by ZSR.

Over 500 examples were built for CD, ZSR and industry with the state railways taking 248 of the class. Many have now been withdrawn – those that remain are mainly used for shunting in locomotive depots. CD class 715 is interesting in that it comprises 4 rack locomotives used on two standard gauge rack railways in the north of the country. Built in 1961, the locomotives have a maximum speed of 31 mph. Two examples are still in existence. CD and ZSR class 720 originally comprised 150 locomotives, a small number of which were converted for use on broad gauge lines. Introduced in 1958, the locomotives have a maximum speed of 37 mph and are used on shunting and light duties. Many locomotives have now been withdrawn. Class 721 was introduced in 1962 as a larger version of class 720 with a higher maximum speed of 50 mph. Over 200 were built for CD and ZSR. Although many of the CD locomotives have been withdrawn, those in ZSR are still used extensively on shunting and light duties. Classes 725 and 726 were introduced in the 1960s with a maximum speed of 44 mph. They were used by CD and ZSR on a variety of duties and the original total of locomotives was almost 200. Most are now withdrawn.

CD class 730 was introduced in two phases in the late 1970s and mid-1980s. The maximum speed of 50 mph makes them useful for shunting in goods

Introduced in 1962, class 721 locomotives are used for freight and shunting work. ZSR's number 721 072, waits at Poprad for its next duty.

Shunting and freight class 725 was used by CD and ZSR but is now largely withdrawn. Locomotive number 725 6092 waits to leave its depot in Bratislava, in August 2000.

Relatively modern shunting and light freight locomotive, CD number 730 007, travels through Decin, in April 2004. The class has a maximum speed of 50 mph which is suited to its role.

CD locomotive, number 731 032, is stabled at Olomouc, in July 2004. This class, introduced in 1988, is also used by ZSR for shunting and light freight work.

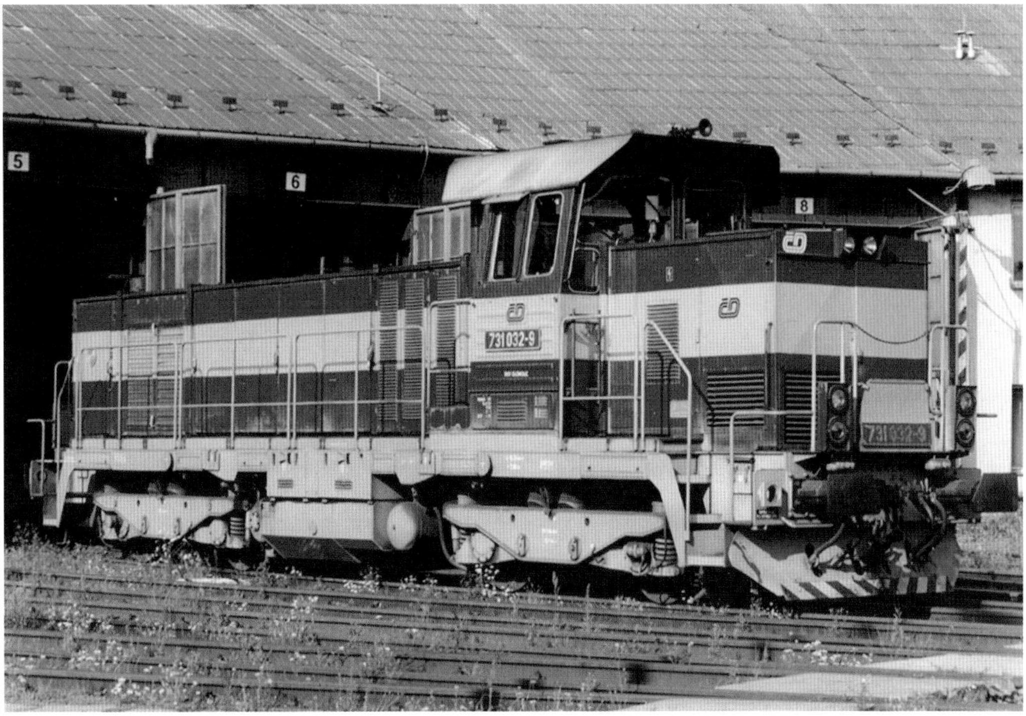

In a quiet country setting, CD diesel locomotive, number 714 207, prepares to leave Tyniste with a local train, in July 2004. This type is a rebuild of older diesel class 735.

Diesel class 736 is a rebuild of class 735 by ZSR for general duties and has a relatively high maximum speed of 62 mph. Locomotive number 736 003 is stabled at Zvolen, in September 2003.

yards and for light freight work. Class 731 is used by CD and ZSR and was introduced in 1988 for shunting and light freight duties and also has a maximum speed of 50 mph. CD and ZSR class 735 comprised almost 300 locomotives for freight and passenger train work. Introduced in 1973, the locomotives have a maximum speed of 56 mph. Most of the class have been withdrawn although a significant number have been rebuilt by CD into class 714 which was introduced in 1992 for use on passenger trains on branch lines. These rebuilt locomotives have a maximum speed of 62 mph. ZSR has rebuilt a small number of 735s into class 736 which was introduced in 1998 as a general purpose locomotive with a maximum speed of 62 mph. One of the largest classes numerically that is still in use is class 742. Over 450 were provided for use by both CD and ZSR with CD taking the largest number. A further batch of 41 locomotives is used by industry. Introduced in 1977, the locomotives are used on shunting duties, freight and passenger trains. The class has a maximum speed of 56 mph. Class 743 is an interesting small class of 10 locomotives designed for freight and passenger train work on steeply graded lines and for work in particular on the Tanvald–Harrachov rack railway in the north of the Czech Republic on which they provide extra support. Introduced in 1987, the class has a maximum speed of 56 mph. The locomotives have a distinctive livery which enhances their appearance. Classes 749 to 753 that follow have been the subject of extensive rebuilding and reclassification as indicated in the text. CD class 749 are passenger train locomotives with a maximum speed of 62 mph.

Standard CD large diesel shunting and light freight locomotive number 742 017, waits to return to work at Plzen, in October 2002.

Class 743 locomotive, number 743 007 is stabled at Ceska Lipa, in April 2005. This type works trains on steeply graded lines.

They are mid-1990s rebuilds of locomotives from class 751 and 752. Class 750 locomotives are allocated to both CD and ZSR and are rebuilds of class 753 completed in the 1990s. They are passenger train locomotives with a maximum speed of 62 mph. Their appearance is quite distinctive as they have a large, "goggles" windscreen. Introduced in 1964, class 751 comprised over 250 locomotives used by CD and ZSR. Initially used on passenger services, most of the surviving members of the class are used on freight work. The class has a maximum speed of 62 mph. Some examples have been rebuilt and reclassified as class 749 or 752. ZSR Class 752 was introduced in 1969 largely as passenger locomotives with a maximum speed of 62 mph. CD created a number of 752s by rebuilding class 751 locomotives in the mid 1990s. CD and ZSR class 753 was introduced in 1968 and over 400 locomotives were built for passenger train work. The class has a maximum speed of 62 mph and also has the distinctive windscreen. A significant number of locomotives has been rebuilt to become class 750 and others have been withdrawn from service. However, other members of the class have been sold to private railway companies in Italy and some have been sold to industrial/private railway companies in the Czech Republic. Class 754 are fast passenger train locomotives used by CD and ZSR. Introduced in 1978, the locomotives have a maximum speed of 62 mph and 86 examples were built. They also have the "goggles" windscreen. Over 100 examples of class 770

Immaculate CD passenger locomotive, number 749 265, poses in the sun at Olomouc, in August 2000. Its innovative livery is one of several different liveries applied to both CD's and ZSR's large diesels.

CD main line passenger train diesel, number 750 234, displays its distinctive "goggle" style windscreen between duties at Plzen, in September 2002. This class is also used by ZSR.

CD passenger train diesel locomotives, numbers 750 333 and 750 224, show off their impressive front ends at Letohrad, in August 2000.

were produced for CD and ZSR. Introduced in 1963 for heavy shunting and freight work, the class has a maximum speed of 56 mph. A small number of the ZSR locomotives have been converted for use on the broad gauge lines to the Ukranian border. The future of this attractive class of locomotives is limited and many locomotives have already been withdrawn. Class 771 was allocated to CD and ZSR and originally comprised over 200 locomotives for freight work. The class was introduced in the late 1960s and

ZSR diesel locomotive, number 751 057, pauses at Plesivec before moving to its next duty, in September 2003. This class is also used by CD.

In supurb condition, CD diesel locomotive number 752 001 poses in the sun at Louny, in April 2000. This class was created by the conversion of class 751 locomotives, in the 1990s.

CD "goggle" diesel class 753 are passenger train locomotives. Number 753 211 pauses between its duties at Plzen, in September 2002.

ZSR passenger train diesel locomotive, number 754 072, is stabled between duties at Zvolen, in September 2003. The class is also used by CD.

ZSR and CD diesel class 754 passenger train locomotives are kept in excellent condition and display a variety of attractive and distinctive liveries. CD locomotive 754 051 is stabled at Plzen, in July 2004.

has a maximum speed of 56 mph. Several ZSR locomotives have been converted for broad gauge use. As with class 770, a number of this class has been withdrawn from service although ZSR undertook a radical rebuild of a small number of locomotives in 1998 to 2001 to provide a modernised locomotive for shunting and general freight work, with a maximum speed of 62 mph. Class 775 and 776 were introduced in 1961 and 44 locomotives were produced that were used by ZSR. The class had a maximum speed of 62 mph. All have now been withdrawn although some examples have been

An impressive line-up of ZSR heavy shunting and light freight locomotives of class 771, at Vrutky in September 2003. Locomotives 771094, 093 and 020 wait in the early morning sun for their next duties.

ZSR diesel locomotive, number 771 143, is stabled at Plesivec in September 2003. CD also has examples of this heavy shunting and light freight class which was introduced in the 1960s.

preserved. Class 781 were Soviet-built locomotives introduced in 1966 and allocated to CD and ZSR. The locomotives are Soviet class M62 and are widely used throughout the old eastern bloc countries. The class has a maximum speed of 62 mph. Virtually all of the CD and ZSR locomotives are withdrawn

Broad gauge diesel locomotive, number 770 811, pauses between freight duties at Haniska, in September 2003. Most of this class are standard gauge.

although some examples are preserved. Other members of the class have been sold to private railway companies in Germany. The major builder of CD and ZSR diesels has been CKD, a Prague-based company that has existed since 1927. It built classes 700, 701, 704, narrow gauge 705, 708, 710, 714, 720, 721, 730, 731, 742, 743, the original locomotives of classes 750 to 754, 770 and 771. It has also built many of the classes primarily used for industrial purposes. This company became bankrupt in 2000 and was acquired by Siemens in 2001 – the new company becoming SKV – Siemens Rail Vehicles. It will be interesting to see if a new range of locomotives emerges from this new company. In Slovakia, Zvolen locomotive works has undertaken the rebuilding of several locomotive classes to produce modern locomotives for ZSR and private companies, in addition to the normal major overhaul of other ZSR diesel classes. Given the cost of new locomotives, it is likely that rebuilding work will continue as a more economical alternative. ZSR has not limited itself to the orthodox rebuilding of locomotives. In the late 1990s, ZSR commissioned the rebuilding of a class 753 locomotive into class 755, which emerged in 1997 as a very stylish, modern looking

Class 781, now withdrawn, were Soviet built diesel locomotives found in several other countries including Germany and Hungary and with some private railway companies. Number 781 600 stands at Sokolov in June 1996.

locomotive. Similarly, ZSR offered a class 771 for conversion into a modern heavy shunting locomotive. The finished locomotive – class 772 – appeared in 1998 and is startling in its appearance in that it has a futuristic styling and is certainly not recognisable as a former class 771. Unfortunately, neither of these locomotives appears to have been a success in that they have not progressed beyond the trial stage. CD has also pursued innovation. Class 759 comprised two prototype locomotives that were designed for express passenger work. Introduced in 1974, the locomotives have a normal maximum speed of 87 mph. However, on tests at the Cerhenice test centre, one of the locomotives achieved 109 mph which remains as the record speed for a Czech diesel locomotive. CD did not pursue any further building of this class, possibly because of the commitment to expand the electrification program and the development of unit type trains. Finally, it is evident that the impact of private railway companies appears to be increasing in the Czech Republic. OKD Doprava started operating coal trains in the Ostrava area in the early 1990s and, subsequently, has extended its operation into other areas. OKD has a large fleet of locomotives, which mainly comprises class 740 locomotives – a class mainly used by industry and not unlike the CD and ZSR class 742 in appearance – class 770s as also used by CD and a number of ex-CD class 753s. Viamont was established in 1992 and is responsible for delivering coal to Dolni Berkovoce power station in the northwest of the country. This company also mainly uses class 740 locomotives. These companies and others in the Czech Republic are now responsible for an estimated 8 per cent of the total freight traffic on the railways operated by CD and this may increase in future years as the "open access" policy makes an impact. The impact of private companies on ZSR is less significant but the Austrian company LTE now has responsibility for some cement and coke freight work using new Vossloth locomotives. US Steel has also taken over the delivery of limestone to one of its plants using its own class 770 locomotives. This company has also acquired a number of rebuilt class 770 locomotives from Zvolen works, which have been designated as class 774.

Italian Railways

Until the middle of the nineteenth century, Italy was still divided between several states, each of which had a different view of their economy and their local public transportation. In the first half of the nineteenth century, the Regno delle due Sicilie (Kingdom of two Sicilys) became the first Italian state with a railway line. The Naples-Portici line was 4.5 mi long and built by the French engineer Armand Bayard. It went on to be inaugurated on October 3 1839 and heralded Italy into the railway age.

The 2-2-2 steam locomotive Bayard, which started working on the section between Naples and Portici, just a few months after the line was opened.

It wasn't long before this was followed by the construction of the Naples-Nocera and Castellammare line, and the Caserta line inaugurated in 1843 – extended the following year as far as Capua – and the Cancello-Nola branch line. The Neapolitan railway network totalled 58 miles in length on June 3, 1846. In 1855 the Kingdom of the Two Sicilies launched an ambitious plan for expansion but only 18 miles were actually finished – the Nola-Sarno and Nocera-Vietri lines.

In the meantime in the Kingdom of Lombardy-Venetia, the Milan-Monza line was inaugurated, on

The Napoli – Portici line was the first railway in Italy and built by a French engineer, Armand Bayard. The name given to this locomotive.

August 17 1840 – the construction of the Milan-Verona-Venice line was also designed. When the first War of Independence broke out in 1848, the Milan-Treviglio and Vicenza-Padua-Mestre lines, totalling 62 mi, were already in operation. The Kingdom of Lombardy-Venetia completed the Milan-Venice line in 1857, and in 1860 extended it as far as Trieste, which was already linked to the line to Vienna. The Grand-Duchy of Tuscany inaugurated the Leghorn/Livorno-Pisa line, on March 14 1844, as the first section of the Leopolda line to Empoli and Florence-Porta al Prato. This was com-

It wasn't long before many other lines opened up. This is a price list of 1857, with a selection of destinations and their prices.

The inaugural ride of August 1867, up the Moncenisio railroad, must have been frightening. Work was carried out in both summer and winter.

pleted on June 10 1848. By the end of that same year and with the Pisa-Lucca, Florence-Prato and Lucca-Pescia lines now open, the Tuscan network exceeded 98 mi. In 1851 the Grand-Duchy completed the line linking Florence to Prato and Pistoia – the Maria Antonia line. The railway network was completed with the construction of the Empoli-Siena line in 1849 – later extended to Sinalunga – and of the Pescia-Pistoia line in 1859. By the end of 1860 Tuscany had 210 mi of track. The Kingdom of Sardinia was the last Italian state to adopt a railway system, with only the Papal States trailing behind it. It was thanks to the farsightedness of Cavour and Carlo Ilarione Petitti, that from the very outset, Piedmont had begun to build a fully-fledged rail network. The main artery of the system was the Turin-Alessandria-Genoa line, of which the first section, Turin-Moncalieri, was inaugurated on September 24, 1848. By 1855, with its 290 mi of line, Piedmont had more track than any other Italian state – increasing it by the end of 1860 to 534 miles. The Papal States, the last to install a railway system, inaugurated the Rome-Frascati line on July 7, 1856, and three years later opened the Rome-Civitavecchia line.

In 1861, with the unification of Italy, the railway network had reached 1,260 mi, which was made up of numerous lines, operated by seven railway companies, with no organic national plan. The newly-created Italian state gave a major impetus to implementing a program to make up for the delays that had built up in the previous decades, keeping Italy behind the more advanced European countries and North America. Several new lines were built, bringing the network five years later up to 2,322 miles in length. Enormous effort was put into building new railway lines, and to push this commitment forward, the newly-founded Kingdom of Italy enacted a law in 1865 to bring all the existing railway lines, and any future line, under four large companies –

A 2-6-0 steam locomotive simmers in the sun and displays its impressive design as it waits to depart with its train.

An old 2-6-0 steam locomotive sits at the platform, waiting for its passengers to board. Italy has recently become much more interested in its railway past.

Preserved class 835 steam locomotive, is pictured in a park at Ancona, in May 2000. These 0-6-0 tank locomotives were introduced in 1906 and over 50 examples still exist.

Societa' Ferroviaria dell'Alta Italia (SFAI), which was given all the northern Italian lines; Societa' delle Strade Ferrate Romane (SFR), which took over the lines along the Ligurian coast (subsequently acquired by SFAI), Tuscany, Campagna, Umbria, Abruzzo and the former Papal State; Societa' Italiana per le Strade Ferrate Meridionali, to operate lines in Campagna (except the Naples-Ceprano line), Molise, Abruzzo, Puglia, and the Bologna-Ancona-Bari-Otranto route; and the Societa' delle Calabro-Sicule, which was given the Taranto-Brindisi, Taranto-Reggio, Metaponto-Potenza-Eboli and the Sicilian lines.

To attract private capital and foreign investment to the railways, Italy adopted the public franchise system of the "concessione," which enabled the companies to earn a good return on operating the lines, and the Exchequer to amortise the costs over a long period. But the public franchise system, under which ownership and operating responsibilities were handed over to the large railway operating companies, did not produce the desired results. In 1885 a new law was therefore enacted completely overhauling the criterion for allocating the lines, and a new covenant was concluded between the state and each of the three large railway companies. This covenant system was based on the principle that the Grantees were only required to operate the railway networks, but the network itself remained the property of the state. Strade Ferrate Meridionali was responsible for the lines down the Adriatic coast and the Rome-Florence line, as well as the lines in the Veneto and part of Lombardy, which totalled 2,582 mi. Società Italiana per le Strade Ferrate del Mediterraneo – known as Rete Mediterranea RM – was given 2,528 mi of line, partly in Lombardy, Piedmont and Liguria, and the long Genoa-Rome-Naples-Salerno-Taranto line, as

Vintage electric locomotive, number 626 248, is stabled at Bologna, in May 2000. This class was introduced in 1928 for freight work.

Diesel shunting locomotive, number 143 3002, waits at Falconara, in May 2000. This class are ex-USA Transportation Corps locomotives built in 1943.

well as the Reggio Calabria-Taranto line around the Ionian coast.

The four largest railway stations – Milan, Florence, Rome and Naples – were jointly managed by them, and each network served major ports and was linked to the foreign railway network. Lastly, Societa Ital-

Class 424 electric locomotives were introduced in the 1940s. Locomotive number 424 318 waits at Ancona with a local passenger train, in May 2000.

Small diesel shunting locomotive, number 216 0043, is stabled in the sun at Falconara in May 2000.This class was introduced in 1965.

iana per le Strade Ferrate della Sicilia was given 368 mi of line in Sicily, mainly comprising the Messina-Catania-Siracusa and the Catania-Caltanissetta-Palermo lines. But even this system proved disappointing as track and rolling stock upgrades and renewals were strictly dependent on increased revenues, and these only began to rise at the end of the century. The covenants were due to expire for the first time in 1905 and the Grantees were unwilling to upgrade the rolling stock, with their contracts about to expire, and did everything possible to keep down their operating costs and raise profits. The freezing of wages, and in some cases wage cuts, created discontent and unease among their employees, while the obsolete rolling stock, which frequently broke down, caused numerous delays and protests from the travelling public. Serious consideration therefore began to be given at the beginning of the new century to the possibility of a full nationalization of the railways. In 1905 this was instigated with the creation of the Amministrazione Ferrovie dello Stato, a state-owned corporation.

The Ferrovie dello Stato was incorporated by Act of Parliament in 1905 and inherited the difficult situation from the three major networks it had acquired. But nationalisation did have its positive side and went some way to meet the demands from different sections of society – the Chambers of Commerce, who had so often complained about the high tariffs that were discouraging exports; the railway workers, who felt more secure both because of their working conditions and improved pay; and the Italian industrialists, who had greater possibilities for acquiring railway tenders now that the engineering industry was able to compete satisfactorily with the most highly developed European countries. Riccardo Bianchi, the former director of the Rete Sicula – Sicilian Network – was appointed to organise, set in motion and develop the new corporation. He embarked on a wide-ranging programme to reorganise the network, modernise the plant and rolling stock, and to upgrade the stations. Service quality began to improve and there were fewer complaints, and all the economic indicators began to rise. The long period of economic expansion in Italy under Giolitti was also helped by the enhanced efficiency of rail transport, which drove the increased demand that continued uninterrupted through to the outbreak of World War I. It was during this period that the tunnel under the Simplon was brought into service and the ferry service over the Strait of Messina, that

In traditional brown livery, electric locomotive number 636 430 prepares to leave Falconara in May 2000. This class is mainly used on freight work.

In new livery, electric locomotive, number 636 241, near Venice in September 2005. This class was introduced in the 1940s and is largely used on freight work although some passenger train duties are undertaken.

had just recently been introduced, came into operation.

But by far the most outstanding event in this period was the large-scale electrification plan for the whole network, which made Italy a European leader in this field. Research began in 1899 into the electrification of the track, and experiments were carried out with accumulators and third rails, using direct current. On the Valtellina line an experiment was carried out that immediately revealed its great potential. The line was electrified using three-phase alternating 3000 v, 15Hz current. This was the first time that such high voltages had ever been used, and in view of the success of the operation it was decided to use the same system for the electrification of the Giovi line, where the gradients were as steep as 1 in 28. The line was electrified with 3600 v 16.7 Hz, three-phase current, and an electric locomotive was designed - the FS E 550 – which delivered an excellent performance. The new train was able to pull 700 wagons a day, compared with only 450 using steam locomotives, and the new train was nicknamed "the Giant of Giovi."

When Italy entered World War I in 1915 thc rail network proved its ability to perform the strategic tasks assigned to it, transporting all the troops and materiel to the Front and taking the wounded troops to hospitals well away from the battlefields, effectively and without interruption.

Between the two world wars, particular attention

Diesel class 345 locomotives are used on passenger and freight duties. Number 345 1079 waits for its next duty near Campobasso, in March 2003.

Modern electric locomotive, number 412 009, is stabled between duties near Milan, in September 2005. This class of triple voltage freight locomotives is designed to work into France, Austria and Germany.

was devoted to the railways. To improve their efficiency, the Board of Directors was dismissed and replaced by administrators. During the Fascist period, wages were cut and railway workers dismissed. Of the 235,500 employees in 1921, 85,000 were sacked during the 1920s and by 1937 there were only 133,100 railway workers left. But the great change occurred in 1924 with the institution of the Ministry of Communications. This was the age of large-scale electrification. The Rome-Naples express line was completed, and after 13 years of work on building the 11-mile-long Great Apennines Tunnel, the Florence-Bologna line was finally inaugurated. With the electrification program, the electrified network was increased from the 280 mi at the end of World War I, to 475 miles in 1928, and by 1939 topped 3212 miles. The electrification program had concentrated mostly on the international links

Electric locomotive for freight work, number 645 042, is stabled at Verona, in September 2005. This class was introduced in 1958.

Electric locomotive, number 646 079, with a passenger service along the beautiful northwest Italian coast, in July 2003.This class was introduced in 1961.

Center-cab diesel locomotive, number 145 1026, is at the head of a light freight train against an impressive mountain background. This class was introduced in 1982 and is also used on shunting duties.

with France, Austria and Switzerland, but had ignored virtually the whole of southern Italy. However, because of the focus on road-building, rail began to lose out against road transport. At the start of the 1930s, Italy had four times as many motorcars and twice as many lorries and trucks on the road than it had a decade earlier.

Before Italy's entry into World War II in 1940, the state railway network was over 10,600 miles long, carrying 194 million passengers and some 66 million tons of freight a year. In the early years of the war these figures rose, as vehicle fuel became scarcer. But during the war, it was the ports and railway lines that were the chief strategic targets and by 1945

Electric locomotive, number 402 012, is stabled at Bologna in May 2000. This class was introduced in 1994 and was initially used on express passenger services. Freight work is now also undertaken.

Class 402.1 is a development of class 402 but shows a radically different design by Pininfarina. Number 402 117 and another member of the class back on to their train at Naples, in May 1998.

A new electric unit is pictured at speed and shows a design that is significantly different from the traditional shape. This type of unit train is increasingly being acquired by other European railways.

One of FS's traditional diesel trains crosses a spectacular viaduct. The train comprises two railcars that are a major feature of local passenger services in Italy.

An electric unit train powers across a viaduct at treetop height. Electric units have been used for some years in Italy and the new Pendolino trains have been designed as units.

One of FS's relatively modern electric train units bends into a curve while passing through spectacular scenery.

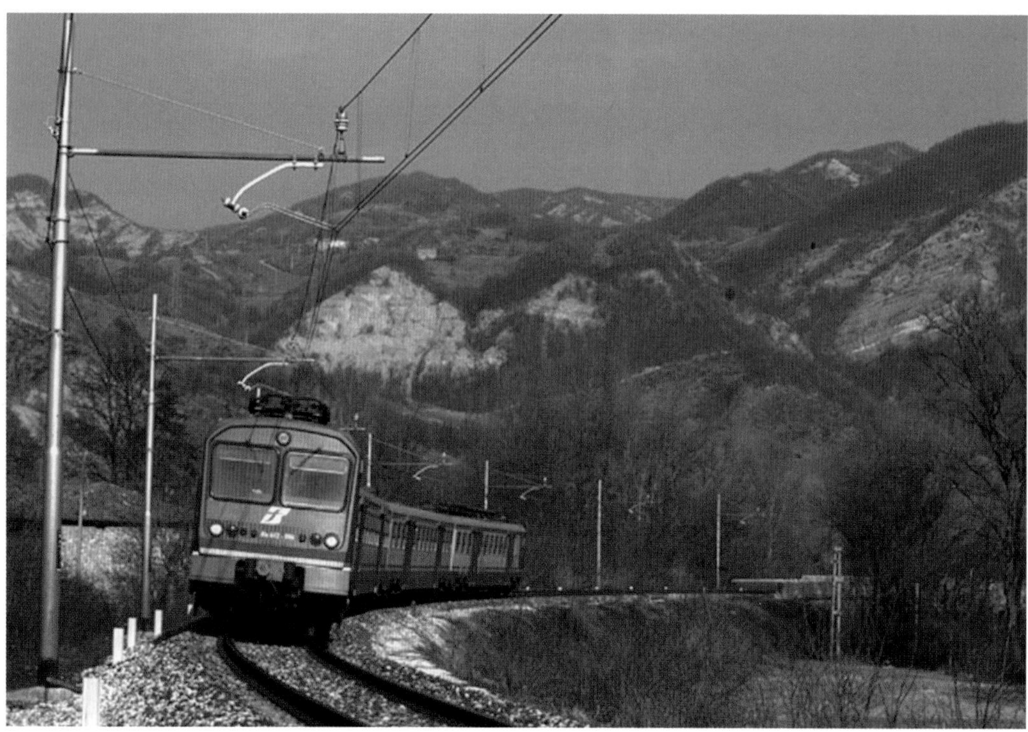

more than 40 per cent of track had been destroyed, and much of the rolling stock too. Just to give some idea of the extent of the destruction, when the war ended Italy had only 1803 locomotives left of the original 4177, and only 1255 of the 8704 passenger coaches.

In the wake of World War II, the railways were once again used to spearhead the huge reconstruction effort and by the end of 1945 the rail network had been restored almost to its original 1940 level. Unfortunately, this massive undertaking never managed to bring any real improvement to the system itself. The network remained virtually unchanged and yet Italians were becoming more mobile. Transporting vast amounts of goods and commodities from one part of the country to the other in a period of all-out economic growth following the traumatic war years, had now become an urgent necessity, but the railways were unable to fully meet this demand. It seemed that as soon as the railway network had been reconstructed, it was already out of date, overtaken by the powerful government-driven policy to introduce and develop private motoring – new roads and motorways were built, increasingly relegating the railways to second best. It took the great oil crisis of 1974, and heightened public concern about the problems of environmental sustainability, to put the railways back to the fore in driving the country's economic development. At the beginning of the 1980s, Italy had an unenviable record in the way that road transport had been allowed to seriously handicap the railways – 85 percent of the public travelled by motorcar from one city to another, while only 12 percent took the train. The situation had not changed by the end of the decade, and the railways were unable to cope with incremental traffic volumes generated in the meantime by increased industrial output.

Meanwhile, abroad – and particularly in France and Germany – the high speed system was already a reality. Italian railways had only just begun to address the problem of upgrading the railway network, by quadrupling the main lines which carried the vast bulk of the national passenger and freight traffic. For traffic capacity could only be increased by embarking on new track construction which would ease congestion on the existing lines, which were by now saturated. Medium-haul and long-haul traffic had to be transferred to the new fast tracks, while simultaneously upgrading local, commuter, and freight traffic using the old network. That is where Italy stands in 2005; it too has developed new commuter and freight trains and also has a high-speed system that will allow it to integrate with the rest of the European rail network.

Belgium and Luxembourg Railways

Although they are not geographically large countries, Belgium (SNCB/NMBS) and Luxembourg (CFL) railways provide an intensive service using an interesting variety of locomotives. Each country has invested heavily in recent years to update the infrastructure and provide new unit type trains and new locomotives.

One of SNCB/NMBS new electric locomotives, number 1357, is pictured at speed with a train of modern coaches.

The first railway in Belgium opened in May 1835 from Brussels to Mechelen. Progress was then rapid to the extent that over 310 mi of lines was in place by 1843 and 620 mi by 1850.

Class 21 is one of Belgium's standard electric locomotives for passenger and freight work. Locomotive number 2140 tilts as it speeds through a curve.

SNCB/NMBS was created in 1926 and the railway by that time had a key role in the economic life of the country. World War II created major problems in terms of the need to reconstruct the railway and it was recognised that the railways had an important role related to the future movement of freight.

Progress continued after the war particularly on the improvement of the infrastructure and the acquisition of a substantial locomotive fleet. SNCB/NMBS

As a part of up-grading the train fleet, SNCB/NMBS has recently introduced new units of which 4101is an example.

now controls 2,186 mi of lines of which over 1,800 mi is electrified including 87 mi of high-speed lines equipped for 190 mph running. In recent years, there has been an investment in new diesel and electric locomotives to support passenger and freight services. A major landmark was the opening of the Channel Tunnel which enabled through passenger services to be introduced between Brussels and London in 1994. This also gave an impetus to the development of a high-speed line through France and into Belgium and enhanced traffic to destinations beyond Brussels. Freight remains particularly important. In 2004, 55 million tonnes of freight was carried and through services are provided into both Germany and France. Freight activity is marketed as B – Cargo, although it remains under SNCB/NMBS control. Organisationally, in 2005 SNCB/NMBS

Preserved steam locomotive, number 29 013, is a 2-8-0 locomotive built in 1945. It is pictured working hard on a special train.

SNCB/NMBS class 11 is dedicated to the Brussels to Amsterdam service. Locomotive number 1184 approaches Brussels Midi station, in July 1995.

created "Infrabel" to be responsible for the railway infrastructure and "Operations" to be responsible for freight and passenger services but they both remain clearly under the overall control of SNCB/NMBS.

To date, the open access policy has not made a major impact in Belgium but some private freight companies are already operating into Belgium and developments are likely over the next few years given the strategic position of Belgium in Europe. There may also be a number of partnerships created, perhaps with DB, NS and SNCF.

The first railways in Luxembourg opened in 1859 with lines from Luxembourg to Arlon in Belgium and Thionville in France. Other lines in Luxembourg itself were opened in the 1860s by a private company, Company Guillaume – Luxembourg (GL) and a second company, Company Prince Henri (PH) built lines in the south of the country in the 1870s.

Class 16 electric locomotive, number 1605, at Oostende in June 2005. This multi-voltage class was introduced in 1966.

Veteran SNCB/NMBS electric locomotive, number 1503, is ready to leave Namur with a passenger train, in September 1993. Following its introduction in 1962, this triple voltage class worked in Holland.

Now withdrawn from service, SNCB/NMBS class 18 locomotives headed express passenger trains. Locomotive number 1802 arrives at Brussels Midi, in September 1993.

SNCB/NMBS class 20 locomotive, number 2005, prepares to leave Luxembourg station with a passenger train, in July 1993.

The GL passed into German control in 1871 when Alsace-Lorraine was acquired by Germany and then into French SNCF control in 1918 when that territory came under French control. The PH remained in control of its area until it became part of German DR in 1918.

Luxembourg Railways CFL (Chemins de Fer Luxembourgeois) came into existence in April 1946 and remains in control of the network.

Today, CFL controls 169 mi of track, the majority of which is electrified to 25 kV ac. There has also been a significant investment in the infrastructure, in new trains including double-deck coaches and in new locomotives.

Although Belgium does not have a national railway museum, a number of steam locomotives have been preserved and are held in storage or at preservation sites.

Preserved class 18 number 18.051 is a 4-4-0 locomotive built in 1905 and based on a design by McIntosh in Scotland. 140 locomotives of this type operated express passenger services principally between Brussels and Antwerp. Another preserved locomotive, class 01 number 01.002 is a 4-6-2 express passenger locomotive, built in 1923. 35 examples were built. In recent years, a Polish class Ty2 "Kriegslok" 2-10-0 was acquired as a working locomotive and was restored for use in Belgium. Originally built in 1943, the locomotive now runs as 26.101.

Passenger and freight electric locomotive, number 2701, is at Liege, in June 1996. This locomotive is the first of 60 in the class.

In distinctive livery, veteran SNCB/NMBS electric locomotive, number 2211, at Monceau, in June 1996. This class was introduced in 1954.

Similarly, Luxembourg operates a "Kriegslok" which was formally OBB number 52.3504 now running as number 5621.

SNCB/NMBS electric locomotive class 23, number 2317, waits in the sun for its next duty at Amsterdam, in February 2000.

Belgium has a significant number of electric locomotives and classes. There is also a mix of single, dual, triple and four voltage types which reflects the nature of a number of through workings into neighbouring countries. Class 11 comprises 12 dual-voltage (1500/3000 v DC) locomotives used exclusively on the Brussels to Amsterdam service. Introduced in 1985, the class has a maximum speed of 100 mph. Another dual-voltage type which uses 3000 v DC and 25 kV AC is class 12. Introduced in 1986, the 12 locomotives were originally express passenger locomotives with a maximum speed of 100 mph. They are now mainly used on freight work within Belgium and into France. Class 15 comprises 6 triple-voltage locomotives using 1500/3000 v DC and 25 kV AC. They originally worked into Holland and France but the introduction of TGV type trains has now largely limited their role to passenger work in Belgium. The class was introduced in 1962 and has a maximum speed of 100 mph. The 8 locomotives of class 16 are able to work to 1500/3000 v DC and 15/25 kV AC and were introduced in 1966. Their work includes throughwork into Holland and Germany although

SNCB/NMBS electric locomotive, number 2553, tilts into the curve at Antwerp with an afternoon freight train, in February 2000.

In immaculate condition, class 26 electric locomotive, number 2612, at Liege, in June 1996. This class was introduced in 1964.

Class 28 locomotives were introduced in 1949 for express passenger train work. Locomotive number 2802 is stabled at Brussels, in September 1993.

New SNCB/NMBS electric locomotive, number 1304, is stabled at Leuven in June 2005. The class works passenger and freight services.

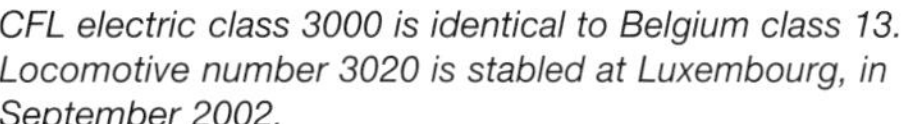

CFL electric class 3000 is identical to Belgium class 13. Locomotive number 3020 is stabled at Luxembourg, in September 2002.

the introduction of more modern trains has curtailed their use to some extent. The class has a maximum speed of 100 mph.

Class 18 is now withdrawn from service although some examples are preserved. Introduced in 1973, the six locomotives had a maximum speed of 112 mph and were four-voltage machines as class 16 with the capacity to work into France and Germany. The class is identical in appearance to SNCF class CC 40100, although they are more powerful than their French counterparts. In 1990, locomotive 1805 achieved 135 mph during high-speed trials – a Belgium record for a locomotive at that time. Class 20 is a single voltage (3000 v DC) class of 25 loco-

A magnificent line-up of CFL veteran class 3600 center-cab electric locomotives at Luxembourg, in January 2000. The class was introduced in 1959 for passenger and freight services and are now being withdrawn.

Several of CFL's class 3600 locomotives carry impressive name plates. The plate from locomotive number 3614 refers to Rumelange in Luxembourg.

motives introduced in 1975 for passenger and freight work and has a maximum speed of 100 mph. These locomotives also work into Luxembourg. The class were the most powerful locomotives in Belgium until the acquisition of class 13. Classes 21 and 27 are identical in appearance and total 120 locomotives used on passenger and freight work. Introduced in the early 1980s, they are both single voltage types with class 21 being the lower powered of the two. Each has a maximum speed of 100 mph. Single voltage class 22 dates from 1954 and comprises 50 locomotives for passenger and freight work with a maximum speed of 80 mph. A number of the class are now stored as new locomotives/train sets have been acquired. Class 23 also dates from the mid-1950s and is largely used on freight work. There are over 80 locomotives in this single voltage class which has a maximum speed of 80 mph. Classes 25 and 25.5 were introduced in 1960 and were both originally intended for passenger work with class 25.5 becoming dual-voltage (1500/3000 v DC) locomotives in

Introduced in 1961, SNCB/NMBS large diesel class 51 are now being withdrawn. Locomotive number 5166 is stabled at Antwerp, in September 1993.

SNCB/NMBS diesel locomotive, number 5401, is stabled at Bertrix, in November 1994. This class was introduced in 1955.

Class 55 diesel locomotives were introduced by SNCB/NMBS in 1961. Locomotive number 5513 is stabled at Liege, in June 1996.

SNCB/NMBS class 59 diesels were introduced in 1955 for heavy freight work. Locomotive number 5924 is stabled at Namur, in February 1992.

the mid-1970s for through working into Holland. Class 25.5 is now largely used for freight work. The combined total of 24 locomotives has a maximum speed of 80 mph. Class 26 totals 35 single voltage locomotives introduced in 1964. The locomotives have a maximum speed of 80 mph and are used on freight work. Classes 28 and 29 were early electric locomotives introduced in 1949 and 1948 respectively. They were used on express passenger services and the class 29s were also used on freight work before they were withdrawn. The class 28s had a maximum speed of 80 mph and the class 29s 62 mph. Two examples of class 29 have been preserved. Class 13 is the most recent locomotive type in Belgium and is also found in Luxembourg as class 3000 (20 locomotives). Introduced in 1997, Belgium has 60 locomotives that have a maximum speed of 124 mph. These dual voltage locomotives work passenger and freight services, including cross-border work into France and Luxembourg. The Luxembourg locomotives have a similar range of work and can often be seen double-heading freight trains with their Belgium equivalents. Luxembourg has three other classes of electric locomotive. Class 3600 was introduced in 1959 and are identical in

Veteran class 62 diesels were introduced in the 1960s and many are still in service. Locomotive number 6231 waits in the sun for its next duty at Antwerp, in February 2000.

Large SNCB/NMBS diesel shunting class 70 locomotive, number 7004, waits at Antwerp for its next duty, in September 1993.

appearance to the French centre-cab class BB 12000. These 25 kV AC locomotives have a maximum speed of 75 mph and are used on passenger and freight services. With the acquisition of new locomotives and train sets, this class is now gradually being withdrawn. Prior to acquiring new locomotives, CFL leased a number of class 185 locomotives for passenger and freight work. Details of this class can be found in the German section of this book. The future use of these locomotives is uncertain following CFL's acquisition of 20 class 4000 locomotives for passenger work. This class is dual-voltage (15/25 kV AC) and are essentially class 185 locomotives built by Bombardier.

Belgium and Luxembourg each have interesting diesel classes. Belgium class 51 was introduced in

Shunting locomotive of class 74, number 7404, waits at Antwerp for its next duty, in January 1995. This class was introduced in 1977.

1961 and comprised almost 100 locomotives largely for freight work. The class has a maximum speed of 75 mph. With the introduction of more modern locomotives, this class is now effectively withdrawn from service. Classes 52, 53 and 54 are Nohab/General Motors locomotives as also found in Hungary (class M61), Denmark (classes MV, MX and MY), Norway (class Di 3a) and Luxembourg (Class 1600). Introduced in the mid-1950s, the locomotives have a maximum speed of 75 mph. They are passenger and freight locomotives although they are now mainly found on freight work. A number of locomotives of each class have been withdrawn although several have been preserved. Class 55 comprises over 40 locomotives for passenger and freight work in Southern Belgium. They also work into

SNCB/NMBS class 82 is typical of several shunting locomotive classes in Belgium. Locomotive number 8273 is stabled at Antwerp, in June 1996.

Luxembourg. Introduced in 1961, the class has a maximum speed of 75 mph. Class 59 was introduced in 1955 for freight work and has a maximum speed of 75 mph. Although they are all withdrawn from normal service, several have been used for hauling trains associated with the building of high-speed lines in both Belgium and France. Several examples have been preserved.

Class 60 was a numerically large class introduced in 1963 and they were all withdrawn from service some years ago. However, a number of examples have been preserved and several were sold to Italian railway infrastructure companies. The locomotives had a maximum speed of 75 mph. Class 62 were introduced in the early 1960s and are used on passenger and freight work. Originally numbering over 130 locomotives, the class has been reduced through withdrawals and some have been purchased by ACTS, a Dutch private freight company. The class has a maximum speed of 75 mph. Classes 70 and 71 are used for heavy shunting work in

SNCB/NMBS shunting locomotive number 8504 at Antwerp, in February 2000. Introduced in 1956, the class is now being displaced by class 77.

The total of over 250 locomotives of classes 80, 82, 83, 84 and 85 are all general purpose shunting locomotives allocated to freight yards throughout Belgium. They were introduced in the 1950s and 1960s and have a maximum speed of either 37 mph (classes 80 and 82) or 30 mph. The work for these locomotives has diminished as class 77 locomotives have been introduced and withdrawals have taken place. Some locomotives of classes 80 and 84 were sold to Italian railway infrastructure contractors some years ago. Class 92 was a class of 25 shunting locomotives with a maximum speed of 28 mph, introduced in 1960 and now withdrawn from service. Similarly, class 91 has been substantially affected by withdrawals. These small shunting locomotives, originally totalling 60 examples, are used in depots and freight yards and have a maximum speed of 25 mph. They were introduced in 1961. Class 77 comprises 170 locomotives introduced in 1999 for shunting and freight work. They have a maximum speed of 62 mph. The locomotives were built by Vossloth/Bombardier and are based on the successful G1200 type locomotives now widely in use throughout Europe. They also have a connection in development terms with the NS class 6400. The locomotives have an attractive grey, white and yellow livery.

Diminutive shunting locomotive class 91 is used for light duties in depots and yards. Locomotive number 9148 is at Stockem, in January 2000.

Antwerp docks. Introduced in 1954 (class 70) and 1962 (class 71), the locomotives have maximum speeds of 30 and 50 mph respectively. Of the smaller shunting locomotives, class 73 is the largest numerically comprising almost 100 locomotives. Introduced in stages between 1965 and 1977, the locomotives have a maximum speed of 37 mph and can be found on both shunting duties and light freight train work. Classes 74 and 75 are two small classes of locomotive used in Antwerp docks. Class 74 was introduced in 1977 and class 75 in the 1980s having previously been class 65 main-line locomotives introduced in 1965. They have a maximum speed of 37 and 51 mph respectively. Class 76 are ex-Dutch NS class 2200s acquired by SNCB/NMBS for work on the new high-speed lines in Belgium. Details of the class can be found in the section of this book related to the railways of Holland.

Class 92 diesel shunting locomotives are now withdrawn from service. Locomotive number 9204 is stabled at Antwerp, in January 1995.

Luxembourg has a number of shunting locomotives and main line diesels. Class 800 are similar in design to American shunting locomotives of the 1950s. There are six locomotives in the class which was introduced in 1954. The locomotives are used for shunting and light freight train work and have a maximum speed of 50 mph. Similar in appearance to French class BB 63000, the eight locomotives of class 850 and 13 of class 900 have a range of duties as class 800. Introduced in the mid-1950s, the loco-

One of SNCB's new diesel shunting and light freight locomotives, number 7721, is stabled at Merelbeke in June 2005.

motives have a maximum speed of 65 mph. Classes 1000, 1010, 1020 and 1030 are small classes of light shunting locomotives introduced in 1972, 1964, 1952 and 1988 respectively. Class 1000 and 1030 have a maximum speed of 37 mph, class 1010 15 mph and class 1020 33 mph. Class 1800 comprises 20 locomotives introduced in 1963 for mainline passenger and freight work. They are virtually the same as SNCB/NMBS class 55 and work into Belgium. The locomotives have a maximum speed of 75 mph.

Now withdrawn class 1600 are classic Nohab/General Motors locomotives as found elsewhere in Europe. Introduced in 1955, they are the same as SNCB class 52 and have a maximum speed of 75 mph. Three examples have been preserved.

Luxembourg has recently leased a small number of modern shunting locomotives and several Vossloth G1200 types. It will be interesting to see if these acquisitions ultimately affect the future of some of CFL's traditional diesel classes.

Class 800 shows its classic American "switcher" design as it prepares to pull empty coaches out of Luxembourg station in July 1993.

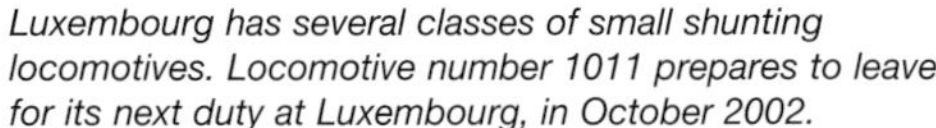

Luxembourg has several classes of small shunting locomotives. Locomotive number 1011 prepares to leave for its next duty at Luxembourg, in October 2002.

CFL class 1000 shunting locomotive, number 1001, manoeuvres wagons at Bettembourg, in July 1993. This class was introduced in 1972.

Introduced in 1963, CFL class 1800 locomotives are used on passenger and freight services. Number 1812 rests at Arlon, in October 1992.

Scandinavian Railways

The railways of Scandinavia consist of the railways of Denmark (DSB), Finland (VR), Norway (NSB) and Sweden (SJ). Each has a railway system that has to operate in extremes of weather over significant distances and over difficult terrain. Each system has a range of diesel and electric locomotives some of which are relatively modern. There is also a range of private railway companies operating in some areas that have an interesting range of locomotive types.

The first railway in Denmark opened in 1847 from Copenhagen to Roskilde and was extended to Korsor in 1856. The line was operated by the Zealand Railway Company. Subsequently, further lines were opened so that, by 1894, the framework of the railway system as it exists today was virtually in place. In 1892, Danske Statsbaner (DSB) was formed and took responsibility for the system. This did not prevent new private railway companies/private lines being created in the years prior to World War II and private railways are still a feature of today's railway system. The period after the war was one of consolidation but, from the mid-1960s, the system began to be improved, particularly in terms of routes to the German border. This culminated with the opening of the Storebaelt bridge link in 1997 and improved links to Sweden with the opening of the impressive Oresund bridge link in 2000.

The builder's plate from DSB steam locomotive number 34 shows that it was built by Henschel and Sohn at Cassel, in 1916.

Preserved Danish steam locomotive, number 34, eases into Aalborg station with a special train of three vintage coaches, in July 2002. This locomotive was built in 1916.

The first line in Finland from Helsinki to Hameenlinna opened in 1862. Railway development tended to focus on the more populous parts of the country in the south and there was a heavy reliance on steam locomotives and latterly diesel locomotives until the first stages of electrification were introduced in 1969. Links with Russia were significant in terms of services and locomotive development.

The first line in Norway from Oslo to Eidsvoll opened in 1854 and NSB has existed since the nineteenth century. The line as far as Bodo in the north was proposed in 1862 and, although sections of the route were opened in the intervening period, the whole route to Bodo was not actually opened until 1962.

The first private railway in Sweden from Orebro to Nora was opened in 1856. In the same year, two state owned lines opened from Gothenburg to Jonsered and from Malmo to Lund, both of which used British built locomotives. In the period from 1862 to 1875, the five state-owned main lines were opened. The last steam locomotives on regular service ceased in 1972 although hundreds of steam locomotives were held in a strategic reserve until 1992.

In 1988, SJ transferred responsibility for the railway infrastructure to Banverket and this organisation has its own fleet of locomotives.

Sweden State Railways introduced electrification in 1915 on the northern iron ore lines and electrification progressed rapidly throughout the 1920s and in the following years. By contrast, Finland was relatively slow in embracing electric power but electrification began in early 1969 with the opening of the electrified line from Helsinki to Kirkkonummi. Despite this progress, steam locomotives were used on regular services until 1975. The first electrified line in Norway was the Drammen line which was converted in 1922 but the majority of Norway's electrification took place after World War II. However, the main line north of Trondheim to Bodo is still not electrified and relies on powerful diesel locomotives for train haulage.

Vintage locomotive number 5 named "Bifrost" is a 4-4-0 tank locomotive dating from 1882. It is shown preserved at Narvik in July 2004.

Denmark's and Finland's systems are electrified to 25 kV ac; Norway and Sweden use 15 kV ac. The construction of the Oresund link and better access to Germany created a need for a class of locomotives with the capacity to work on a dual-voltage basis and this is provided by DSB's class EG locomotives.

Today, Denmark has over 1,600 mi of lines of which 25 per cent are electrified. Finland has over 3,500 mi of lines of which 45 per cent are electrified. Norway has just over 2,400 mi of which 60 percent are electrified and Sweden has almost 7,100 mi of which over half are electrified.

There has been a wide range of steam locomotive types in use in Scandinavia. Denmark's first line, opened in 1847, used five British built 2-2-2 "Odin" class locomotives. DSB's K class locomotives were 4-4-0s introduced in 1894. Over 100 were built. DSB class D1 was introduced in 1902 and 41 of these 2-6-0 locomotives were built. A significant number of the class were still at work in the 1960s. Class P1 was a 4-4-2 type introduced in the early 1900s for express passenger work. Two examples are preserved.

Finland's class Tk2 were broad gauge 2-8-0 wood burning locomotives based on an American Baldwin design and introduced in the early 1900s. These locomotives worked into the late 1950s. Class Tv1 were 2-8-0 freight locomotives introduced in 1917 that had a successful working life into the late 1960s. Class HR1 were 4-6-2 express passenger locomotives introduced in 1937. Twenty-one were built and lasted into the 1970s, ending their working life on freight duties. In addition to those steam locomotives preserved in Finland, several have been imported into Britain for preservation.

Norway has preserved an interesting locomotive at Narvik. Number 5 "Bifrost" is a 4-4-0 tank locomotive built in 1882 and later acquired for use on iron ore trains at Narvik. It was withdrawn from service in the 1950s. Class 18 were NSB's first 4-6-0 locomotives introduced in 1900. They were followed by class 27 in 1910 and these locomotives were responsible for passenger services until the 1930s. Class 49 were 2-8-4 powerful locomotives for working on steeply graded mountainous routes. Introduced in 1935, the class worked until the 1950s and one example has been preserved.

The plate from locomotive number 5 "Bifrost" showing that it was built in 1882 and acquired by LKAB at Narvik in1901.

LOKOMOTIVET "BIFROST"
BYGGET AV NYQVIST & HOLM I TROLLHÆTTAN, SVERIGE I 1882.
KOM TIL NARVIK, LKAB I 1901.
TEKNISKE DATA: TOTALVEKT 21 TONN
TREKKRAFT 2 "
TOTALLENGDE 7,2 METER
VANNBEHOLDNING 1,5 M3
KULLBEHOLDNING 0,8 TONN
SYLINDERDIAMETER 31,0 CM
SLAGLENGDE 44,5 CM
DRIVHJULSDIAMETER 86,8 CM

NSB vintage 4-6-0 steam locomotive class 30a, number 271, is preserved near Oslo where it is pictured in September 2004. This locomotive was built in 1914.

Sweden's class G was introduced in 1867. These British built 0-6-0s were freight locomotives and worked into the 1920s. One example has been preserved. Class MA was introduced in 1902 and these 2-8-0 locomotives worked the iron ore trains in the north of Sweden and into Narvik in Norway. Class F was introduced in 1914 for express passenger services. Fifteen examples were built and worked until 1937 when the class was sold to DSB becoming class E. A further 25 examples were built in Denmark. One of the original locomotives has been preserved in Sweden.

Each country has a number of electric locomotive classes. With the exception of the Danish EG class, all locomotives are single-voltage types.

DSB has two electric locomotive classes. Class EA comprises 22 locomotives introduced in two batches in the mid-1980s and in 1992. They are used on passenger and freight work and have a maximum speed of 175 kph. Class EG was introduced in 1999 and comprises 13 dual-voltage locomotives for freight work. They are similar in appearance to Germany's class 152 locomotives although this is rather disguised by their distinctive DSB GODS (goods) livery. The class has a maximum speed of 87 mph and can be seen on regular workings into Germany and Sweden.

DSB electric locomotive, number 3017, prepares to move to its next duty with another member of the class, at Fredericia in July 2002.

VR electric locomotives are all 1524 mm broad gauge. Class Sr 1 was introduced in 1973 and is used for passenger and freight work. The class has a maximum speed of 87 mph. There are over 110 locomotives in the class, which were mainly built in Russia with some of the work being completed in Finland. Class Sr 2 comprises 46 locomotives introduced in 1996 for passenger and freight work with a maxi-

New DSB electric locomotive, number 3107, prepares to depart Fredericia with a freight train, in July 2002. This class was introduced in 1999.

VR standard electric locomotive class Sr1, number 3019, has arrived at Helsinki with a passenger train, in October 1994. This class is broad gauge and was introduced in 1973.

mum speed of 124 mph. This class is similar in appearance to Swiss Railways class 460 and NSB's class EL 18.

NSB has a number of electric locomotive classes. Class 9 was an early class of locomotives that worked on the famous Flam Railway. Locomotive 9.2063 has been preserved. The 30 locomotives of class El 14 were the first modern electric locomotives introduced in the late 1960s. They are powerful locomotives and were originally used on passenger train work over mountainous routes. They are now mainly freight locomotives and have a maximum speed of 75 mph. Class El 15 is a small class of six locomotives that work on the iron ore trains that operate between the north of Norway and Sweden. They were introduced in 1967 and have a maximum speed of 75 mph. They are now operated by LKAB/MTAB, the iron ore company. These locomotives are part of the Rc type found in Sweden. Class El 16 is also part of the Swedish Rc family and was introduced in 1977 as passenger and freight locomotives with a maximum speed of 87 mph. A

Preserved vintage electric locomotive, number 9.2063, worked on the Flam Railway. In immaculate condition, it is pictured at Flam station, in June 2004.

This ex NSB locomotive is owned by Swedish company TKAB. Re-numbered as 24, ex NSB 16.2209 is at Sunsvall, in September 2004.

NSB number 17.2228 is one of the class that works on the Flam Railway in Norway. In its attractive green livery, the locomotive waits to leave Flam with its train to Myrdal, in June 2004.

Modern NSB electric locomotive, number 18.2259, backs onto its passenger train at Bergen station, in June 2004. This class was introduced in 1996 and is similar to types found in Switzerland and Finland.

The LKAB/MTAB iron ore company, operating in the north of Sweden and Norway, has retained veteran locomotive class Da number 889 at Kiruna, where it is pictured in September 2004.

SJ class Dm are three section locomotives now operated by LKAB/MTAB. They haul heavy iron ore trains to and from Narvik. Locomotive 1228 with 1227 and 1243 at Narvik, in July 2004.

LKAB/MTAB twin locomotives, numbers 107 and 108, take an empty train through Narvik station, in July 2004. These impressive locomotives were introduced in 2001 and are among the world's most powerful electric locomotives.

SJ electric locomotive class Rc3, number 1052, waits in the sun before leaving Linkoping with its passenger train, in July 2002.

number of these locomotives have been sold to a Swedish private railway company, TKAB, for passenger work. Class El 17 is an interesting class in that a number of locomotives work on the famous Flam railway and have a distinctive green livery. Introduced in 1981, the class has a maximum speed of 93 mph. Although the class is still operational, one example has already been preserved. Class El 18 are the most modern electric locomotive class operated by NSB and are similar in appearance to Swiss class 460 and VR class Sr 2. Introduced in 1996, the 22 locomotives have a maximum speed of 124 mph. They are designed for passenger and freight work but in practice are mainly used on express passenger services.

SJ has a substantial fleet of electric locomotives. Classes Ud, Ue and Uf are locomotives for shunting, the earliest examples of which were introduced in the 1930s. Most examples have been withdrawn but some remain in use in the Stockholm area and others have been preserved. Class Da originally comprised 90 locomotives for passenger and freight work introduced in the 1950s. Few examples now remain although one locomotive has been retained by LKAB/ MTAB, the iron ore company operating in the north of Sweden. Classes Dm/Dm3 are impressive three-section machines introduced in 1963 to work iron ore trains in the north of Sweden and into Narvik in Norway. They are powerful locomotives with a maximum speed of 47 mph. They are now part of the LKAB/ MTAB fleet.

SJ electric locomotive class Rc2, number 1196, parades its attractive Green Cargo livery at Hallsberg, in July 2002, before moving to its freight train.

SJ locomotives of class Rc4, numbers 1298 and 1193, are stabled at Borlanger, in July 2002. This class was introduced in 1975 and the type can be found in the USA, Austria and Norway.

LKAB/MTAB has acquired some equally impressive new locomotives to work on iron ore traffic. They are double-section locomotives and are amongst the most powerful electric locomotives in the world. Introduced in 2001, they are nine double locomotives with a maximum speed of 50 mph.

SJ's classes Rc 1 to 6 are the result of SJ's decision in the 1960s to upgrade its electric locomotive fleet. The class has been a major success and examples have been exported to a number of countries including the

One of SJ's successes has been the introduction of express tilting trains. A Linx express leaves Stockholm, in July 2004.

DSB has several small shunting locomotive classes. Frichs built shunting locomotive, number 269, is stabled at Copenhagen between duties, in August 1999.

USA, Iran, Austria, Norway, Bulgaria and Romania. Class Rc1 was introduced in 1967 and originally comprised 20 locomotives. Class Rc2 consists of 100 locomotives introduced in 1969 and class Rc3 was a small class of 11 locomotives introduced in 1970. Class Rc4 comprises 130 locomotives introduced in stages from 1975 and class Rc5 (later converted to class Rc6) was introduced in 1982. The Rc classes

Two of DSB's modern shunting locomotives, numbers 604 and 611, are stabled at Fredericia, in July 2002. Although there were originally 25 locomotives in the class, several have recently been sold by DSB.

Classic DSB Nohab diesel locomotive, number 1135, at Copenhagen, in August 1999. This type can also be found in several other countries.

DSB main line class MZ diesel locomotive, number 1454, waits to leave Copenhagen with a passenger train, in July 2002.

DSB class ME diesel locomotive, number 1507, poses in the sun at Copenhagen, in August 1999. This class is used for passenger train work.

There is a wide range of diesel locomotive types in use throughout Scandinavia. Denmark's small shunting class of Frichs built locomotives was introduced in the 1960s and has a maximum speed of 28 mph. Class MK comprises 25 locomotives introduced in 1996. These new locomotives are mainly used by DSB's freight division although several locomotives have been acquired by operators in Germany and Luxembourg.

DSB class MY and MX are classic Nohab locomotives as found in a number of other countries including Norway, Hungary, Belgium and Luxembourg. They were introduced in 1954 and 1960 respectively for passenger and freight work. They are all withdrawn

NSB small shunting locomotive, number 220 212, pauses at Bergen, in June 2004 before moving to its next duty.

were originally mainly passenger locomotives but can now also be found on freight duties and in some cases the locomotives have been fitted with remote controls for shunting duties. Classes Rc1, 2 and 4 have a maximum speed of 84 mph. The other classes are able to run at 100 mph. Class Rm was introduced in 1977 for iron ore traffic. They are Rc type locomotives able to generate more power but with a lower maximum speed of 62 mph. SJ class X2 are designed to power express X2000 tilting trains. Introduced in two batches in 1990 and 1994, the locomotives have a maximum speed of 124 mph.

One of VR's large main line diesel locomotives of class Dr13, number 2307, enters Helsinki station with a passenger train, in October 1994.

NSB small battery powered shunting XSka class shunting locomotive, number 223 402, is stabled in the sun at Oslo, in September 2004.

Ex NSB Nohab class Di 3a locomotive, number 3 605, heads a small freight train at Kristinehamn in Sweden, in September 2004.This type, introduced in 1954, can be found in several other countries.

from DSB service although several examples are now owned by Danish, Swedish and German private railway companies and other examples have been preserved. The classes had a maximum speed of 83 mph. Class MZ was introduced by DSB in the period 1967 to 1978 for passenger and freight work. Some of the original 61 locomotives have now been withdrawn with some others being sold to Swedish and Spanish private railway companies. The first batch of locomotives has a maximum speed of 89 mph with the later locomotives having a maximum speed of 100 mph. DSB class ME are used on push-pull passenger services and were introduced in 1981. The 37 locomotives have a maximum speed of 109 mph.

Powerful NSB large diesel locomotive of class Di 4, number 4654, waits to leave Trondheim with a passenger train for Bodo, in June 2004.

NSB Cargonet locomotive, number 66 406, is stabled near Bodo, in June 2004. This General Motors type is now widely used throughout Europe.

SJ diesel shunting locomotive, number V5 158, is ready for its next duty at Borlanger, in July 2002. This class was introduced in 1975 and is used throughout Sweden.

VR has several classes of small shunting locomotives and Classes Dr 12 to 16 are classified for main-line use. Dr 12s are the largest class numerically (almost 200 locomotives) and were introduced in 1964 in three different series. They are passenger and freight locomotives with a maximum speed of 78 mph. Class Dr 13 comprises 54 locomotives introduced in 1963 for express passenger work. They have a maximum speed of 87 mph. Class Dr 16 was introduced in 1987 for passenger and freight work. The 23 locomotives have a maximum speed of 87 mph and are the most powerful diesel locomotives in Finland.

SJ diesel locomotive, number T43 231, at Copenhagen, in August 1999. The locomotive is in the attractive Banverket (Swedish infra-structure Company) livery.

SJ large diesel shunting and light freight locomotive, number T44 356, is stabled at Stockholm, in July 2004. This class dates from 1968.

SJ Green Cargo small diesel shunting locomotive, number Z70 724, is stabled between duties at Gallivare, in July 2004. The class was introduced in 1961.

NSB has a series of small shunting locomotives in service, the smallest of which are battery powered and there are several classes of main-line diesel locomotives. Classes Di 3a and 3b are Nohab types, of which a few remain in service. Examples of this class can be found throughout Europe (see DSB MY and MX above). The class has a maximum speed of 65 mph and was originally used on passenger and freight services. A small number of ex-NSB machines are in use in Sweden with private railway companies.

NSB class Di 4 of five locomotives was introduced in 1980 for passenger services on the non-electrified routes principally from Trondheim to Bodo. These powerful locomotives have a maximum speed of 87 mph. Class Di 8 was introduced in 1995 for heavy shunting and freight duties and the 20 locomotives have a maximum speed of 74.5 mph.

Danish private railway OHJ/HTJ locomotive, number 103, is stabled at Copenhagen, in July 2002. This locomotive was previously DSB MX 1010.

NSB's latest acquisition for Cargonet are six class 66s which are the same as other General Motors of that type widely in use throughout Europe except that they have been modified to cope with severe weather.

SJ's diesel locomotive fleet includes several classes of small shunting locomotives and a number of main-line locomotives. Classes V 4 and V5 are shunting locomotives introduced in the 1970s with a maximum speed of 43.5 mph. Classes T 43 and T44 are freight locomotives introduced in 1961 and 1968 respectively. They have a maximum speed of 62 mph. Class Z70 date from the 1960s but were rebuilt in the 1990s as a shunting locomotive with a maximum speed of 43.5 mph.

A particular feature of both Denmark and Sweden is the number of private railway operators that exist using a variety of diesel and electric locomotives, some of which were acquired from DSB, NSB and SJ.

Danish private railway SB (Skagensbanen) locomotive number 11, is stabled at Aalborg, in July 2002. This locomotive was previously DSB MX1009.

In Denmark OHJ/HTJ is responsible for a 100 km railway based on Holbaek to the west of Copenhagen and also operates on a small part of the DSB network. It is now known as the Vestsjoellands Lokalbaner (VL). The railway has used an ex-DB class 323 shunting locomotive and has a number of ex-DSB Nohab class MX diesel locomotives acquired in the late 1980s. These locomotives were originally built in the early 1960s and have a maximum speed of 83 mph. The railway also has a class 24 diesel locomotive built by Frichs in 1952 and now stored. Also in Denmark, the Skagensbanen (SB) operates on 25 miles of line from Skagen to Frederikshavn – the DSB terminus – and has a number of locomotives including ex-DB class 323 and 332 shunting locomotives and ex-DSB class MX Nohab locomotives acquired in 1992 and 1994. One of these MX locomotives was acquired from the OHJ/HTJ. The railway provides passenger and limited freight services and is now a part of NJ, the Nordjyske Jernbaner that provides services in the north of Denmark.

TAGAB is based at Kristinehamn in Sweden and uses a variety of locomotives including ex-DSB MX and MZ diesels, several ex-SJ class T43 diesels, ex-OBB (Austria) class 1043 electric locomotives and a number of small shunting locomotives. It operates freight trains on the Kristinehamn to Persberg and Strotorp to Laxa routes for SJ.

TGOJ is a significant freight railway organisation in Sweden carrying steel, minerals and container traffic. It was created in 1931 and became wholly owned by SJ in 1989. When SJ created business divisions in 2001, it became TGOJ Trafik AB and it is now a subsidiary of Green Cargo which took over SJ's freight operation. It also operates some passenger services.

TGOJ owns a sizeable electric locomotive fleet consisting of ex-SJ and NSB locomotives and ex-OBB class 1043s. Of particular interest is ex-SJ class Ma numbers 401 – 409, introduced in 1954 and still operating following modifications in 1980. This class has a maximum speed of 65 mph. There are over 20 other Ma class locomotives in the fleet, all dating from the 1950s and with a variety of number ranges. TGOJ also operates several ex-SJ class T43 diesels and acquired two General Motors class 66 locomotives of the same family as the British class 66s and as owned by a number of other European railways. TGOJ owns several shunting locomotives of classes Z65, V10 and V11.

Ex DSB MY class Nohab diesel locomotive displays its stylish and attractive Great Northern livery, at Kristinehamn, in July 2002.

Diminutive TAGAB diesel shunting locomotive, number Z1 201, rests between duties at Kristinehamn, in July 2002. This locomotive was built by Deutz.

TAGAB Rc2 electric locomotive, number 006, poses in the sun at Kristinehamn, in July 2002. This locomotive was previously OBB number 1043 006.

TGOJ veteran electric locomotive, number 407, displays its immaculate and attractive livery, at Gothenburg, in July 2002. This locomotive was built in 1954.

Bulgarian Railways

Bulgarian Railways (BDZ) operates a number of electric and diesel locomotive classes. A new diesel train from the Desiro range will service the destination from the Black Sea city of Varna to the town of Dobrich in north eastern Bulgaria in 2006. This is the fourteenth Desiro diesel train to be been put into operation and another three are expected in the country by the end of January.

The first railway in Bulgaria opened in 1866. It ran from the Danube port of Ruschuk to Varna on the Black Sea – a distance of 140 miles, and was a mainline route. Subsequently, the main cross-country line from the Yugoslavian border to Sophia and Svilengrad was opened, and this formed part of the classic Orient Express route.

BDZ was formed in 1888 and has controlled the network since that time. Today, BDZ has almost 2,672 miles of lines of which over half are electrified to 25kV ac. The figure includes a number of non-electrified narrow gauge lines.

A classic BDZ 2-8-2 steam locomotive shows its impressive silhouette. This is one of many BDZ steam locomotives that have been preserved.

One of BDZ's preserved steam locomotives is number 148 – one of four British built locomotives that worked on Bulgaria's first railway. The 0-6-0 locomotive was built in 1865 and was bought by a Turkish railway in 1873 before returning to Bulgaria in 1888. Class 900 – later class 19 – comprised 70 locomotives introduced in 1913 for passenger and freight work. Examples of this 2-10-0 class worked into the 1960s. Class 46 was introduced in the 1930s and originally comprised 12 locomotives. A further eight locomotives were built in the 1940s. These massive 2-12-4 tank locomotives were designed for heavy freight work. The 22 locomotives of class 11 were built in the 1940s and were designed for passenger and freight work. The locomotives had a 4 10-0 wheel arrangement and performed well on steeply graded lines.

BDZ has several classes of electric locomotive. Class 41 originally comprised 41 locomotives built in the early 1960s and they were followed in the late

BDZ electric locomotive, number 41 102, progresses through Sofia station with a mixed freight train, in October 1993. The class was introduced in 1960.

1960s by 90 class 42 locomotives, which were introduced in stages. Class 42 is equivalent to Czech Railway's (CD) classes 23 and 240 and has a maximum speed of 68 mph. Classes 43, 44 and 45 are Czech built locomotives developed from classes 41 and 42. They are passenger and freight locomotives introduced in the 1970s and early 1980s. These classes are now BDZ's principal electric locomotives. A total of over 200 locomotives was built and, with the exception of class 45 (68 mph), have a maximum speed of 81 mph. Class 46 was introduced in

The plates on the side of BDZ electric locomotive, number 41 102, show the impressive crest and BDZ ownership in Cyrillic lettering.

BDZ class 43 locomotives work passenger and freight services. Locomotive number 43 191 waits at Sofia with a passenger service, in October 1993.

the mid-1980s and comprised 45 locomotives, built in Romania and equivalent to CFR's class 46. The locomotives have a maximum speed of 81 mph.

Diesel class 04 was introduced in the early 1960s and originally comprised 50 locomotives. The class is Austrian Railway's (OBB) class 2020 and were the first main-line diesels in service. They are used on passenger and freight work and have a maximum speed of 74.5 mph. Class 06 was introduced in the late 1960s and originally comprised 130 locomotives built in Romania and equivalent to Romanian Railway's (CFR) class 060. Class 07 comprised 91 locomotives introduced in the 1970s and built in Russia. The class is part of the German Railway's (DB) class 230/231/232 family. Class 51 originally comprised 71 locomotives for shunting work. Introduced in the 1960s, the locomotives are equivalent to Hungarian Railways' (MAV) class M44. Class 52 was introduced in the mid-1960s and is

BDZ class 44 electric locomotives are one of BDZ's principal classes. Locomotive number 44 123 is about to leave Sofia station to pick up its next train, in October 1993.

BDZ large diesel locomotive, number 04 048, progresses past Sofia station, in October 1993. This class was introduced in the 1960s.

equivalent to DB class 346. 116 of these shunting locomotives were built. Class 55 comprised 160 shunting locomotives introduced in 1969. Class 60 comprises four locomotives introduced in 1960 and used for shunting work. Class 61 are centre-cab locomotives introduced in the mid-1990s and used for shunting and freight train duties. The 20 Czech-built locomotives have a maximum speed of 50 mph. BDZ has a number of locomotive classes to work its narrow gauge lines. Classes 75, 76, 77, 80 and 81 were introduced from the mid-1960s through to the 1980s and originally totalled approximately 40 locomotives.

Class 06 is one of BDZ's standard diesel classes and is equivalent to CFR's class 060. Locomotive 06 012 is at Sofia, in October 1993.

A BDZ diesel locomotive of class 07 progresses a freight through the countryside. This class is the same as DB class 230.

BDZ has acquired new unit type trains to update the passenger train stock. Two of the units are pictured showing the modern design and the good window visibility.

Swiss Railways (SBB CFF FFS)

Often described as the most efficient railway system in the world, Swiss railways comprise a mix of the state-run main railway network and many independent railways that operate on a variety of systems, often in vastly different natural environments. Swiss railways are characterised by impressive feats of engineering, notably a number of significant tunnels and spectacular lines.

One of the new diesel unit railcar sets gives its passengers a spectacular view as it crosses a typical Swiss viaduct. Railcars and units are a feature of Swiss private railways.

Both the state and independent railways operate a range of diesel and electric locomotives and there are several lines that use steam locomotives. Although the designation of the railway is SBB CFF FFS to reflect the fact that German, French and Italian are spoken in Switzerland, SBB is used in this book to denote the main Swiss railway system.

The first railway in Switzerland ran from Zurich to Basel and opened in 1847. In 1848, the Government asked Robert Stephenson, the British engineer, to devise the framework for a national railway network. He proposed a line from Zurich to Geneva via Lausanne and this line is the core of the SBB system today.

One of SBB's double-deck trains winds its way through a maze of tracks. These trains are spacious, well designed and have a significant passenger number capacity.

A more recent design of double-decker train, waits for departure.

Given its location, it is not surprising that Switzerland sought to link its network with those of neighbouring countries but this necessitated finding ways to cross the Alpine ranges. The first solution was the Gotthard line into Italy but this created a problem of steep gradients for locomotives. To surmount this difficulty, a system of spiral tunnels was adopted and the Gotthard Tunnel opened in 1882. Even today, this remains a remarkable feat of engineering.

The Glacier Express passes through some of Switzerland's most spectacular scenery. Here it crosses one of the many rivers on the route.

The more orthodox Simplon Tunnel was opened in 1906 on the line from Geneva to Italy. At Brig that line joins with the private Bern, Lotschberg and Simplon railway (BLS) which had built the Lotschberg Tunnel on the ascent from Spiez.

The steam locomotive Breithorn is the only engine of the former BVZ to have survived into the 21st century. It was rebuilt to burn light oil in 2001.

The Swiss were early pioneers in railway electrification. The Simplon Tunnel was electrified after its opening in 1906 and the BLS line in 1913. The Gotthard line was electrified after the First World War. The metre gauge Rhaetian Railway (RhB) from Chur to the Alpine resorts is a spectacular, sharply curved and difficult line which purpose built locomotives use without any apparent difficulty. The RhB owns over 224 miles of routes. It includes the famous and photogenic Landwasser viaduct that carries the line 213 feet above the valley floor and then into the Landwasser Tunnel. The famous Glacier Express runs from Zermatt to St Moritz and uses the metre gauge former BVZ (Brig, Visp and Zermatt Railway) and FO (Furka Oberalp Railway) lines and the RhB from Chur to St Moritz. This train is a classic way of seeing the Swiss scenery at its best and experiencing a variety of locomotive traction on the train. The most important initiative taken by SBB in recent years was the adoption of the Rail 2000 plan, which recognised the importance of the railways. It

A single deck push-pull train at speed. Such trains are normally the responsibility of class 460 locomotives.

A regional train of the Swiss Central Rilways, whisks its passengers between the towns of Meiringen and Interlaken, with views of the magnificent mountains in the background.

Preserved class Eb3/5 2-6-2 tank locomotive, number 5819, at Biel in June 1997. This locomotive was built in 1912.

In a magnificent mountain setting, 1910 built narrow gauge class HG3/3 0-6-0 tank rack locomotive, number 1067, is at Meiringen, in June 1999.

dealt with the renewal of the railway and introduced new train frequencies and improved speeds, including the use of tilting trains. The main objectives of phase 1 of the plan had largely been achieved by 2005. Today, SBB has almost 1,864 miles of lines all of which are electrified to 1500 V ac. This total excludes lines owned by independent railways which comprises over 1,243 miles. All of the SBB lines are standard gauge except for the 1000 mm Brunig line from Interlaken to Luzern. In organizational terms, SBB became a limited company in 1999 with responsibility for long distance passenger and freight traffic and is structured into individual

Class Re4/4 electric locomotive, number 10013, is stabled at Lausanne, in June 1997.This locomotive was built in the mid-1940s.

units responsible for infrastructure, passengers and freight respectively. SBB Cargo has established subsidiaries in Germany and Italy.

One of the steam locomotives that operated on the first Swiss railway was "Limatt," a 4-2-0 German built locomotive. A replica of this locomotive was built in 1947 for the Swiss railway centenary and can be seen today in "preservation."

Class A3/5 4-6-0 locomotives performed well on steeply graded routes. Introduced in 1902, over 110 examples were built, one of which has been preserved. Class C4/5 was introduced in 1904 and the locomotives were equally successful. The last of these 2-8-0 locomotives ran until 1957.

Class Eb3/5 was introduced in 1911. Thirty-four of these 2-6-2 tank locomotives were built for suburban and country line work and several have been preserved. Class C5/6 was introduced in 1913 for passenger and freight work and comprised the most powerful steam locomotives in Switzerland. Several of these 2-10-0 locomotives have been preserved.

Preserved electric locomotive, number 10700, is at Lausanne, in June 1997. This class Ae3/6 locomotive was built in the mid-1920s.

Vintage class Ae4/7 electric locomotive, number 10976, is in immaculate condition at Basel, in June 1997.This locomotive dates from the late1920s and the last class members worked in normal service until 1996.

Class HG3/3 meter gauge steam locomotive 1067 was built in 1910. This 0-6-0 tank rack locomotive is one of several that have been preserved.

SBB has a significant number of electric locomotives. Class Re4/4.1 was derived from a class of motor luggage vehicles and was introduced in 1946 for passenger services. Fifty were built but most have now been withdrawn. Some have been preserved and others carry out empty coaching stock work. The class has a maximum speed of 78 mph. Classes Ae3/6.1, 11 and 111 were introduced in the 1920s as passenger and freight locomotives with a maximum speed of 110, 100 and 90 kph respectively. Examples of each class have been preserved. There were over 120 locomotives in class Ae4/7 which was introduced in 1927. The locomotives were mainly used on passenger services and many examples were still working until the class was

Class Ae4/7 electric locomotive, number 10964, is stabled at Basel, in June 1994 – two years before the class was withdrawn from service.

With a spectacular mountain background, several locomotives of class Re4/4 await their next duty at Bellinzona, in June 1999.

Class Re4/4 electric locomotive, number 11349, is stabled at Olten, in June 1995. The locomotive is in its original green livery.

Class Re4/4 locomotive, number 11184, is stabled at Geneva, in June 1994. This locomotive is in the later red livery.

Class Ae6/6 electric freight locomotive, number 11424, waits in the sun for its next duty at Bellinzona, in June 1999.

Class Re6/6 locomotive, number 11667, at Bellinzona, in June 1998. This powerful class was designed for work over mountain lines.

Vintage 1922 class Ce6/8 electric locomotive, number 14270, is preserved against a mountain background at Erstfeld, in February 1996.

Preserved vintage 1926 class Ce6/8 electric locomotive, number 14305, prepares to leave Yverdon with a special train, in June 1997.

Zurich S-Bahn locomotive, number 450 001, waits at Zurich for its next duty, in June 1995. This class works double-deck trains in the Zurich area.

Class 460 was introduced in 1991 for express passenger and freight train work. Locomotive number 460 038 arrives at Bellinzona, in June 1998. Similar locomotives are also found in Norway and Finland.

withdrawn in 1996. Several examples have been preserved. The class had a maximum speed of 62 mph.

Class Re4/4 comprises over 270 locomotives and there are some design differences within the class. Built over a twenty-year period from 1964, the locomotives have a maximum speed of 87 mph. They are used on passenger and freight services. Class Ae6/6 was introduced in the 1950s for work on the Simplon and Gotthard lines but the locomotives now work throughout the system. The class has a maximum speed of 78 mph and is mainly used on freight trains. Some locomotives have been withdrawn as new classes entered service. Class Re6/6 was introduced in the 1970s. The locomotives are used on passenger and freight work and have a maximum speed of 87 mph. They are especially suited to mountainous routes but are found throughout the network. Class Ce6/8 comprised two subclasses and was introduced in the 1920s and the locomotives are affectionately known as "Crocodiles" because of their appearance. The locomotives have a maximum speed of 40 mph. Several examples have been preserved. The Zurich S-Bahn class 450 locomotives are modern locomotives introduced in 1989. They work push-pull double deck trains in a wide area around Zurich. The class has a maximum speed of 81 mph and comprises 114 locomotives. Class 460 comprises 118 locomotives for express passenger and freight services, introduced in 1991. The locomotives have a maximum speed of 143 mph and are similar in appearance to Norway's class El 18 and Finland's class Sr2. Many of the class are painted in livery advertising products, services and public awareness type messages. SBB and its Cargo organization have invested heavily in new locomotives for freight work as a means of improving freight services both within Switzerland and into Germany and Italy. Class 482 comprises 50 locomotives which are essentially DB class 185 locomotives, details of which are in the

German railway section of this book. They were introduced in 2002.

Class 484 comprises 18 locomotives and was introduced in 2004. Class 474 has only recently been introduced and comprises 18 locomotives. Both classes are dual-voltage locomotives (1500 v AC and 3000 v DC) to enable them to work into Italy. SBB also has several classes of electric shunting locomotives. Classes Te 1, 2 and 3 are small electric locomotives introduced in stages from 1927 (Te2), 1937 (Te1) and 1941 (Te3) with further locomotives of Te 2 and 3 being built in the 1960s. Classes Tem1, 2 and 3 are interesting in that they are electric and diesel powered shunting locomotives, introduced in the 1950s and 1960s. Class Te4 is a class of three locomotives introduced in 1980. Class Ee3/3 are larger center-cab shunting locomotives introduced in 1928 with additional locomotives built in the 1930s,

Some class 460 locomotives are decorated in "advertising livery." Locomotive number 460 034 is at Lausanne in June 1997, publicising a railway workshop.

Class Te3 electric shunting locomotive, number 154, is at Olten, in July 1999 alongside class Tm3 diesel electric shunting locomotive, number 924.

Class Ee3/3 electric shunting locomotive, number 16425, is stabled at Bern, in June 1994. This class was introduced in 1951.

Large class Eem6/6 diesel shunting locomotive, number 17003, is at Biel, in July 1999. This class was introduced in 1970.

SBB class Am4/4 were previously DB class V220 diesels. Locomotive number 18465 heads a line of the class at Biel, in June 1997.

1950s and early 1960s. There are design differences between the locomotives within the overall class with some locomotives being single-voltage, others being dual-voltage and the final batch being four-voltage machines. Classes Ee6/6 1 and 2 are heavy shunting locomotives introduced in 1952 and 1980 respectively. They are used in the main freight yards and have a maximum speed of 28 (6/6 1) and 53 mph (6/6 2). Class Eem6/6 comprises six heavy shunting locomotives introduced in 1970 as electric and diesel powered locomotives with a maximum speed of 40 mph. In 1984, they were converted to diesel electrics.

SBB has several classes of main-line diesel and diesel shunting locomotives. Class Am4/4 locomotives were acquired in 1987 from Germany, having previously been DB class V200, details of which are in the German section of this book. They are now withdrawn from SBB service, although examples

Class Am 841 are shunting and light freight locomotives, introduced in 1996. Locomotive number 841 020 is at Olten, in July 1999.

Shunting locomotives of class Bm4/4 are also used on light freight work. Locomotive number 18429 is at Basel, in January 2000.

Class Em3/3 shunting locomotives are widely used throughout the SBB system. Locomotive number 18807 is at Basel, in June 1995.

Class Tm3 shunting locomotive, number 918, is at Lausanne in June 1994. These locomotives are diesel electrics, introduced in 1958.

Diminutive locomotive number Ta 969 is battery powered. It was introduced in 1911 and is pictured at Yverdon, in June 1997.

Class Tm4 are diesel shunting locomotives, introduced in 1970. Locomotive number 8757 is stabled at Olten, in June 1995.

Class Tm235 was introduced in 1991 for line maintenance work. Locomotive number 235 001 is at a snowy Erstfeld, in February 1996.

have been sold to German private railway companies. Class Am 841 comprises 39 locomotives, introduced in 1996. The locomotives are used for shunting and light freight train work and have a maximum speed of 50 mph. The two locomotives of class Am 842 were acquired from a private railway contractor in 1994, having been built in 1992. They are similar to class 6400 found in Holland and have a maximum speed of 50 mph. Class Am 842.1 are two locomotives built in 2003 of the Vossloth G1000 type. SBB Cargo acquired six Vossloth G2000 locomotives for freight work, in 2003. They are designated class Am 840.
The 73 locomotives of class Am 843 were introduced in 2003 for shunting work and have displaced a number of the older large shunting locomotives. Class Em 831 are three locomotives introduced in 1992 as prototypes for a new type of diesel shunting locomotive. Class Bm4/4 was introduced in 1960 for shunting and light freight work. The 46 locomotives have a maximum speed of 48 mph. Classes Bm6/6 and Am6/6 are shunting locomotives introduced in 1954 and 1976 respectively. Class Em3/3 are 41 shunting and light freight locomotives introduced in 1959 with a maximum speed of 40 mph. SBB also has a range of small shunting locomotives. Classes Tm 1, 2 and 3 were introduced in the 1950s and are significantly different in terms of their design and appearance. They are used for light shunting in depots, stations and freight yards.
Class Ta are very small shunting locomotives powered by batteries. They are used in SBB locomotive works. They vary in design and appearance and the earliest example was built in 1911. Class Tm 4 was introduced in two stages in the 1970s and comprises over 80 locomotives used on shunting duties in sta-

Brunig line class HGe 101, introduced in 1989, are orthodox and rack system locomotives. Number 101 964 is at Meiringen, in June 1999.

Brunig line class De110 was introduced in 1941. Locomotive number 110 004 is departing with its train from Meiringen, in June 1999.

With a spectacular mountain background, Brunig class Te3 electric shunting locomotive, number 203, moves to its next shunting duty at Meiringen in July 1999.

tions and on engineering trains. They have a maximum speed of 19 mph and 37 mph (second batch). Class Tm3 was also introduced in two stages in the late 1970s and early 1980s and are fitted with a hydraulic platform for overhead line work. The second batch also has a hydraulic crane fitted. The class

BLS class Re4/4 electric locomotive, number 161, is at Lausanne, in June 1997. This class was introduced in 1964.

has a maximum speed of 37 mph. Class Tm 235 was introduced in 1991 for line engineering work. This class has a maximum speed of 50 mph and is fitted with a platform for carrying equipment. Class Tm 234 comprises 37 locomotives for shunting work. They were introduced in 2000 and have displaced several small shunting classes.

The Swiss independent railway companies have a fascinating range of locomotives running on a mix of

Modern BLS electric locomotives of class 485 regularly work into Germany. Locomotive number 485 007 is at Mannheim, in April 2004.

gauges and using a variety of systems. Until comparatively recently, there were over 60 independent companies and, although there have been some amalgamations and other rationalizations, a significant number remains. Although actually run by SBB, the Brunig line from Luzern to Interlaken deserves to be mentioned in the context of separate railways since it is meter gauge and incorporates a section of rack railway. Class HGe 101 are electric locomotives introduced in 1989 that are capable of using the orthodox lines and the rack section. Class De 110 are motor luggage vans introduced in 1941 with a maximum speed of 40 mph that at one time also had rack equipment fitted. This was removed and push-pull equipment was fitted, which now limits their use to the non-rack lines. The Brunig line also has several small shunting locomotives of classes Te1, Te 3 and Tm 2 that are metre gauge versions of their SBB equivalent classes. Two locomotives of class Tm 2 are fitted for rack operation.

The BLS group has a number of electric locomotives including some vintage types. Class Re4/4 is the standard locomotive and 34 examples exist. Introduced in 1964, the class has a maximum speed of 87 mph. Class Re465 was introduced in 1994 and is similar to SBB class 460. The 18 locomotives have a maximum speed of 143 mph. BLS class 485

Built in 1973, RhB class Ge4/4 electric locomotive, number 614, prepares to leave Chur with its passenger train, in June 1999.

is the latest class of electric locomotive and can be seen throughout Switzerland and also working into Germany. They were introduced in 2002 and are the same as SBB class 482 and DB's class 185, equipped to work into Switzerland.

The RhB also has a wide range of locomotives. Class Ge4/4 comprises three subclasses introduced in

RhB class Ge6/6 electric locomotives were introduced in 1993. Locomotive number 644 slowly approaches a waiting train near Chur with a passenger service, in June 1998.

1947, 1973 and 1993. The first 10 locomotives are passenger and freight locomotives with a push-pull capacity. Class Ge6/6 was introduced in 1925 and are "baby crocodile" configured locomotives now regarded as working preserved locomotives. Classes Abe4/4 and Be4/4 are electric railcars introduced in 1939 and 1971 respectively. The RhB also has a number of shunting locomotives used in freight yards and stations. The remaining independent railways vary in size and have different types of steam, diesel and electric locomotives.

The BVZ is a metre gauge system with a variety of electric locomotives. Class HGe4/4 was introduced

RhB class Be4/4 locomotive, number 513, waits at Landquart with its passenger train, in June 1998. This class was introduced in 1971.

Class Te2/2 is one of the RhB's shunting locomotive types. Number 72 was built in 1946 and is at Davos, in June 1998.

One of BVZ's class Deh4/4 electric locomotives leaves Brig with a passenger service, in June 1998. This class was introduced in 1975.

in 1929 and has a maximum speed of 28 mph. Class HGe4/4.2 are five locomotives built in 1990 and with a maximum speed of 56 mph. Class Deh4/4 was built in the mid-1970s and has a maximum speed of 40 mph. All classes are rack-equipped.

The FO Railway is now combined with the BVZ and is also a meter gauge line. It has a similar range of locomotive classes as the BVZ, and most locomotives are rack equipped.

The Montreux Oberland Bernois Railway (MOB) has a variety of electric and diesel shunting locomotives including locomotives of classes Gm4/4 introduced in 1976, class GDe4/4 (1983) and Ge4/4 built in 1995. It also has three Tm2/2 shunting locomotives introduced in 1938, 1953 and 1954 respectively.

The Regionalverkehr Mittelland (RM) is an amalgamation of three railways, one of which was the Emmenthal, Burgdorf and Thun Railway (EBT). This railway has a number of locomotives including vintage electric class Be4/4 introduced in the 1930s and with a maximum speed of 50 mph.

One of the smaller lines which also uses its locomotives over a small part of the SBB network, is the RVT which is based in the west of Switzerland. The line has two locomotives including a 1983 Tm shunting locomotive and a class Be4/4 electric locomotive, built in 1951.

One of the RhB shunting locomotives, number 86 of class Tm2/2, waits at Davos for its next duty, in June 1998.

MOB is based in Montreux and has a variety of locomotives including class Tm2/2 locomotive, number 2, pictured at Chernex, in June 1999.

RVT class Be4/4 electric locomotive, number 1, is at Neuchatel, in June 1997. This locomotive was built in 1951.

Spanish (RENFE) and Portuguese (CP) Railways

Spain and Portugal are mainly broad gauge railway systems although they also have narrow gauge lines. Additionally, Spain has some standard gauge lines. Each country has a range of electric and diesel locomotives, including a number of relatively modern classes.

The first railway in Spain was the line between Barcelona and Mataro that opened in 1848.

The Spanish AVE trainsets are made in France with some Spanish components added. It derives directly from the French TGV trains.

Apparently, the line was broad gauge because this was specified in a Royal Decree, that also specified that the state should be heavily involved. The decision on the gauge may have inhibited future development because it was inconsistent with the gauge of most railway developments elsewhere in Europe. New railway companies were established to build new lines but financial pressures limited progress. Finally, in 1924, the state agreed to provide funding for the restoration of the system but the company income returns were not sufficient in subsequent years to enable them to run an effective service or to develop the infrastructure. The Civil War in 1936 resulted in the destruction of railway infrastructure and the state took control of the railways in 1943 and established the railway operator RENFE.

In Portugal, the first railway between Lisbon and Carregado was opened in 1856. Subsequently, private funding developed the national network using broad gauge and the lines were equally divided in terms of being private or state owned. In 1926, the state leased its lines to the private company but in 1947 the whole system was brought under CP control with the private company having an agreement to continue to work the lines previously leased.

Today, Spain has a total of over 9,134 miles of lines. The majority of broad gauge lines are electrified at 3000 v DC. RENFE has also invested heavily in high-speed standard gauge lines all of which are electrified at 25 kV AC. Portugal has almost 1,864 miles of lines of which a significant percentage is electrified to 25 kV AC. CP has also invested in new high-speed lines.

The last steam locomotives ran until the 1970s in both Spain and Portugal and each country had a

RENFE class 276 are broad gauge versions of SNCF class CC7100. Locomotive number 7652 is pictured at Barcelona, in October 1998.

range of interesting steam locomotives. Class 030 in Spain was introduced in 1857 and many of these British and French built 0-6-0 locomotives worked into the 1950s. One example has been preserved.

The RENFE Garratt class was introduced in the 1930s. The six locomotives were 4-6-2 and 2-6-4 and were very successful in hauling passenger

RENFE electric locomotive, number 269 402, at Malaga station with a TALGO train, in April 1996. This locomotive is dedicated to this service.

Electric locomotive, number 279 002, is stabled in the sun at Irun, in August 1995. This class was introduced in 1967.

RENFE modern electric locomotive, number 252 060, backs onto its train at Malaga, in April 1996. The class works passenger and freight services.

trains over steep gradients. They worked until 1970 and one example is preserved at Barcelona Museum. RENFE class 141F were 2-8-2 locomotives built in the 1950s and used on fast freight and passenger work. Over 240 locomotives of the type were built.

Portugal's class E were 2-4-6-0 tank locomotives introduced in 1911 for work on the metre gauge Douro valley lines. They worked into the 1970s. Class 020 were broad gauge 2-8-4 tank locomotives introduced in 1925 for suburban train work around Lisbon and Oporto. They worked into the 1960s.

CP veteran electric locomotive, number 2514, is stabled between duties at Lisbon, in April 1995. This class was introduced in 1956.

CP electric locomotive, number 2609, is stabled at Lisbon, in April 1995. The styling of these locomotives is identical to SNCF class BB15000.

RENFE diesel class 316/1600 was introduced in 1955. Locomotive number 1616 poses at Barcelona in its attractive COMSA railway constructor livery.

Preserved RENFE class 318/1800 locomotive, number 1801, is stabled at Barcelona, in October 1998. This class was introduced in 1958.

RENFE electric locomotive class 276 was introduced in 1956 and some examples were rebuilt in 1993. The class originally totalled 136 locomotives and are broad gauge versions of SNCF class CC7100. This class is now largely withdrawn. Numerically speaking, Class 269 is the largest class of electric locomotives and they were introduced in stages from 1973. They work passenger and freight trains and have different gear arrangements to match the work being undertaken. Some examples are allocated to work specific types of passenger services. The class has a maximum speed of 81 mph although this reduces if the low gear arrangement applies. Class 279 was introduced in 1967 and are dual voltage locomotives (1500/3000 v DC) for work on the Spanish and French border. They are now mainly used on freight trains. Classes 250, 251 and 252 were introduced in the 1980s and early 1990s. Some examples of class 252 are standard gauge and others broad gauge. Approximately half of class 252 are dual-voltage locomotives (3000 v DC and 25 kV AC). The class works passenger and freight services. CP has a number of electric locomotives. The two groups of class 25 single-voltage locomotives were introduced in 1956 and 1963. They work on passenger and freight duties and have a maximum speed of 75 mph. There are two groups of class 26 introduced in 1974 and 1987 mainly for passenger work. The locomotives are identical in appearance to SNCF's class BB15000 and were built in France and Portugal. The class has a maximum speed on passenger services of 100 mph. Class 56 are more modern locomotives introduced in 1993. They work on passenger and freight duties and have a maximum speed of 124 mph.

RENFE diesel class 1600 (later class 316) was introduced in 1955 and rebuilt in the 1970s. They worked passenger services and had a maximum speed of 75 mph. The class is now withdrawn although some examples are used by railway infrastructure contractors and one has been preserved. Class 1800 (318) was introduced in 1958 and comprised 24 locomo-

Powerful RENFE diesel locomotive, number 319 247, pauses between duties at Algeciras, in August 2004. This class is used on passenger and freight work.

RENFE veteran 1960s diesel shunting locomotive, number 308 025, waits to move its train at Barcelona, in October 1998.

Relatively modern RENFE shunting locomotive, number 309 011, prepares to leave for its next duty at Hendaye, in August 1995.

RENFE class 310 shunting and light freight diesel locomotive, number 310 021, moves to its next duty at Malaga, in April 1996.

CP class 1200 diesel locomotives were introduced in 1961. Locomotive number 1209 waits to leave Lagos with a local service, in April 1995.

tives mainly for passenger services. The locomotives had a maximum speed of 75 mph. They have all been withdrawn but one example has been preserved. Class 319 was introduced in 1965 and has a maximum speed of 75 mph. They are used on freight and passenger work and when introduced, some of the class were standard gauge. Classes 352, 353 and 354 were introduced in the 1960s and 1980s (class 354) to work TALGO passenger services. With the opening of high-speed lines, their work has diminished and they are now mainly withdrawn.

CP class 1300 diesel locomotives were acquired from RENFE (ex class 313). Two examples are pictured at Barreiro, in April 1995.

CP diesel locomotive, number 1446, waits to depart from Barreiro with a local train, in April 1995. This class also works freight duties.

RENFE has several classes of shunting locomotive including class 308, introduced in the 1960s, and classes 309 and 310 introduced in the 1980s. CP class 1200 were introduced in 1961 for passenger services and are based on SNCF class BB634000. They have a maximum speed of 50 mph. Class 1300 were acquired from RENFE in 1989 having been built in 1965 as class 313. The locomotives have a maximum speed of 75 mph. Classes 1400 and 1500 were introduced in 1967 and 1948/1955 respectively. They are passenger and freight locomotives with a maximum speed of 65 and 75 mph respectively. British built class 1800 was introduced in the 1960s and are based on British Rail class 50. The class worked on passenger and freight duties and had a maximum speed of 87 mph. They are now withdrawn although examples are preserved. Classes 1900, 1930 and 1960 were introduced in 1973 (class 1962) and the 1980s. The 1900s are freight locomotives with the other two classes specialising in passenger work. The freight class has a maximum speed of 62 mph and the others 75 mph. Class 1150 is the latest class of shunting locomotives introduced in 1966 with a maximum speed of 36 mph. Classes 1001, 1051 and 1101 are classes of small shunting locomotives introduced in 1948, 1955 and 1949 respectively.

Both Spain and Portugal have independent railways operating to standard and narrow gauge in Spain and narrow gauge in Portugal. The systems use mainly diesel locomotives although the Estoril line in Portugal has a number of veteran electric locomotives built in the 1920s and 1940s that use a 1500 V dc electrification system.

CP diesel locomotive, number 1505, prepares to leave its stabling point at Barreiro, in April 1995. The class works passenger and freight trains.

CP diesel passenger and freight locomotive, number 1552, is stabled in the sun at Barreiro, in April 1995.

Now withdrawn CP class 1800 locomotive, number 1807, is stabled at Barreiro, in April 1995. This class was introduced in the 1960s.

The French styling of CP diesel locomotive, number 1940, is unmistakable as it prepares to leave Albufeira with a passenger service, in April 1995.

CP diesel shunting locomotive, number 1172, pauses between duties at Lisbon, in April 1995. This particular locomotive was introduced in the 1960s.

Slovenian Railways

Previously part of the old Yugoslavia, Slovenia became an independent republic in 1991 and its railway system reflects that of a number of republics that were also a part of Yugoslavia.

Slovenian Railways (SZ) has a range of steam locomotives that have been preserved together with an operational fleet of electric and diesel locomotives.

The first line in what is now Slovenia was opened in 1846 and ran from Sentilj to Celje, now a part of the route from Graz in Austria to Trieste in Italy. It was opened by the Imperial Royal Southern State Railway which was taken over by the Imperial Royal Privileged Southern Railway Company in 1857. This company remained in existence until 1924 and, during that time, owned the principal lines in Slovenia. The latter part of the 1800s saw the opening of a significant number of lines and this process continued until World War I. In 1918, the Kingdom of the Serbs, Croats and Slovenes took over the railway system and, in 1929, the Yugoslavian State Railway (JDZ) came into existence operating through regional administrations, one of which was Ljubljana, now the Slovenian capital.

Class 118 2-8-2 tanks were passenger locomotives introduced in the 1920s. 118 005 is preserved at Nova Gorica and is pictured in the early morning sun, in September 2005. This locomotive also worked in Italy as FS number 940 015.

Ex German Kriegslok, number 52 4936, worked in Slovenia as class 33 110. It is shown preserved at Nova Gorica, amongst the trees, in September 2005.

World War II caused major damage to the railway system which had to be repaired in succeeding years. In 1952, the railway became JZ and in the 1960s over 12 percent of the now Slovenian system was closed. Following the creation of the Slovenian Republic in 1991, Slovenske Zeleznice (SZ) was created to run the railway system. Today, the SZ network comprises over 1200 km of lines of which over 310 mi are electrified to 3000 V dc which is the same as neighboring Italy. There are plans in place to include Slovenia in the network of high-speed lines, using Italy as the point of connection. SZ already has acquired tilting and new unit type trains. Slovenia is now a member of the European Union and it will be interesting to see the extent to which the "open access" policy impacts on Slovenia.

Class 125 0-6-0 locomotives were freight locomotives dating from the 1890s. Preserved number 125 037 is pictured at Pragersko, in September 2005.

SZ has a significant number of preserved steam locomotives most of which are held at the excellent railway museum in Ljubljana. Others are displayed on plinths at railway stations and locomotive depots. The former Yugoslavian President Tito's special train is one of the three class 11 locomotives kept at the museum. This magnificent locomotive is a 4-8-0 built in 1947 in Hungary. Class 118 locomotives were 2-8-2 tank locomotives built in the 1920s for passenger train work. Locomotive 118.005 has been preserved and this locomotive also worked in Italy as FS 940.015. Class 33, of which a number of examples have been preserved, were previously German "Kriegsloks" 2-10-0s built in the 1940s and used as versatile passenger and freight locomotives. Class 125 were 0-6-0 freight locomotives built in the 1890s. One example has been preserved that also previously worked in Hungary as MAV class 326. Class 06 were 2-8-2 locomotives used for passenger train work and built in 1930. Three examples have been preserved. Class 25 were 2-8-0 freight locomotives introduced in the 1920s that also saw service in Italy. Several examples have

SZ electric locomotive class 342 are passenger and freight locomotives. Number 342 039 is responsible for a solitary restaurant car at Ljubljana, in October 2002.

Several class 342 locomotives have been sold to Italian private railway companies. FNM locomotive, number 640 03 is at Milan, in September 2005.

1960s SZ electric locomotive, number 362 038, is pictured at Ljubljana, in October 2002. This class is used on passenger and freight work.

been preserved. SZ has used four classes of electric locomotive. Class 361 comprised 17 ex-Italian railway (FS) class 626 locomotives built in the late 1920s and acquired after World War II. They were finally withdrawn from service in the late 1970s. Class 342 comprises 40 passenger and freight locomotives introduced in 1968. A number of these

SZ electric locomotives 363 023 and 029 wait at Jesenice, in October 2002.The steam locomotive water crane is a pleasant reminder of the past.

locomotives are now in Italy, having been sold to Italian private railways. Class 362 comprises 17 locomotives built in the early 1960s and are used on passenger and freight duties.

Class 363 are 39 locomotives based on French SNCF class CC 6500 and their appearance reflects their French styling. They are passenger and freight train locomotives. Currently, SZ is evaluating locomotives of German Railways' (DB) class 189 and it is possible that some locomotives of this type will be acquired. SZ has several classes of diesel locomotives. Class 642 comprises 18 shunting locomotives introduced in 1961 and built in Yugoslavia to the same design as SNCF class 63400 locomotives. The locomotives have a maximum speed of 50 mph. Class 643 are similar but more powerful locomotives introduced in 1967 and built in France.

Class 644 consists of 20 Spanish built locomotives introduced in the mid-1970s and used for freight work on local lines. They have a maximum speed of 56 mph. Class 664.1 are the most powerful diesels in Slovenia and were introduced in 1984. The class comprises 20 General Motors locomotives assembled in Yugoslavia. They are used on passenger and freight work and have a maximum

SZ diesel shunting locomotive, number 642 200, is stabled at Maribor, in September 2005. This class was introduced in 1961.

SZ diesel shunting locomotive, number 643 014, powers through Ljubljana in October 2002. This class was introduced in 1967.

speed of 65 mph. Class 661 originally comprised 3 locomotives of class 661.0, two locomotives of class 661.1 and two locomotives of class 661.4. The locomotives were introduced in the 1960s and the early 1970s. Today, only the 661.4s remain in service and are used on freight duties. They have a maximum speed of 77 mph. Classes 731 and 732.1 are shunting locomotives introduced in 1960 and 1970 respectively. SZ has five class 731s and 23 locomotives of class 732 although some of these locomotives were given to Bosnia-Herzegovina to assist with the rebuilding of the railway in that country.

SZ class 661 diesel, number 661 415, rests at Maribor, in September 2005. This small class of locomotive is used on freight duties.

SZ's spanish built diesel, number 644 015, is stabled at Ljubljana in September 2005. This class was introduced in the 1970s.

One of SZ's most powerful passenger and freight train diesel locomotives, number 664 118, is stabled at Nova Gorica, in September 2005.

Shunting locomotive, number 732 178, awaits its next duty at Maribor, in September 2005. This class was introduced in 1970 and some examples were donated to Bosnia-Hercegovina to help with railway re-construction.

Polish Railways (PKP)

Poland is a large country geographically and has a sizeable fleet of steam, electric and diesel locomotives running on a mix of broad, standard and narrow gauge lines

The first railway in Poland opened in 1842 when the territory was actually shared between Germany and Russia, and this arrangement lasted until 1919. This did not prevent the development of the railway system, although lines in the Russian area were broad gauge (1542 mm) and those in the German area were standard gauge.

A Polish 2-10-0 is silhouetted against the skyline as it speeds through the countryside with its passenger train.

During World War I, the Germans and Austrians took over the Russian area, and some of those railways became standard gauge after the war.

The Polish state came into being in 1921 and PKP was created in 1926. The period before the Second World War enabled improvements to be made to the railways. Although some lines had been electrified in what later became Poland, the first official electrified line opened in 1936, and other lines rapidly followed. The lines were British built and the locomotives used came from Britain and were supplied as part of the contract. The Second World War created major infrastructural problems, with many of the locomotives and much of the rolling stock being destroyed. The post-war period saw the creation of new lines, including narrow gauge, and a commitment to electrification. Today, PKP has over 14,790 mi of lines, the majority of which are electrified at 3000 V dc. PKP has now created a number of business sectors including PKP Cargo – responsible for freight activity. Poland also has a significant number of private railway operators.

Unfortunately, PKP has been beset by financial problems in recent years. Poland is now a member of the European Union and there is a possibility that European funding may help with the cost of essential development and renewal work.

Poland still has a number of operational steam locomotives and has a number of preservation sites. Working classes include the 01.49s, 2-6-2 locomotives introduced in the 1950s for passenger and freight work, Ty2 and Ty42s, which are 2-10-0s introduced in the 1940s. There are also several classes of narrow gauge steam locomotives. One of these is actually preserved in the Cook Islands in the Pacific Ocean!

An early example of PKP's large class of electric locomotives, number EU07 117, moves around its train at Chabowka, in October 2005.

A later built example of class EU07, number 448, prepares to leave Gdansk with its passenger train, in October 1996.

PKP electric locomotive, number EP09 013, moves on to its train at Krakow, in October 2005. This class was introduced in the 1980s.

PKP has a significant number of classes of electric locomotives and the total fleet numbers many hundreds of locomotives. The principal classes include EU07 introduced in the period 1963 to 1992 and used mainly for passenger train work. They are derived from British built class EU06 introduced in 1961. Class EP09 was introduced in the mid-1980s for express passenger train work. This small class of 47 locomotives has a maximum speed of 100 mph. Class ET22 originally comprised 1200 locomotives with a maximum speed of 78 mph. The class was introduced in 1971 for freight work but they also see passenger train use. Classes ET40, 41 and 42 are double unit locomotives introduced in the 1970s for freight work.

PKP double unit electric locomotive, number ET40 43, moves slowly through Gdansk station, in October 1996. This class dates from the 1970s.

Impressive PKP double unit electric locomotive, number ET42 007, waits for the signal to change at Gdansk, in October 1996.

PKP also has a sizeable fleet of diesel locomotives. Class SM30 are shunting locomotives introduced in 1959. Classes SM42, SP42 and SU42 are shunting and light freight locomotives introduced in 1963. Some are also used for passenger train work. Class SU45 locomotives are modernised class SP45s introduced in the 1960s and used on passenger and freight work. Class ST43 and ST44 are numerically large classes introduced in the 1960s. Class SU46

PKP small diesel shunting locomotive, number SM30 250, pulls a works train through Gdansk station, in October 1996. This class dates from 1959.

were introduced in 1974, mainly for passenger train work, and are PKP's most powerful diesels. Class SM48 are Russian built locomotives introduced in 1976. PKP has classes of narrow gauge locomotives for a variety of gauges, introduced in the 1960s and 1970s. Some of these are still operational although others are now out of PKP service, having been acquired by the Welsh Highland Railway in Britain!

A PKP large diesel shunting and light freight locomotive of class SM42 speeds through Gdansk station in October 1996.

The attractive class and number plates on PKP narrow gauge diesel locomotive number LYd2 58. This locomotive is now at the Welsh Highland Railway.

The builder's plate from PKP narrow gauge diesel number LYd2 58 showing that it was built in Romania in 1979.

Other European Railways

Several other European countries and countries that have strong railway links with neighboring European countries have interesting locomotives, some of which are types found throughout Europe.

Croatian (HZ) diesel locomotives, number 2063 014, sports an attractive blue livery as it waits on the Croatia/Hungarian border, in September 2004.

Croatian Railways (HZ) class 2063 locomotives are former Yugoslavia Railways (JZ) class 663. Built by General Motors in the early 1970s, these impressive locomotives work passenger and freight services. They are now painted in an attractive blue livery. Electric class 1141/1142 locomotives are based on the Swedish (SJ) class Rc family of locomotives found in a number of countries including Austria (class 1043), Bosnia and Macedonia (class 441). Details are given in the Swedish railway section of this book.

Greek Railway (OSE) modern electric locomotive, number 120 027, is pictured shortly after delivery in late 2005. This class is being built in Germany.

Romanian (CFR) class 60 are also found in several European countries. Some were sold to a German railway company KEG and locomotive 2105 (CFR number 60 0905) is pictured at Rheine, in May 2001.

Greece has class 120 locomotives, which were previously class H-561. They are Greek Railway's (OSE) first electric locomotives and six locomotives were introduced in 1998. Subsequently, a further 24 locomotives were ordered and are currently being delivered. The locomotives operate off 25 kV ac and have a maximum speed of 124 mph

Romanian Railways (CFR) class 60 locomotives are a successful diesel class that has been used in a number of other countries including Poland (class ST43), Bulgaria (class 06) and China (class ND2/3). The class was introduced in 1960 and over 1400 examples were built for CFR out of a total build of approximately 2500 locomotives. The class is used on passenger and freight work and has a maximum speed of 62 mph. In recent years, CFR had a surplus of this class and examples were sold to Germany (KEG private railway provider), Spain and Italy.

The Ukraine Railway, formerly a part of the USSR but now independent as UZ, class TE steam locomotives were previously German "Kriegsloks" 2-10 -0 locomotives built in the 1940s and acquired after the war by the USSR. An example – TE 3915 – has been preserved at the Speyer Museum in Germany and was previously German locomotive 52. 3915. UZ also has heavy freight electric locomotives. Class VL11 sub-class m is a double unit locomotive built in the 1980s and using the 3000 V dc electrification system. The locomotives are part of a total build in the USSR of over 1000 locomotives in the broader family of class VL11. These broad gauge locomotives have a maximum speed of 62 mph and work in conjunction with Slovakian Railways (ZSR) class 125 broad gauge locomotives, which work freights to and from the Ukrainian border.

Many German Kriegsloks were retained in the USSR. Locomotive 52.3915 became Ukrainian TE 3915 as shown at the German Speyer museum, in May 2002.

The ex USSR states inherited locomotives on achieving independence. Ukraine operates electric double-unit freight locomotives and locomotive VL11 m 106 is at the Slovakian/Ukraine border with a freight train, in April 2005.

Siemens AG has been asked to supply GP NPK Electrovozostroeniya, a locomotive manufacturer in the Ukraine, electrical equipment for 100 locomotives. The units are jointly developed by the two companies, for the Ukrainian railroad company Ukrzaliznizija.

Baltic States Railways

The Baltic states comprise Estonia, Latvia and Lithuania. Until each country achieved independence, they were a part of the Soviet Union (RZD) Railway and the locomotives used on each system still reflect the typical RZD types. The locomotive fleets contain some varied locomotive classes that have been augmented, in Estonia, by the acquisition of second-hand locomotives from the USA.

Estonia became a part of Russia in 1721 but won its independence in 1920. Following wartime occupation by the Germans and later the Soviets, the country became a part of the Soviet Union and remained so until independence was achieved in 1991. The first railway opened in Estonia in 1870 and was a broad gauge line from Narva to Paldiski. Other major lines followed in the latter part of the nineteenth century and in the first few decades of the twentieth century. Some of these were narrow gauge but they were eventually converted to broad gauge. In 1963, the three Baltic states became a part of the Pribaltiiskaya Railway, one of 15 zones of RZD. Estonian Railways (EVR) came into existence in 1991 and was privatized in 2001 with the state retaining a 33 percent interest. EVR now runs freight trains with other business units having responsibility for passengers. The total network comprises over 600 miles of which just over 80 miles is electrified to 3000 V dc.

Latvia has mirrored Estonia in terms of its achievement of independence and its previous involvement with the Soviet Union. Latvian Railways (LDZ) comprises over 1240 miles of lines of which over 150 miles are electrified at 3000 V dc. As also applies in the Estonian organizational arrangement, from 2003 LDZ retained responsibility for freight with another business unit being responsible for passenger services.

Lithuania also achieved independence with the other two states but the railway system run by LG does not follow the same business unit type arrangement and

Over 4200 examples of L class 2-10-0 locomotives were built in the Soviet Union. Locomotive 1646 at Tallinn in Estonia is fired up to provide steam for a laundry, in October 1994.

Class M62 locomotive, number M62 1286, is stabled at Tallinn in Estonia, in October 1994. This locomotive type is used by several other countries.

LG controls all services. LG has over 1180 miles of lines of which 76 miles are electrified at 25k V ac. The overall line total includes the Panevezys to Rubikiai (ASG) narrow gauge line. LG has recently ordered new diesel locomotives to upgrade its services. All three states are now members of the European Union and may seek funding to ensure the development of their respective systems.

In October 1998, class M62 locomotive, number M62 1597, prepares to leave Vilnius station in Lithuania, with a passenger service.

There are several classes of steam locomotive that have survived and that are now preserved, in some cases as working locomotives, or used as stationary boilers for a variety of heating purposes. The most common class are the L class 2-10-0s built in the late 1940s/early 1950s that were the main post-war design of freight locomotive. These reliable locomotives, of which 4200 examples were built in the Soviet Union, had a maximum speed of 56 mph. There are several Su class 2-6-2 locomotives, introduced in 1925 for passenger train services and with a maximum speed of 70 mph. There is also at least one example of the class TE 2-10-0 locomotives, introduced in Germany in 1942 as Kriegsloks and retained by the Soviet Union after the war. These locomotives had a maximum speed of 50 mph.

Locomotive M62 1700 waits at Vilnius in Lithuania with a passenger train, in October 1998. A class TEP 60 locomotive waits on another platform with its passenger service.

Latvian double unit freight locomotive, number 2M62 0894, powers its train through Riga station, in October 1997.

There are no electric locomotives used in any of the three systems although unit type electric train sets are used for passenger services.

The Soviet type diesel locomotives in use in all three states include: Class M62 which was originally developed for Hungarian Railways but later sold to

A class 2M62 locomotive at Riga in Latvia with a freight train, in October 1997. This type is actually two linked M62 units.

many other European countries including Germany, Poland, the Czech Republic and Slovakia in addition to exports to North Korea, Cuba and Mongolia. Developed in the 1960s, the locomotives have a maximum speed of 62 mph. They are used for passenger and freight train work. Class 2M62 is, in effect, two M62s modified to create a double unit locomotive. Production of these locomotives started in 1976 and each has a maximum speed of 62 mph.

Class 2M62 locomotive, number 0230, uses the power of its two units to accelerate its freight through Vilnius in Lithuania, in October 1998.

They are used for freight work. Class 2M62U is also used which is an improved version of the earlier classes, introduced in 1987. Class ChME3 was introduced in 1965 and has a number of sub-classes. A massive total of over 7400 of these locomotives was produced until the 1990s and they are in use in several other countries including the Czech Republic and Slovakia. The locomotives are mainly used for shunting and freight train work and have a maximum

Locomotive number 2M62 0027, at Vilnius in Lithuania, in October 1998. The configuration of two linked class M62 locomotives can clearly be seen.

Class ChME3 was introduced in 1965 and over 7400 were built. Locomotive number 4512 is at Tallinn in Estonia, in October 1994.

ChME3 locomotive, number 7185, catches the afternoon sun as it waits for its next duty at Vilnius in Lithuania, in October 1998.

Class TEM2 was introduced in 1967 for shunting work. Locomotive number TEM2 330 prepares to pull empty coaching stock out of Vilnius station in Lithuania, in October 1998.

Class TEP60 was introduced in 1961 for passenger train work. Locomotive number TEP60 0339 is stabled at Tallinn in Estonia, in October 1994. The red star on the front shows its previous Soviet ownership.

Powerful express passenger class TEP70 was introduced in 1978. Locomotive number TEP70 0320 is stabled at Tallinn in Estonia, in October 1994 with another member of the same class.

speed of 59 mph. Class VME1 was introduced in 1958 and is used for shunting. The locomotives have a maximum speed of 50 mph. At one time, they were used on suburban passenger traffic in the Tallinn and Riga areas of Estonia and Latvia respectively. Class TGM3 was introduced in 1959 for shunting and passenger train work. The class has a maximum speed of 44 mph. Class TEM2 was introduced in 1967 and is a shunting locomotive with a maximum speed of 62 mph. Class TEP60, introduced in 1961, are passenger train locomotives with a maximum speed of 100 mph. Some examples are now withdrawn from service. Class TEP70 are powerful passenger locomotives introduced in production format in 1978. The locomotives have a maximum speed of 100 mph. Class 2TE116 is a double unit freight locomotive, introduced in 1972. The locomotives have a maximum speed of 62 mph. Over 1600 of these locomotives had been built by the mid-1990s. Class TV2 comprises 12 narrow gauge diesel locomotives used on the ASG narrow gauge line.

Based on their experience of the traditional types and given reduced availability of locomotives, EVR decided soon after privatisation to acquire a different, more reliable and effective locomotive fleet. As a result, a decision was taken to acquire 77 class C36.7i and 7ai second-hand diesels from the USA to be used for freight work. The locomotives were originally built in the 1980s by General Motors. The availability of these relatively modern locomotives has enabled EVR to withdraw locomotives of classes TEP60, M62 and 2M62 from service.

In terms of new locomotives, LG has ordered 34 new Siemens DE20 type locomotives for delivery in 2007. This type is the same as Austrian Railways (OBB) class 2016. The LG experience of these locomotives may initiate similar acquisitions by the other two states.

TEP60 locomotive number TEP60 0992 powers out of Vilneus station in Lithuania with a passenger train, in October 1998.

Irish Railways

Ireland has some 1,430 miles of public railways, all 1600 mm – five foot, three inch gauge. Irish Rail – Iarnrod Eireann – the state railway system in the Republic, has 1,208 miles, and Northern Ireland Railways operates another 222 miles with most of the system carrying predominantly passengers. Freight traffic is light compared to international standards, with some lines, particularly on the NIR system, carrying no freight at all.

The stylish lines of Great Northern Railway 4-4-0 steam locomotive number 171 are evident as it simmers at Dublin, in August 1996. This locomotive was built by Beyer Peacock in 1913.

The history of rail transport in Ireland began only a decade later than that of Great Britain. The first railway to be built in Ireland was the Dublin and Kingstown – now Dún Laoghaire – Railway (D&KK) and it travelled over a distance of six miles. William Dargan, the builder of the line, was also instrumental in the construction of many other lines too. It was on December 13 1834 that the locomotive Hibernia travelled the length of the route from Westland Row – now Pearse station – through to Dunleary, near Kingstown. The route used the four foot, eight and a half inch gauge and still remains part of today's Dublin Area Rapid Transit, electrified commuter rail system. The track gauges chosen by the first three railways were all different but the chosen gauge for the mainline railways of Ireland became five foot, three inches, which is an unusual gauge but can also be found on some Australian lines and in Brazil. By the early 1920s, both the route mileage – about 7,450 miles – and the traffic levels carried were at their peak, but competition from road traffic began to make inroads into railway traffic from here onwards. While most of the system was 1600 mm gauge, many rural areas were using narrow gauge – 914 mm in size. In the north-west, County Donegal was almost entirely served by two large narrow gauge systems, totalling some 186 miles.

The main lines between Dublin and Cork, Belfast, and Belfast-Derry, received a fair amount of investment over the years, and locomotives, carriages and services were as good as anywhere in Europe. Rural and western lines received little new investment, especially during the lean years of the 1920s – 1930s. In 1923, the Keady-Castleblayney line, in County Armagh, was closed after only 10 years, and by the early 1930s a number more rural lines had followed the same route, most of which were in the south and west of the country.

Many narrow gauge lines of three foot size were also constructed on the island, but most have closed down today, including what was the biggest both in Ireland and in the United Kingdom. By the begin-

Preserved IE diesel locomotive, number B113, is stabled at Dublin, in August 1996. This class was introduced in 1950 and was withdrawn in 1977. The locomotives had a maximum speed of 49 mph.

IE class 201C was introduced in 1956 and were withdrawn in the mid-1980s. Locomotive number C231 is at Dublin, in August 1996.

ning of the twentieth century, several mainline railways had opened and even more independent lines were working too.

Although the railway system survived independence, it was hit harder with the Irish Civil War (1922-1923), when bridges and rails were damaged and destroyed. In 1925, all the railway companies whose lines fell wholly on the southern side of the newly created border – between Northern Ireland and the Republic – were amalgamated as the Great

IE class 421 are small diesel locomotives, introduced in 1962. Locomotive E428 is at Dublin in August 1996.

Southern Railways. By the late 1940s, Ireland still had an extensive railway system which was almost entirely steam operated, and one short branch line in County Tyrone remained horse-driven until its closure in 1957.

The Second World War also took its toll on the Irish railway. Having taken a neutral stance during the war, Britain was no longer obliged to supply coal,

Northern Ireland class 111 are General Motors locomotives introduced in 1980. The locomotives of the class originally worked Belfast to Dublin passenger services into Connolly station where number 113 is shown in August 1997.

IE class 071 was introduced in 1976. They were originally express passenger train locomotives but are now also used on freight services. Locomotive number 087 leaves Dublin Connolly station, in August 1999.

and so it had to make do with inferior Irish coal or even wood if available. If these were not available then the trains didn't run at all. Following nationalisation of CIE (the state transport company in the Republic) in 1950, many of the lines that were not making money were closed, and others reduced to freight-only status. Meanwhile, in the North, the Ulster Transport Authority – state owned railway and general public transport in Northern Ireland 1949 to 1967 – closed almost 80 percent of the railway system under its control, and introduced diesel railcars to the rest. Both economic circumstances and political interference had resulted in the closure of most of the Great Northern Railway system in 1957. The remainder was divided between the two state companies. CIE took over the remaining lines in the Republic, and the UTA took over what was left in the North – only to close over half of it by 1965. It was at the end of 1962, following the delivery of more diesel locomotives and further branch line closures imminent, that the CIE eliminated steam traction for good.

In the North, dieselization had followed a different pattern; no mainline diesel locomotives had been acquired at all, and practically all passenger trains were railcar formations. Freight traffic had been abolished by the UTA in 1965, apart from cross-border traffic to and from Belfast and Derry, and yet further closures of lines had taken place. In 1967, the UTA was split up into road and rail undertakings and the railways became the Northern Ireland Railways system. Steam lingered on in the form of a remaining few ex-NCC W class 2-6-4Ts until 1970, when the last two were withdrawn. The last public mainline passenger train in both Ireland and the British Isles had operated on Easter Monday, 1970. After that, NIR began a gradual program of renewal.

Class 071 locomotive, number 085, heads a short freight near Dublin, in August 1995. This class was introduced in 1976.

With a lack of proper maintenance, there is always the risk of danger and accidents, which is what happened at Sligo. On August 1, 1980 a diesel express running between Cork and Dublin was derailed, with 18 people killed and 62 injured. As ever it takes an accident for people to realize that the system is in need of attention. Following the accident, the CIE and the Irish government, under pressure from the public, were obliged to upgrade the older coaches for new British Rail Mark 3 models. Cutbacks were also experienced at this time with the closure of more lines – some that were not in use were left to rot. The new north to south commuter line, the Dublin Area Rapid Transit – DART – was introduced in 1984 after the electrification of

In 1994 IE introduced class 201 for passenger and freight train work. Locomotive number 228 is at Dublin, in August 1995.

the line. Further expansion was due but didn't happen until the mid-1990s, when the Republic experienced an economic boom. New locomotives from General Motors, new carriages from De Dietrich and a general upgrading of signalling and track changed the whole face of the railways. NI Railways purchased 23 new trains as part of an £80 million (approximately 117 million Euros) investment approved in December 2000 by the Northern Ireland Assembly, and 14 of these new C3k trains are now in public service on Northern Ireland's rail network. The introduction of the new trains marks an important milestone for rail service in Northern Ireland. Translink, who runs the trains, has plans for further investment in the delivery of a modern, high quality railway network for the wider local community.

IE class 121 are General Motors built locomotives, introduced in 1960. The locomotives operate push-pull passenger services and work freight trains. Locomotive number 127 is shown at Dublin, in August 1995.

IE General Motors built class 181 was introduced in 1966 and the locomotives are used on passenger and freight services. Locomotive number 187 is stabled at Dublin, in August 1997.

New Zealand Railways

The national rail network of New Zealand is currently run by the government-owned organisation ONTRACK – the New Zealand Railway Corporation. The railways used to be administered by the government's Railways Department, with responsibility being held by a Cabinet Minister of Railways. In 1981 this was changed and it was reformed into the New Zealand Railway Corporation. For 1990, core rail operations were reconstituted as New Zealand Rail Ltd, with non-core assets retained by the New Zealand Railways Corporation. New Zealand Rail was privatized in 1993, with the new owners adopting the name Tranz Rail in 1995. There was some unrest with the way Tranz Rail was operating the system and as confidence and shares of the company started to dive, so the government had to intervene. In the end Toll Holdings of Australia made a successful take-over bid for Tranz Rail, which was accepted.

The actual rail services in New Zealand are now run by private companies of which the prime operator is

Class D16 were 2-4-0 tank locomotives, built in 1878. One example has been preserved at the Pleasant Point Railway where it is pictured in February 2002 at the head of a passenger train.

the Australian-owned Toll Rail, with Connex operating the commuter services in Auckland. As New Zealand's largest operator Toll Rail handles containerised freight, consolidated general freight and the transportation of logs, coal, milk, steel, aggregates and fertilizers. It provides shuttle trains specifically designed for container movement along with other types of freight. It can also provide customers with a hook-and-tow facility for their own equipment. Connex on the other hand, is the brand name of the international transport services division of the French-based multinational company Veolia Environnement. They have a presence in many countries around the world and employ some 55,000 workers worldwide.

New Zealand saw its first railway in 1862 on South Island, when two Carriages were pulled on a three foot gauge track, by horsepower rather than by steam engine. The first steam train ran from Christchurch a year later, on a larger five foot, three inch, gauge line. Following several experiments and gauge sizes, a four foot, six inch gauge was chosen as the standard. Double Fairlie locomotives started running at Duneadin on September 1872. Along with having an extraordinary selection of gauge sizes, New Zealand also bought several different types of steam engines, but as most of the lines were short and radiated inland from the ports, the most popular engine became the F class 0-6-0T saddle tank. There were a good number of American locomotives too, Rogers locomotives was one supplier of their K class from 1878, and Baldwin Locomotive Works also supplied their Pacific locomotives from 1901. Tank engines were also popular on the Islands and several 4-6-4TW class models were running alongside the heavier engines. During World War II, some 40 J class locomotives were delivered to the New Zealand Railways for their less busy lines. At its peak period during the 1950s and 1960s, the railway network had some 100 different lines operating around the country, but it was in the late 1960s and the 1970s that large-scale closures of branch lines was instigated.

Until the 1950s most lines on the national network ran steam trains, although there were some sections that ran on a 1500 volt DC electrical system, and which still do today. During the 1940s, some diesel engines were used for shunting duties, but the first mainline locomotives were introduced in 1954, when the DF class came into service. Like many countries, by the mid-1960s many steam trains had been, or were starting to be, phased out. The South Island though did remain faithful to the steam cause up to the 1970s. Today several privately-owned

Magnificent 2-4-2 steam locomotive, number 92, is pictured at Kingston, in February 2002. This preserved locomotive was built by Rogers in 1878 and shows classic American styling of the time.

A detailed view of the front of Roger's built steam locomotive, number 92, showing the builder's plate which confirms that it was built at Paterson, New Jersey.

Ab class 4-6-2 locomotive, number 778, prepares to leave Kingston with the "Kingston Flyer," in February 2002. This locomotive was built in 1925.

J class locomotive, number 1211, is shown on a special train at Auckland, in February 2002. This 4-8-2 locomotive was built in 1939.

A detailed view of the front of 4-8-2 J class locomotive, number 1211. The builder's plate confirms that the locomotive was built in 1939.

steam and diesel trains do operate, but mainly as tourist attractions.
Long-distance passenger services are operated by a subsidiary of Toll Rail, TranzScenic. Where back in the 1950s and 1960s there was an abundance of services, today there are only four main routes – the Overlander, which travels between Auckland and Wellington; the Capital, which connects Wellington to Palmerston North; the TranzCoastal, which runs between Picton and Christchurch and the TranzAlpine, which connects Christchurch; with Greymouth. Between 2002 and 2004, some less popular services, like the Southerner – which ran from Christchurch to Dunedin and Invercargill – and the Northerner night service, were eliminated from the schedule. As far as suburban services are concerned, TranzMetro, again a subsidiary of Toll rail, operate passenger services in the Wellington area. Here there are four lines, 90 percent of which have been electrified. EMUs are used mainly on these services along

Diesel locomotive, number 1429, was built by English Electric in 1952. It is preserved at Ferrymead where it is pictured in February 2002.

Class DX diesel locomotive, number 5500, at Christchurch, in February 2002. This is the most powerful diesel class in New Zealand.

Diesel shunting locomotive, number 2680, waits for its next duty at Christchurch, in February 2002. This center-cab class was introduced in 1962 and was built in Britain.

Class DJ locomotives, numbers 3211 and 3286, wait with their trains at Dunedin, in February 2002. These former NZ locomotives were built in 1967 and are now used on the Taieri Gorge Railway.

Class DFT locomotive, number 7199, waits at Auckland for its next train, in February 2002. The class, introduced in 1979, can be found on both New Zealand islands.

Class DC diesel locomotive, number 4726, at Christchurch, in February 2002. This class, introduced in 1961, was re-built in the 1970s.

with some diesel locomotives. Today Wellington still runs all-electric trains – it was the first city in New Zealand to install electric trains in the 1930s – and is reputed to have the best passenger rail service in the country. TranzMetro lost their franchise for the Auckland lines in 2004, which are now under the control of Connex Auckland, who run the suburban lines. These lines use diesel operated engines – DMUs and locomotive hauled trains – and there are plans to electrify the system to improve the service. There are about 60 groups that run heritage lines and/or museums around New Zealand. Rail preservation really started in the 1960s as the steam trains were starting to be phased out and lines closed down. Heritage lines and museums vary from the simple half-mile lines with trains being displayed in museums, to the considerably longer lines that focus much more on the actual use of the line and its locomotives.

Current operations of the heritage railway type include the Bay of Islands Vintage Railway, Glenbrook Vintage Railway, Bush Tramway Club, Waitara Railway Preservation Society, Weka Pass Railway and Taieri Gorge Railway. The Taieri Gorge Railway, which is operated as a Local Authority Trading Enterprise of the Dunedin City Council, is 37 miles in length, making it the most ambitious project of its type to date. All other lines are operated by voluntary societies. The Weka Pass Railway at 8 miles is the most lengthy of these; although the Bay of Islands Vintage Railway is 7 miles in length, it is in poor condition and has been closed since 2002.

Small diesel shunting locomotive, number 943, is stabled at Dunedin, in February 2002. This class was introduced in 1973.

Ex NZ class TR diesel shunting locomotive, number 350, is now used at the Kingston railway where it is shown, in February 2002.

Australian Railways

It's difficult to imagine the social and industrial impact that the steam locomotive must have had in those early days, when the means of transportation were animals, wagons, stage coaches and the like. Suddenly there it was, a huge, steaming, noisy, metal machine, that could take you from one end of the country to the other, in a time never imagined before. The fear it must have generated in some must have been traumatic.

This early photo shows an odd arrangement, the rear wheels are driven from the cylinders, and in turn the front wheels via a connecting rod. Not a happy bunch by the look of it!

Australia is a vast country and even with today's modern transport, it takes a good chunk of time to get from one side of the landmass to the other. Like so many other countries, the first rail journey was horse-drawn, and this took place in 1854, over a 7-mile stretch, between Goolwa and Port Elliott, in South Australia. In this same year a steam train ran 2 miles from Melbourne to Port Melbourne, and a further line of 14 miles was opened between Sydney and Parramatta. Two years later a 8 miles line was opened to Adelaide and by 1860 a line was opened to the Kapunda copper mines. Lines started to open large tracts of the country and railway building started to take off – in 1861 there were 242 miles of line in Australia, by 1871 there were 1,029 miles, and by 1881 there were 4,012 miles in six colonies.

Not much thought went into linking isolated towns and seaboards; railway lines were built to link ports with local hinterlands, rather than city with city. Each colony jealously developed autonomous economies and railway systems, with different gauges and little thought of transcontinental travel. This would be a problem that the planners would have to face in the future – for example, it took another 100 years before gauges on the national rail network were standardized.

The Kimberley 0-4-0 class A Steam loco, was built in 1922 and operated from the early 1950s in Carnarvon, Australia. It was replaced by diesel powered locos in 1958.

As settlers dared to venture further inland looking to set up their farms, and miners searched for gold deposits, it was essential to have a means of transport to move the produce back to the cities and ports. It was these early inland lines that created the foundation for what would eventually become Australia's transcontinental railways of today.

There had been much talk of building a transcontinental line, north to south, even as early as 1858 but it was rejected by the South Australian government – it has to be remembered that Australia was still split into colonies at that time. Finally a Bill authorised the building of a line from Port Augusta to Government Gums – later renamed Farina. Barry, Brookes and Fraser, were given the contract, and in 1891 the line reached Oodnadatta, which remained the railhead until it was extended to Alice Springs in 1929. From here onwards, lack of money, lack of enthusiasm and even a tornado that destroyed Darwin, left the line still unmade. Although some progress was made, huge amounts of money were squandered on the project with little to show for it. It wasn't until 1997 that the AustralAsia Railway Corporation was established by the South Australian and Northern Territory governments. They sent out tenders for the railway and in June 1999 it was announced that the Asia Pacific Transport Consortium had been selected as the preferred bidder to build and operate the railway. Prime Minister John Howard, South Australian Premier John Olsen and Northern Territory Chief Minister Denis Burke turned the first sod for the project at a ceremony in Alice Springs in July 2001. In February 2004, the line between Alice Springs and Darwin was finally completed.

This is a Government Railway locomotive from 1880, in the Queensland area. It ran on the three foot, six inch gauge tracks, and is a Dobs built 2-4-2 tank engine.

By the 1950s, the total railway mileage was in the region of 28,000 and all but a very small percentage was state-owned. An east to west transcontinental line was completed in 1917, which linked Port

Engine E18, a classic Stephenson long boiler design 0-6-0 locomotive. This engine is currently at the Thirlmere Rail Heritage Centre at New South Wales Rail Transport Museum.

This is K1, an 0-4-0+0-4-0 articulated Garratt. One of a pair built in 1909 by Beyer Peacock for the North-East Dundas Tramway, Tasmania.

The makers plate – the name Garratt derives from the engineer Herbert William Garratt, who devised the type, and developed it in association with the Manchester firm of Beyer Peacock.

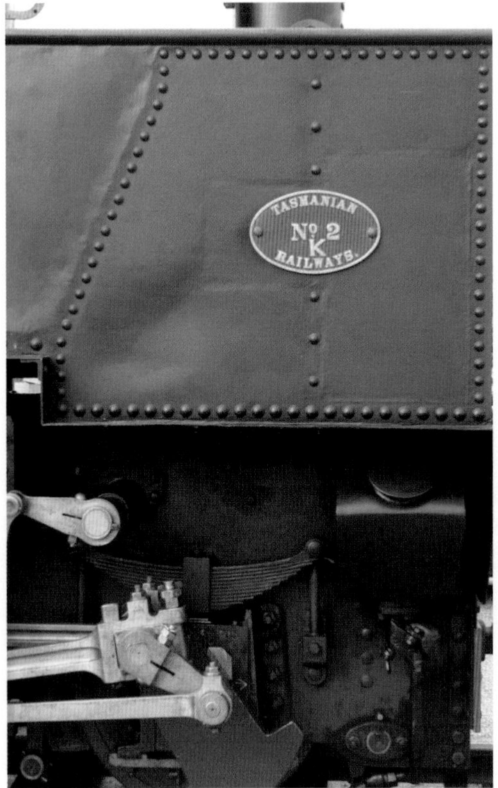

Augusta with Perth and served the goldfields of Kalgoorlie and linked with the north to south transcontinental at Alice Springs.

By the 1950s, steam trains were starting to be phased out and new cleaner diesel and electric locomotives began to appear. Diesel trains are still used for freight, and on some country routes, but the majority of trains in the built-up areas are electric-powered. Most of the trains brought in were derivatives of those used in Europe and America, which were modified to suit track, climatic conditions and of course gauge – of which there were a good selection even in the late 1950s. Once lines started to expand and move into other states, a problem of gauge size arose. Because each state had decided on their own gauge, which was probably not the same as their neighbor's gauge, there was an incompatability problem. Quite often both freight and passengers would have to change trains, depending on what state they were in. For example, in 1917 in Brisbane, a person who wanted to get from Perth to Brisbane on an east to west journey, found themselves having to change six times due to the track gauge! There is more uniformity today but there are still some smaller lines, and of course enthusiast lines, that are narrow gauge and do not conform.

In 2005, most of the big electric and diesel locomotive builders supplied Australia with their trains – English Electric, Alco, and GM. There are some amazing journeys to be travelled across different parts of Australia, in comfort and at speed. The Ghan

Standing strong in its yellow and green livery, this is Diesel locomotive CLP 16, with Co-Co wheel arrangement; built in 1971 by Clyde Engineering, Granville, New South Wales.

– an abbreviation of the word Afghan, and a reference to the camels that were once used along with their drivers – takes you from Adelaide in the south, through Alice Springs and up to Darwin in the far north. The journey crosses several landscapes which take you from temperate Adelaide, through to the

Another stop for commuter locomotive number 3913 on its long journey to Cairns, Northern Australia.

A local articulated commuter train seen at Belford, South Australia. Train number NP23, model EA2501 makes its way through local countryside.

The Ghan, it's an odd name for a train but in Australian history it is a living legend. You can board The Ghan in Adelaide or Darwin.

arid Red Centre, then on to the unique Katherine region, and finally on to tropical Darwin. The Indian Pacific takes you from Sydney on the Pacific Ocean in the east, through to Adelaide and then on to Perth on the Indian Ocean in the west. It is one of the world's longest railway journeys and covers over 2,835 mi. It takes three days and nights through the stunning Blue Mountains, the Nullarbor plains and through the historic towns of Broken Hill and Kalgoorlie.

South American Railways

Argentina

A line was opened in 1857 between Parque and Floresta and the locomotive took the name of La Portena. It was a four-wheeled engine which had been used during the Crimean War. Argentina had a large spread of lines over the country and with it a large array of locomotives and gauges. Most were run by the British and so much of the rolling stock was imported from Britain. These locomotives allowed the country's economy to thrive, with trains transporting large amounts of meat, grain and fruit all over the country for shipment abroad. As with many of the South American countries, diesel power is now dominant and engines are supplied by British and Italian companies.

Argentina had the largest population of steam locomotives in South America, like this Sentinel. Most were imported from England and were often fired by Welsh coal.

Brazil

Rio de Janeiro saw the first short line open in 1854. The first locomotive to run was the Baroneza, which used a 2-2-2 wheel configuration. Most of the tracks laid were of the one-meter gauge and most early locomotives supplied were from America, such as the Baldwin 2-8-0.

Unlike Argentina, the Brazilian railways were equipped with mainly American locomotives but again these helped to transport goods all over this vast country and abroad. Some British locomotives were imported for their one-meter gauge lines.

Brazil also had a rich collection of steam locomotives, like this strange looking plantation engine. Many locos were modified to suit their workload.

Mexico

A line was opened in 1873 between the capital Mexico City and Veracruz. A selection of engines were supplied, for example Fairlie 0-6-6-0 and Johnstone articulated – it seems that this locomotive was so big it had to be dismantled on its delivery journey from North America.

Paraguay

Equipped with mainly standard gauge lines, these link the capital city Asuncion with Encarnacion, on the Argentine border. Again, the locomotives are mainly British, in particular Moguls from the North British Works in Glasgow, Scotland.

An Edwardian mogul locomotive, built by North British of Glasgow, Scotland, puffing its way from Asuncion to the Argentinean border town of Encarnacion.

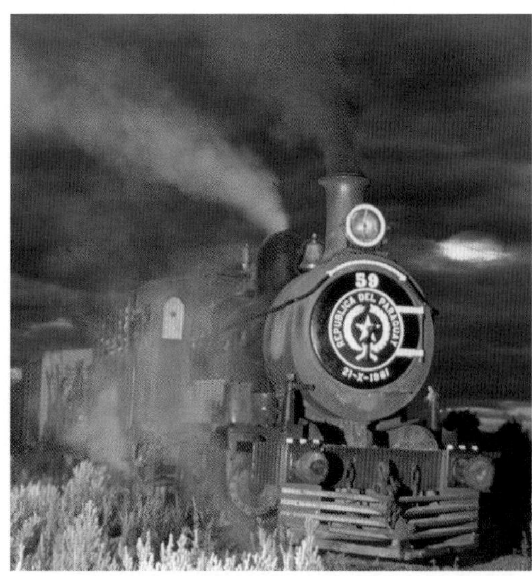

Bolivia

Bolivia is locked between several other South American countries – Brazil to the north-east, Paraguay and Argentina to the south Peru and Chile to the east. Connections to these other countries was made, but over some of the densest forests and highest mountains. Locomotives from many European, American and British companies survive in this country. Recently the Bolivian government has pursued capitalization of the railway sector. In December 1995, it concluded the disposal of a 50 per cent interest in the shares of the Bolivian railway company ENFE, which was previously divided into two separate companies – one covering the Andean network and the other covering the eastern country network. An offer made by the Chilean company, Cruz Blanca, was selected for both networks.

Chile

Positioned right on the southern coast of South America, Chile has had railways since 1851. Today the country has a total of 4115 miles of railway lines which are split into: 1770 miles of broad gauge; 1047 miles of meter gauge; 2,346 miles narrow gauge. 823 miles of the meter gauge is now electrified. Both electric and diesel-powered engines now carry out the work of passenger and freight transportation, once done by the steam engines. There is a goodly range of engines from several different countries like Russia, Italy and of course America.

Once the transporters of gold and nitrates to Pacific ports, this last surviving Kitson-Meyer 0-6-6-0 locomotive is now working in Chile's Atacama Desert.

A modern electric train used on local Santiago commuter lines. Their website informs people to book at least one week ahead. Not the greatest service!

Columbia, Ecuador, Peru and Uruguay

All these countries relied on both British and/or American locomotives and none had traditional builders of engines. Today Peru has replaced its steam engines for diesel-electrics of which most come from GM. Their long mineral trains scale the heady heights of the local Andean mountains.

This is a T class 2-8-0, heading for the meat canning port on the Uruguay river. It is the last surviving of its class in the Uruguayan Railway roster.

South African Railways

Mr Harrison Watson, chairman of the Cape of Good Hope Western Railway, banker and merchant, announced in 1845 that his company had plans for a railway. Unfortunately the reaction of the people around him was not as enthusiastic as he was and the venture never took off. So therefore the first running railway was not founded in Cape Town but somewhere else. The Natal Railway Company was initiated in 1859 and a line – just two miles in length – was opened on June 26, 1860. The track was laid along the Bluff in Durban, the capital of Natal, and it was oxen that pulled vehicles along the track prior to the locomotive "Natal" – but it seems even this was not the first to run in South Africa. By 1857 and after long administrative delays and some interference by other competitors, a contract to build the first railway line in the Cape of Good Hope was awarded to the Cape Town Railway and Dock Company on August 6, 1858. The first proposed line was to be from Cape Town to Wellington – a short but important line of 45 miles – that would serve the wine-growing districts of the Western Cape. Construction started on March 31, 1859, and the first trains in the Cape Colony started running on the Cape Town to Eersterivier section, in February 1862. The 0-4-2 locomotive used during the construction, and built by Hawthorn & Company of Leith, Scotland, was credited as being the first train to run on rails in South Africa.

The Wynberg Railway Company, formed in 1861, looked at building a line from Cape Town to Wynberg, which finally opened in 1864. The first working railway line in the Transvaal is credited to a route named the Rand Tram, a line running from

This is South Africa's first steam locomotive which operated in Cape Province in 1859. This 0-4-2 was built by Hawthorn & Co, at their works in Leith, Scotland.

Many locomotives of this type are used for the different mining activities carried out in South Africa, in particular mines like the East Daggafontein Mines Ltd.

Another steam locomotive transports its load to the factory, this is one of several owned by the Albion colliery.

Johannesburg to the Boksburg coal mines. It was completed in 1890 and then extended to Krugersdorp and to Springs later that same year. By 1892 several lines had linked up. The Cape Government Railway from Port Elizabeth and East London reached Bloemfontein in the Orange Free State, whilst both the Cape Town and Bloemfontein lines had reached the Transvaal, therefore opening three ports to the Rand gold fields. On November 2, 1894 the Transvaal railway line from Pretoria to Delagoa Bay – later named Lourenco Marques and since renamed Maputo, in Mozambique – was opened and by December 16, 1898, the Natal government line also linked into the system. 1900 saw the establishment of the Imperial Military Railway, which came into being after the second Anglo-Boer war and the defeat of the Afrikaner Republics. The railway was left under the supervision of Lieutenant-Colonel Sir Percy Girouard and it wasn't long before the IMR took control of all lines of what was now the Transvaal and Orange River Colony, becoming the Central South African Railway – CSAR. 1916 saw the Union of South Africa formed which consisted of the former four colonies – Cape of Good Hope, Natal, Orange River and Transvaal. In 1916 all the railways in South Africa became a unified state-owned system when the CSAR, CGR and NGR were merged by an Act of Parliament, from which South African Railways and Harbours – SAR&H – was born. The big split happened in 1961, when the Union of South Africa ceased being a part of the British Empire and became the Republic of South Africa. Further changes were made to restructure the SAR&H so as to prepare it for privatization. By now the group included more than just the railways – harbour, road transport, aviation and pipelines management were also a part of this group. In 1981 this

Chucking out plenty of smoke, these two Garratt GMA class 4-8-2+2-8-4 locomotives struggle to get their load under way. These engines were made in the mid 1950s.

Most of the locomotives used by the collieries and mines were supplied by North British of Glasgow, and generally were 4-8-2 wheel configuration.

South African Railways were to become the largest users of Garratts in the world, even though they bought a good many from other builders. Seen here is another GMA class loco.

An SAR locomotive class 24, 2-8-4 Berkshire, takes the scenic route between George and Knysna, skirting the Indian Ocean. These engines were introduced in 1948.

complex group of services came under the name of South African Transport Services – SATS, and was split into units with emphasis on localised management. Then 1989 saw the transformation of SATS from a government department into a public company and just one year later it received company status, under the TRANSNET name. Transnet Limited is a public company of which the South African government is the sole shareholder and incorporates the country's largest transport business and consists of eight major divisions. Metrorail and Spoornet are just two divisions of Transnet. Metrorail operates the urban commuter train services in South Africa's main urban areas, namely greater Johannesburg, Cape Town, Durban, Tshwane, East London and Port Elizabeth. Spoornet is a South African company providing transport and logistical solutions, contributing to Africa's economic renaissance – Spoornet provides its customers with inclusive freight transport solutions.

Locomotive class E61, seen on the Trans Karoo Express line at Worcester in Cape Province. This train runs from Cape Town to Pretoria and can take up to twenty-six hours.

Diesel locomotive 33.056 makes a scheduled stop. These more modern diesels are ideally suited for pulling long distance commuter trains.

Seen here is a Spoornet long distance train. They are the largest division within Transnet, who presently operate rail freight and long distance passenger transport.

North African Railways

Africa would without doubt be a much richer place if more thought had been put into the railway system, right from the very start. The railways have always played a major part in the transportation of materials over vast areas of land and a Pan-African attitude, rather than the slightly narrow view taken, would have benefited the system greatly. All the same, the railways have played and are still playing a major role with the movement of materials and people.

Situated on the north coast of Africa, Algeria is the second largest country of the continent. It covers more than 900,000 square miles – about four-fifths of which is in the Sahara Desert. The country had been an integral part of metropolitan France since the French had occupied it in 1830.

Algeria's first railway was completed in July 1862, and was a thirty-mile standard gauge line, running southwest from Algiers. Not long after it had been completed the line was taken over by the French Paris-Lyon-Mediterranean company, and in 1871 they completed the line through to Oran. In 1870 the Algerian Eastern Railway built a line between Algiers and Constantine and in 1904 this line became state owned and run by the PLM Company. In 1910 a narrow gauge – forty-two inch/1055 mm – line was constructed to connect the coal producing area of the country with the desert settlements at Colomb-Bechar. The Algerian Western Railway – between Oran and the Moroccan border – was completed in 1922, after which more lines opened between the Sahara Desert and the coastal areas of the country.

Prior to the Second World War, the Algerian section of the Trans-Sahara Railway was started where it joined the Moroccan section – completed in 1931 – at Bou Arfa. It continued through Algeria, to connect with the narrow gauge line at Colomb-Becher. Due to the war, work on the line had to be stopped and it didn't continue after the war either. A joint railway administration – Chemins de Fer Algeriens

Algeria is planning to invest $50 billion in infrastructure over the coming years, and a large portion of this will go towards its railway network and rolling stock.

Switzerland and Algeria are very close when it comes to trade, and it looks like Switzerland will take a leading role in the modernisation of the Algerian State run railways.

An impressive Tunisian Railway class 91 mainline diesel locomotive stops the traffic as it progresses slowly into the station at Sousse, in August 2001.

Tunisian Railway class 91 diesel locomotive, number 553, enters Sousse station with a passenger train. This class was built by General Motors in Canada and was introduced in the 1990s.

– was created in 1933, to oversee and unify the Algerian Railway system, of which the French State Railways was the major partner. They were then nationalised and became separated from the French system in 1939 and took the title of Societe Nationale Chemins de Fer Algeriens – SNCFA. In 1976 this was changed again to Societe Nationale des Transports Ferroviaires – SNTF. Algeria has some 2600 miles of lines, of which about 1500 is standard gauge and the remainder is narrow gauge. A small section of this is electrified and is used to transport materials from Tebessa to the El Hadjar steel mills near Annaba. This has helped Algeria to become independent as far as steel was concerned – prior to the connection and building of these mills the country relied on imported steel. Other lines are starting to open up too, linking the once deserted areas of the country with its heartlands. It is the railroads that are becoming the lifelines of the country and helping its future development and prosperity.

History accounts for Tunisia as far back as the Phoenician traders in the twelfth century BC, with Carthage being a great trading post for the Western Mediterranean in 814 BC. The Romans conquered the Carthaginians, who in turn were ousted when the Arabs came in 693 AD. In 1854 Tunisia then joined

Large Tunisian Railway diesel locomotive, number 60 312, heads an early morning freight train through Sousse station, in August 2001.

the Crimea War with the British and French, after which a French "puppet" Turkish ruler was put in power in 1877. Tunisia was finally given independence in 1956, in the interim remaining under French rule.

Tunisia saw its first railways built during the last years of Turkish rule, in 1874. these were standard gauge lines and served the capital Tunis. A standard gauge line was completed to the Algerian border in 1877, whilst other lines to the south of Tunis were

Tunisian Railway class 040 DM locomotive, number 262, on manoeuvring duties at Sousse station, in August 2001.

Twisting its way through the mountains of Morocco on the Casa - FES line, this train is on its way to Bab Tissra. Morocco knew no railway at all before 1908.

constructed as one-meter gauge lines. The first of these – finished in 1897 – was owned by the Gafsa Phosphate and Railroad Company and travelled between the phosphate mines near Gafsa to the port of Sfax. In this same year the capitol was connected to the coast at Sousse and in 1912 this was extended to Sfax. Other lines to various industrial areas followed. Nationalization happened in 1965 and nearly all lines came under the new organization of the Tunisian National Railroad Company – Societe Nationale des Chemins de Fer Tunisiens – SNCFT. They inherited 1243 miles of line, of which most was meter gauge. The rest of the system, which is in the northern part of the country, is standard gauge and connecting lines that will allow inter-country exchange have been planned. The phosphate mines

You can practically feel the heat. A train makes a successful stop at the station at Rabat Ville. Most trains in Morocco are now electrically powered, as is this one.

have taken advantage of this situation and both supply of materials and the transport of them via railroads has benefited the country as a whole. Commuter lines too have been increased in the capital city of Tunis.

Morocco lost its independence in 1912, becoming a French Protectorate, which also influenced the choice of railways. It was about now that the French Army started building a 600 mm gauge line that was to connect all the principal cities of the region, which was opened in 1915. The route started at Oujda and ended in Marrakech, taking in Fes, Rabat and Casablanca, some 580 miles long. Initially a car was modified to travel on the lines at a maximum speed of 15 mph, which must have been tedious to say the least. The military lines were upgraded to standard gauge in 1923 along with newly laid lines. Major cities and industrial areas began to be connected with new lines in the following few years. In 1935 enough lines had been connected, internally and externally, that one could travel from Marrakech, in the west, through Morocco and Algeria, to the Tunisian capital of Tunis in the east. This was all standard gauge rail and covered some 1500 miles. The expansion of the railway saw Tunisia develop its industries and this continued through to the 1970s, when the country saw the beginnings of electrification. 1963 saw nationalization of the railways, which was run under the new Office National des Chemins de Fer du Maroc – ONCFM. Traffic increased over the following years and new modernisation plans had to be brought in to help with the replacement of outdated stock and congestion. By the 1980s, both electric and diesel engines were being used widely for passenger and freight transportation. Today at least 50 percent of the system is electrified; it is modern with 3 Kv overhead connections and the non electrified sections are covered by diesel engines.

Egypt was for many years an important part of the "overland route" to India and the East, which was established in 1842. In 1851 the then Khedive of Egypt, Abbas I, anxious to encourage traffic by this important overland route, entered into negotiations with Robert Stephenson for the construction of a railway from Alexandria to Cairo. This was the first railway on the African continent, and the first section, begun in 1852, was opened to Kafr-el-Zayat in 1854; a further section through to Cairo was opened two years later. This length of 120 miles involved the construction of two bridges over the Nile, one at Kafr-el-Zayat and one at Benha. From Cairo the railway was carried on to Suez, thus completing the overland route by rail. Until the opening of the Suez Canal in 1869 it was a source of considerable revenue to the Egyptian State Exchequer. More and more lines started to appear and old military lines were converted. With British influence much in evidence, plenty of British locomotives were used. Many of the express passenger services saw the Atlantic 4-4-2s pulling coaches with Moguls taking on other mixed traffic work. During the Second World War, in particular during the Africa campaign, the trains were essential to the military. Although much damage was done to the system during the war which left it in some disarray, British Steiner 8F 2-8-0 locomotives were ordered and before too long, lines were back up and running. Over the years lines have been electrified and new diesel engines have been put into operation. Today new lines are being built, old ones are being reopened and new diesel locomotives are being implemented by Egyptian State Railways.

The first lines were laid in 1852 in Egypt, and the locomotives came from England. There was extensive use of 0-6-0 locomotives, which had outside frames and inside fitted boilers.

Chinese Railways

China didn't have a great start to their railway system. There was great suspicion and opposition to those strange smoking machines. The first railway was opened for only a short time in the province of Kiangsu. The line was about five miles long, used a two foot six inch gauge and ran between Shanghai and Wusung. The locomotive used was the Pioneer, built by Ransome & Rapier of Ipswich, England. It seems that not long after it had opened, a man was fatally injured, after which riots ensued and the line was closed. A second attempt was made to run locomotives on the line using two nine-ton 0-4-0STs named Celestial Empire and Flowery Land. Unfortunately these had an unhappy ending too, when the Chinese authorities ordered they be dismantled.

The next attempt to start a railway line was in the northern province of Hopeh, when a mining company built a line between Kaiping coalfield, near Tangshan, and the canal that connected with the Pehtang River. Although initially mule power was used, a locomotive was built by the resident engineer, C W Kinder, who had to construct it with parts assembled from redundant locos, and the like. Word leaked out about its construction and for several weeks the engine had to be concealed from the Chinese authorities, until Viceroy Li Hung Chang eventually gave the word for construction to quietly continue. The result of Kinder's efforts came to fruition on June 9, 1881, when the home-made 0-6-0 tank engine, christened the Rocket of China, entered service on the tramway. The highly successful introduction of Rocket saw two further 0-6-0 tank locomotives being ordered from Robert Stephenson & Co. of Newcastle, England. Two locomotives were exported to China from Britain by Dubs & Co of Queen's Park in 1886, named Speedy Peace and Flying Victory. Dubs & Co were founded in 1863 and built locomotives for railways in many parts of the world. The company gained a good reputation for the reliability of their engines, but the first locomotives

Rocket of China is generally considered to be the first locomotive built in China. The picture here depicts Claude Kinder, British engineer, alongside a modified Rocket.

The first two locomotives exported to China from Britain were built by Dubs & Co at Queen's Park in 1886 and named Speedy Peace, shown here, and Flying Victory.

The China Express newspaper of January 13 1888. Note at the bottom, a large advertisement by Black, Hawthorn & Co of Gateshead-on-Tyne for their locomotives.

VIA MARSEILLES.]

The London and China 新聞紙 Express.

VOL. XXX.—No. 1,275.] LONDON, FRIDAY, JAN. 13, 1888.

INTERNATIONAL INVENTIONS EXHIBITION.
ONLY GOLD MEDAL.
MINING MACHINERY
T. B. JORDAN, SON AND COMMANS,
52, GRACECHURCH STREET,
London, E.C.

JOHN NORMAN & CO.
KEPPOCHHILL ENGINE WORKS,
GLASGOW,
Engineers, Millwrights, and Boilermakers,
HIGH & LOW PRESSURE STEAM ENGINES.
Plant for Distilling, Refining, and Cooling Paraffin and other Oils.
HYDRAULIC AND FILTER PRESSES.
Flour, Corn, and Rice Mill Machinery, Roller Plant,
Water Wheels and Gearing for transmitting Power,
LAND AND MARINE ENGINES.

SUBMARINE VESSELS. STEAM AND ELECTRIC LAUNCHES YACHTS, &c.
J. F. WADDINGTON & CO.,
SEACOMBE, NEAR LIVERPOOL.
Shipbuilders Marine, and Electrical Engineers.
High-Speed Engines.

JAMES RUSSELL & SONS LIMITED
CROWN TUBE WORKS. WEDNESBURY, ENGLAND.
INVENTORS, PATENTEES, AND FIRST MANUFACTURERS OF GAS TUBING.
MOST EXTENSIVE FIRM IN THE TRADE.
IRON OR STEEL TUBES UP TO 4 FEET DIAMETER.
IRON OR BRASS VALVES, COCKS, AND OTHER REQUISITES.

BLACK, HAWTHORN & CO., GATESHEAD-ON-TYNE.
TANK LOCOMOTIVES.
LOCOMOTIVE ENGINES AND TENDERS.
STEAM TRAMWAY AND LIGHT RAILWAY LOCOMOTIVES. MARINE SCREW AND PADDLE ENGINES.
GAS ENGINES AND TORPEDO BOATS.

Probably only used on fine days and high days, this early Chinese steam engine is ready for refurbishment. Many early engines were imported from the USA.

Only a little British design lasted with China's railways, mainly American locomotives were to see import to the country, although British moguls did play their part.

Dubs sent to China in 1886 didn't have very long lives. Although these 0-4-0ST engines were not the first locomotives to be seen in China, they caused some anxiety with the locals, who saw them as steam-breathing monsters. The engines ran on tracks near a cemetery and the locals claimed that the burial grounds of their ancestors were being desecrated, and

As recently as the 1930s, China had less than10,000 miles of track but the country was influenced by American imports, due to similarities in their terrain and landmass.

duly threw people in front of the locomotives. After some twenty people had been killed, the line was closed and the engines scrapped.

Although a rather stuttering start for these initial railways, some success followed and by the late 1890s, engines were being imported from the Baldwin works in America. These were much bigger locomotives than those previously seen, with 84 inch driving wheels and cylinder sizes of 19 x 24 inches. By the early part of the 1900s, China was building its own engines, based on earlier American types. It wasn't long before they were also building rolling stock and lines too, but much of China's railways were hugely disrupted and destroyed during this period from wars and unrest and fighting over territory in which these lines operated.

Even by the 1930s, China only had some 10,000 miles of railway track, but probably the most important part of the system was the Manchurian Railway – the Chinese Eastern Railway (CER) as it was known – which connected China and the Russian Far East. The southern part of this was known as the Southern Manchurian Railway and became the focus for several wars – the Russo-Japanese War and Second Sino-Japanese War. The main administration of the CER was from Harbin and construction of the line was started in 1897 and completed, from end to end, in 1916. Parts of this line were fought over vigorously and changed hands on several occasions. The locomotives used on these lines came mainly from America, an influence dictated by Japan, who owned the Railway. The JF Mikado was one of the most significant classes in Chinese railway history, being introduced in 1918 by the Japanese, as they consolidated their hold over Manchuria. The JF became the standard freight locomotive in the north-east and the railways of Manchuria played a pivotal role in the

Huge China Railway QJ class 2-10-2 locomotive, number 2655, is preserved at the Speyer Museum in Germany where it is pictured in May 2002. The class was introduced in 1956.

The builder's plate for China Railway's QJ class steam locomotive, number 2655, showing that it was built in 1978 – over 20 years after the class was introduced.

rapid industrialisation of Japan in the run up to the Second World War. The Japanese relied on the railways to keep its forces supplied as they progressively overran the rest of China, and many new JF locomotives were built during this period. Following the Liberation in 1949, the construction of the first locomotive without foreign involvement was viewed as a significant step in the development of the "New China." That first locomotive was a JF and over 400 more were built after the class was adopted as the standard freight design by the People's Republic. Production ceased at the end of the 1950s but a few JF models remain in use even in 2004.

Steam trains have disappeared from most countries today – except for those in captivity – but China still had a large contingency of them running on mainlines up to 1996. Due to China's centralization plan, there were five types, and of the main-liners, most are QJ class 2-10-2s, followed by JS class 2-8-2s, JF class 2-8-2s, SY class industrial type and then there are the standard gauge 0-8-0s of the 762mm gauge lines. Most of these are American engines and date back to the First World War.

In 2005, China's extraordinary industrial growth saw their railway system being updated and expanded. Many of the older steam trains are disappearing and new technology is finally kicking in, with new trains and new train systems. The railway network plan by 2020 outlines, among other things, that the railway operating length will increase from 45,360 miles in 2003, to 62,000 miles by 2020. Passenger and freight traffic will be separated on busy trunk lines and a rapid passenger-dedicated railway network and heavy-duty freight transport corridors will cover China's major cities. That's looking to the future, but some will say that losing the steam-operated trains will be a dreadful shame. Progress can sometimes be hurtful, although necessary.

Although steam locomotives had started to be phased out in the 1950s and most had been illuminated by the 1970s, China was still building new ones.

A giant QJ class engine steams out of Sangkong, leaving a trail of smoke and steam. These locomotives are still running in China and give much pleasure to enthusiasts.

In 2005 as people become more pollution conscious, these lovely steam engines are being scrapped or put into museums, even in China where there are still a good number running.

In 2000 the Chinese government ordered a Transrapid track to be built connecting Shanghai to its Pudong International Airport. It was inaugurated in 2002 but low passenger numbers has hampered the line.

Japanese Railways

The ruling Tokugawa Shogunate, which had kept Japan in international isolation for 260 years, was replaced by the Meiji government in 1868. This marked the beginning of Japan's modernisation with the new government, ending feudalism and introducing Western ideas.

Construction of railways, particularly between Tokyo and Yokohama, and Osaka and Kobe, was suggested several times by foreigners and some Japanese prior to the Meiji government.

In 1869, Harry Parkes, the British Minister to Japan, advocated that railways would help modernise Japan, insisting that the government build them as soon as possible. The Meiji government agreed to build railways for political reasons, to put an end to feudalism and centralize power in Japan. On December 7, 1869, Harry Parkes met the heads of the Meiji government to discuss basic measures for introducing railways and telegrams in Japan. Two of the ministers present – Shigenobu Okuma (Vice Minister of Finance) and Hirobumi Ito (Assistant Vice Minister of Finance) – later took charge of building railways. It was decided to build the country's first railway over the 18-miles distance between Tokyo, Japan's capital, and Yokohama, one of the few ports open for international trade at that time. The preliminary survey work began on April 25, 1870. The terminal in Tokyo was to be built at Shimbashi and the terminal in Yokohama at Noge Kaigan. These two places were chosen because they were close to the city sections and the foreign settlements. The trains were to run on the three-foot, six inch gauge tracks used in many British colonies at that time. The first shipment of 10 tank locomotives and 58 two-axle passenger carriages from Britain arrived in Yokohama in September 1871. On June 12, 1872, two daily train services started between Shinagawa and Yokohama, marking the start of regular passenger trains in Japan. The Meiji Emperor attended the opening ceremony on October 14, 1872 at Shimbashi and Yokohama stations making a round-trip on the train between the two terminals. There were four stations on the line: Shinagawa, Kawasaki, Tsurumi, and Kanagawa. It took 35 minutes from one terminal to the other. Freight services started on September 15, 1873. On August 25, 1870, surveying work began between Osaka and Kobe and

Japanese triptych print shows a view of Ueno-Nakasendo railway from Ueno station, Tokyo, with trains at the station and travelling along tracks through the city and landscape.

regular service started on May 11, 1874. The first wrought-iron bridge and tunnel in Japan – running under a raised-bed river – were built in this section. The line was later extended to Kyoto in 1876 and to Otsu in 1880. This section included the Osakayama Tunnel – 2119 feet long – Japan's first mountain tunnel and the first tunnel to be designed and built by Japanese engineers.

In 1881, Nippon Railway was authorized to run between Tokyo and Tohoku, and the first private service began in 1883 between Ueno, on the north side of Tokyo, and Kumagaya. By 1891, the company had completed its line between Ueno and Aomori through northeastern Honshu. In the following years more and more lines sprang up and when completed, the linking of the two largest cities of Tokyo and Kyoto/Osaka, the Tokaido railway was the first major step in the development of railways in Japan. A large number of British engineers were hired by the Japanese government in the early stage of Japanese railways and during those years, foreign engineers taught basic techniques and valuable know-how to their Japanese counterparts. In May 1877, the Engineer Training College was opened at Osaka Station and by 1880, there were enough capable Japanese engineers to replace foreigners in most key posts except in designing steam locomotives and bridges, where foreigners continued the design work until the 1890s. These included Richard Francis Trevithick and his brother Francis Henry Trevithick, grandsons of Richard Trevithick, the inventor of the steam engine.

Japanese triptych print - one section only - showing a steam train passing through Shiodama (Shimbashi), Tokyo station with Japanese and foreign people in the foreground.

The robust Japanese economy created by the success of Masayoshi Matsukata's financial reforms, and the success of Nippon Railways, the first private railway, led to the establishment of a number of other private railways after 1885 until the 1890 economic recession. Railway mania had arrived and by July 1889, Japan's railway networks totalled 547 miles for government railways and 522 miles for private railways. In May 1890, Tokyo Electric Light Company – the first electric company in Japan and incorporated in 1884 – laid a 500 meter track at the Third Internal Industrial Exposition held in Ueno Park, Tokyo, and operated two Spragne electric tramcars, imported from Brill & Co. of the USA. This was the first time electric trams operated in Japan. Blueprints of electric railways boomed in various cities, but many were just speculative projects lacking sound technical resources and backup. The

A Japanese triptych print, showing foreigners watching a train that is carrying passengers and going by Western battleships. Japanese sailboats sail in the Yokohama harbour.

first commercial operation was started by Kyoto Electric Railways on February 1, 1895, running on a 4.3 mile route connecting Kyoto station and Fushimi, along the Yodo River. The line was later extended to the inner city and many railways quickly followed suit.

The locomotives, passenger carriages and wagons used in Japan's first railway between Tokyo and Yokohama, which went into service in 1872, were all made in the UK. The design of ten imported tank locomotives was entrusted to British locomotive builders, who were provided only with simple specifications and performance requirements. The 1B 2-4-0 wheel arrangement was used for all the locomotives. Tender locomotives and more powerful locomotives, capable of running on gradients, were imported along with tank locomotives for use in the railway built between Kobe, Osaka and Kyoto after 1874. In 1876, two C 0-6-0 tender locomotives with a driving wheel diameter of three feet seven inches for freight transport were converted into 2B 4-4-0 tender locomotives, with a driving wheel diameter of four feet six and four-fifths inches for passenger transport.

The first railway in Hokkaido was constructed for shipment of coal between Temiya (Otaru) and Horonai coal mine. The line went into service between Temiya and Sapporo, in 1880, and was extended to the mine in 1882. Since this railway was designed and built like an American frontier railway under the direction of JU Crawford, an American engineer, 1C 2-6-0 tender locomotives, manufactured by Porter Inc. (H.K. Vertec) of Pittsburgh, USA, were used. These locomotives were famous, because they were named after Yoshitsune and Benkei – popular heroes in the Japanese medieval period. The Iyo railway, which went into service in 1888 between the outer port and inner city of Matsuyama, Shikoku, was a narrow-gauge railway using two feet six inch gauge tracks for the first time in Japan. 7.8-ton, B 0-4-0 tank locomotives, manufactured by Lokomotivfabrik Krauss of Munich, Germany, were used. In the early twentieth century, tender locomotives with a 2B 4-4-0 wheel arrangement were used mainly for long-distance passenger trains, 1B1 2-4-2 or 1C1 2-6-2 tank locomotives were used for short-distance, general-purpose trains, and 1C 2-6-0 or 1D 2-8-0 tender locomotives and C1 0-6-2 tank locomotives were used for freight trains and trains running on steep gradients. Although the use of compound locomotives and Mallet articulated locomotives still remained at an experimental stage, Sanyo Railway introduced a large number of Vauclain compound locomotives – 24 in total – of which 12 were manufactured at the railways Hyogo works. The first locomotive manufactured in Japan was a Worsdell compound tank locomotive with a 1B1 wheel arrangement. It was test manufactured at the government Kobe works in 1893 and designed and built under the supervision of R F Trevithick, a locomotive superintendent at the works. In 1895, a 1C 2-6-0 tender locomotive, similar to the Yoshitsune model, was manufactured at the Temiya works of the Hokkaido Tanko Railway. The locomotive was named Taisho-go (Great Victory) to commemorate Japan's victory in the Sino-Japanese War. Although it was the only locomotive manufactured at that

This Illustration is one part of a series depicting the Siberian War. Part 6 shows the brilliant exploits of the Noshido Infantry Company destroying the railroad, by going around the back of the enemy.

works, subsequently, copies of imported locomotives were manufactured at some domestic works. Full-scale domestic production of locomotives started after 17 major private railways were nationalised from 1906 to 1907. German Schmidt system superheated locomotives, which were developed originally in Japan, were promoted as the standard model.

歩兵第十四聯隊第十二中隊之殊勲敵の背後に迂廻し鐵道を破壊し装甲列車を鹵獲す
救露討獨遠征軍畫報（其六）
THE ILLUSTRATION OF THE SIBERIAN WAR.

The Railway Nationalization Bill was introduced to the House of Representatives in March 1906. It passed unchanged, but was amended in the House of Peers and sent back to the House of Representatives. The amended bill finally passed the House of Representatives at the end of a Diet session that was in such an abnormal state that deliberation was omitted and all opposing members walked out. Although this bill stipulated nationalization of 17 private railways within 10 years, the government had plans to buy them as soon as possible, and all 17 were nationalised within 2 years – 1906 and 1907.

The reason why Japanese railways use narrow gauge (1067 mm) is not clear. But, considering that the railways constructed in New Zealand in the same period by British engineers are also narrow gauge, there may have been a policy of some sort. The wish to change from narrow to the international standard gauge (1435 mm) had been expressed since 1887 by the military authorities who wanted more efficient military transportation. A proposal for standard gauge railway construction passed the Diet, and a Gauge Investigation Committee was established in the Ministry of Communications to investigate the matter further. However, in 1898, the military changed its policy from standard gauge to nationalization, and the issue was left untouched for a while. Railway nationalization meant unified management and operation of railways throughout Japan, which led naturally to unification under the narrow gauge system. This didn't end the dispute but after much discussion and debate, in 1919, the new Seiyukai Cabinet under Premier Hara formally rejected the standard-gauge plan. The 1067-mm narrow gauge remained the standard in Japan until JNR opened the Tokaido Shinkansen Line at the international standard gauge in 1964.

In a period from August 1910 when the Light Railway Act was enforced to March 1911 when fiscal 1910 ended, 23 new companies were licensed to operate light railways. In addition, 17 railway companies opened under the Private Railway Act, and nine other private railway companies under planning or construction changed their legal status to light railway by the end of the fiscal year. Many of the new light railways used the two feet six inches gauge in addition to the three feet six inches gauge of the government railways.

In Japan, the 1920s saw the beginning of automobile transportation. In those days, Japanese roads were in a poor condition, but bus networks still expanded rapidly throughout the country. Early Japanese buses had poor performance with a carrying capacity of less than 20 person; nevertheless, short local private railway lines were defeated in competition with bus lines and many went out of business.

When World War I broke out, Japan could not easily import locomotives, and Amenomiya Works (which developed from Dainihon Tramway, Tokyo) and Nippon Sharyo (Nagoya) became the main domestic suppliers.

Chikugo Tramway in northern Kyushu first used an internal combustion engine locomotive for operation of commercial trains in 1905 with a locomotive powered by a single-cylinder hot-bulb engine, of about 10 hp, designed for a fishing boat. The hot-bulb engine was manufactured by Fukuoka Iron Works in Osaka, and large numbers of engines of this kind were supplied to railways in northern Kyushu.

Yoshima Railway in Fukushima Prefecture commercially operated gasoline-engined rail-cars for the first time in 1921. The government railways used its first gasoline-engined rail-cars in 1929, but it was a failure because of low output and poor performance. However, highly reliable gasoline engines of 100-150 hp were manufactured domestically in 1933 and afterwards, and rail-cars powered by them were mass-produced for local lines and short trunk lines throughout the government railway network. After nationalization, government railways purchased a few large tender 2C1 type locomotives from the UK, the USA, and Germany. They developed domestic standard locomotives based on these imports. After establishing standards and manufacturing methods a 1C type locomotive for express passenger trains – Class 8620 – and a 1D type locomotive for freight trains – Class 9600 – were completed. After World War I, two new models were developed to meet rapidly-growing traffic volumes on trunk lines, the 18900 – later renamed C51 - for passenger trains and the 9900 – D50 – for freight traffic. In 1930 C51 started hauling Tsubame limited express train on the Tokaido Line, connecting Tokyo and Osaka in 8 hours and 20 minutes. In 1934, completion of the Tanna Tunnel reduced the travel time to 8 hours. On the other hand, the 9900, built from 1923, brought a breakthrough in freight transport by increasing hauling capacity to 950 tons, compared to 600 tons offered by the 9600.

The most notable innovations improving transportation efficiency were air brakes and automatic

Umekoji Steam locomotive Museum, outside Kyoto station, was opened in 1972. The roundhouse houses a number of steam locomotives, including C581, the Imperial Train. The gold disc is the Imperial chrysanthemum.

The D51 series was a large-scale freight locomotive, of which 1,115 examples were manufactured, between 1936 and 1945. It acquired the nickname Namekuji, meaning slug, due to the dome running along the top of the boiler.

This is the plate from locomotive number C581, the Imperial Japanese train, parked at the Umekoji museum in Kyoto.

couplers. In 1919, the government railways decided to use air brakes in place of traditional vacuum brakes and started to develop a local model based on technology from Westinghouse. All freight cars were equipped with pneumatic brakes by 1930, followed by passenger cars in 1931. Similarly, the use of American-type automatic couplers was decided in 1919. Government railways started operating electric multiple-unit trains when it acquired a private railway in Tokyo – Kobu Tetsudo, now Chuo Line. It immediately noticed their advantages in urban transport and decided to expand operations. In 1915, electric multiple-unit trains were introduced between Tokyo and Yokohama. This development of electric multiple units formed the basis of high-speed EMU trains in later years. Geographical expansion of sections served by EMU trains and improvement of service through higher frequency, allowed government railways to become the major provider of public transportation in the Tokyo area.

Despite the political instability, Japan's economy recovered from the Depression in the mid-1930s and demand for transportation began to grow. There was significant technical progress and improvement in railway services, although the narrow-gauge track caused limitations.

The Sino-Japanese war started in 1937 as an "incident," not a declared war, but it spread to many parts

Locomotive C571 seen at high speed. Constructed in 1937 by the Kawasaki Locomotive Company, it has a chequered history. Although it was involved in a derailment in 1961 it has been restored back to original condition.

The B20 locomotive design sprang from the Second World War and B2010 was made in 1946 by the Teteyama Heavy industries Company.

of China. As Japan's relations with other countries worsened, she tried to seek a better position by joining the Nazi Germany and Fascist Italy Axis. Such behavior destroyed relations with the USA and the UK and in 1941, Japan declared war against them, marking the beginning of World War II in the Pacific arena. The Japanese economy came under wartime controls; the introduction of the National Mobilization Law in 1938 reorganized all industry for wartime production. Transportation demand for the war efforts increased and government and private railways had to increase their capacities while suffering from shortage of materials. An urgent need at that time was to strengthen the transport link to the Asian continent and so a decision was made in 1939 to build a new standard-gauge railway called the New Trunk Line – Shinkansen – from Tokyo to Shimonoseki at the western tip of Honshu island. Construction had just started when the entire project was suspended by the war. It was more than 25 years later, in 1964, that JNR actually started Shinkansen services, using some land purchased much earlier for the proposed Bullet Train right-of-way.

The railways that survived the war were badly damaged and almost totally unmaintained, due to material and manpower shortages. All the facilities were in poor condition due to wartime abuse. Rail accidents such as collisions and derailments were common between 1943 and 1945.

The Japanese Government Railways were reorganized as a public corporation called Japanese National Railways (JNR) on 1 June 1949. This was a major change in the history of Japan's railways, and is as important as the nationalization in 1906/7 and the privatisation in 1987.

Postwar Japan was run by the Allied Occupation Forces from General Headquarters (GHQ). A letter from General MacArthur dated July 22, 1948, instructed the government to reorganize the Japanese Government Railways and other state monopolies into public corporations, leading to the births of JNR. Railway operation in postwar Japan faced a serious dilemma between the fast-growing need for transportation, and a capacity that had fallen to less than 30 percent of the pre-war level. Transportation demand rose rapidly as people flocked to trains; soldiers returning from Manchuria, Korea, etc., schoolchildren evacuees returning from the countryside, GIs, foreigners, and hungry people going to farming villages in search of food. A heavy burden was placed upon railways because motor and coastal transportation was still unrestored. A series of bad accidents resulted from worn-out facilities and lack of funds to maintain them. However, despite the burden, the railway authorities did all they could to restore services and modernize. They resumed limited express train operations and introduced electric and diesel trains. The first five-year plan in 1957 initiated serious investment in railway facilities.

The start of the Korean War in 1950 turned Japan into a UN military base. Demand for transport of military supplies increased sharply, leading to rapid economic growth. As the economy gained momentum, the capacity of the Tokaido Line soon reached its limit. The Tokaido Line was (and still is) the most important traffic market in Japan ever since its completion in 1889. In 1950, it represented only 3 per cent of total route mileage, but accounted for about 24 percent of transport volume. The completion of the long-awaited electrification in 1956 between Tokyo and Osaka to improve capacity did not solve the problems and, so in 1958, the Japanese government and JNR agreed to construct the Tokaido Shinkansen on the international standard gauge (1435 mm). The project was started with financing from the World Bank and was completed six years later in 1964. The project had been first envisaged in 1938 before the war when it was called the Bullet Train Project. In the late-1950s, some 10 years after World War II, Japan's economy had recovered to the pre-war level and started remarkable growth. The share of railways in the domestic transport market was still so large that the economic growth called for increased passenger and freight capacities. Heavy investment was made in the 1960s to hasten modernisation of trunk lines.

Up to the war's end, the Japanese government railways (JNR after 1949) had relied on steam power, whereas private urban railways had already been

A typical suburban station, Tanakura is on the Nara line, which was not electrified until 1984. Seen here is an EMU pulling into the station.

EF-66 is an electric train, built in 1966. Japan is split in half electrically, with 1500v DC; 2000v AC and multi-voltage locos to cover both.

Whilst Japanese workers carry out repairs, Tobu Railway 11655 creeps past on its way out of Sengenda, avoiding any chance of an accident.

The Midosuoi line, Nakamozu service approaches Momoyamadai station at Suita City, Osaka, which is run by the Kita Osaka Kyoko Railway.

The Yamanote Line originated in 1885. Today it is one of the busiest in and out of Tokyo, with services provided by 205 series trains, introduced in 1985, and the newly introduced E231 series.

Japan's first permanent capital was established at Heijo, known today as Nara, which is served by Kintetsu Railways. This is Mo 30200 with Nara – Namba Express.

Nagoya has a population of 2.1 million and needs a good train system to shuttle people to their work. This is train 1235, on the suburban Kinetsu-Kinki Nippon Railway line.

A freight train EF 200 is seen at Yamazaki – between Osaka and Kyoto. The 200 series are a special 6000kw loco built for JR Freight in the early 1990s, with B-B-B wheel arrangement.

The EF66 series was introduced in 1966, for mixed traffic use and with B-B-B wheel arrangement. An EF66-100 Series was introduced in 1988, for the then new JR Freight which still had wheel arrangement B-B-B.

The ED79 Series locomotives were introduced in 1985. This series was rebuilt from the ED75 series and is used in the Seikan tunnel. B-B wheel arrangement is used but the mouse face is optional!

A very different design of locomotive from the local commuter trains, this long distance EMU is departing from Osaka, transporting it's passengers to the far flung corners of Japan.

The Romance Car is the Odakyu line's name for its limited express services. Romance seats are two-person seats, without separating armrests, when one-person seats were the norm. The Odaky-Odawara Line is known for its Romance Car train.

This is a local JR commuter train of the Geibi Line, taking people to and from the city and into the countryside. This one is travelling out, just north of Hiroshima City.

Osaka has a monorail line in its northern Prefecture. It runs on an elevated line between Osaka International Airport and Kadoma City. Current total length is 14.8 miles, but an extension is due to open by spring 2007.

A commuter EMU making its way to Minami on the Musashino Line, run by JR East.Through trains run over the Keiyo Line at Nishi-Funabashi to continue to Tokyo station, with some going onto Minami-funabashi.

electrified. After the war, electrification was promoted chiefly on the major trunk lines. The Tokaido Line between Tokyo and Osaka was completely electrified in 1956, the Sanyo Line in 1964, the Tohoku Line in 1968, and the Kagoshima Line in 1970. The total length of JNR's electrified sections increased from 1677 miles in 1960 to 3741 miles in 1970, then to 5228 miles in 1980. In addition to the 1500-volt DC system the AC system, which became common in post-war Europe, started being adopted in Japan in the late 1950s. Japan has two power frequency zones – the Tohoku Line in the east mostly uses 50 Hz, 20 kV, while the Kagoshima Line in the west operates on 60 Hz, 20 kV. In addition to locomotive-hauled trains, EMUs also began operating on the electrified lines with JNR's first long-distance EMU starting operation on the Tokaido Line between Tokyo and Numazu in 1950. In 1958, JNR started operating express trains with a maximum speed of 68 mph between Tokyo and Osaka. While major trunk lines were electrified, DMUs with under-floor diesel engines were put into operation on sub-trunk lines and secondary lines. A nationwide service of express trains with DMUs or EMUs was formed after JNR's first DMU made its debut in 1960. For freight traffic on non-electrified lines, steam locomotives kept playing a substantial role through the 1960s – steam locomotives did not go out of daily use until 1976.

Construction of the Tokaido Shinkansen was started in 1959 and the line was opened on October 1, 1964 in time for the Tokyo Olympic Games. For the first time in the world, the Tokaido Shinkansen routinely topped 124 mph and demonstrated the high safety level of railways. The Tokaido Shinkansen became the forerunner of high-speed railways worldwide, such as the French TGV.

Private vehicle ownership was becoming common in the 1970s as typified by the Japanized phrase "mai kaa" (my car). Private cars formed 28 percent of the domestic passenger market, striking another blow at rural railways. Private railway lines were quickly replaced by private bus services but JNR lines could not be closed due to local resistance, although their unprofitability was obvious. By 1980, the railway's share of domestic freight was just 8 percent and had even fallen to only 40 per cent of the passenger market. By 1980, private cars represented 39 percent of the passenger market. Although the Japanese transport market was experiencing massive structural changes, JNR still continued making profits through the 1950s and early 1960s, but this was because Japan was 10 years behind Europe in entering the age of car ownership. JNR stunned the world by opening the Tokaido Shinkansen in 1964, at a time when railways were generally viewed as a declining industry. This year JNR went into the red for the first time and things went from bad to worse as the government decided to continue investment. By 1987, the deficit totalled 25 trillion yen, similar to the combined national debts of several developing countries. A proposal

This is the series 281 Haruks train, which links Kansai International Airprt with Kyoto. the 281series uses a 1-inverter/1-motor VVVF control system and the standard configuration is 1M2T. Designed for airport users it has specific storage areas.

recommended privatizing and dividing JNR into six regional passenger railway companies – the JRs – and a freight company – JR Freight – and a number of other smaller companies in the information, telecommunications and R&D fields. But it was realised that these would have problems maintaining profitability due to their small customer base, whereas JR East, JR Central, and JR West would be profitable due to the large number of commuters and customers using the Shinkansen. The new JRs became reality on April 1, 1987 and their operating balances soon improved dramatically compared to the JNR days. The booming economy at the time of JNR privatization was lucky for the JRs, but the subsequent serious depression has made it impossible to sell the land held by JNRSC, delaying the debt redemption. This remains a serious issue and the current debt of 28 trillion yen is equivalent to approximately 200,000 yen for every man, woman, and child in Japan, or about 5 percent of the total national debt.

The Tokaido Shinkansen, the world's first inter-city, high-speed railway system, began operations on its route between Tokyo and Osaka more than 30 years ago, in 1964.

Narita Airport, is located in the city of Narita in Chiba Prefecture and about 35 miles outside of Tokyo. The fastest option to get to Tokyo Station is the JR Narita Express (NEX).

Indian Railways

Although a steam locomotive by the name of Thomason had been used for hauling construction material in Roorkee, for the Solani viaduct in 1851, the first commercial passenger service in India set off at 3.35pm on April 16, 1853. The train, with 14 carriages and 400 guests, left Bombay's Bori Bunder for Thane, with a 21-gun salute. It was hauled by three locomotives – the Sindh, Sultan, and Sahib – and the journey took an hour and fifteen minutes. These locomotives were followed up by the Falkland, which was used for shunting work on the first line being built out of Bombay, and which later became the Great Indian Peninsular Railway (GIPR) locomotive number 9. Vulcan was another locomotive present in 1852, which was also being used for shunting duties. Whilst the GIPR started in Bombay, the East India Railway (EIR) was started in Calcutta, and in March of 1870 the lines from the two cities were joined via the Thull Gat. During 1871, south-east of Kalyan, the GIPR line was extended over the Bhore Ghat to reach Raichur, connecting with the Madras Railway, whose branch line out of Arakkonam now also reached Raichur. By now EIR trackage had reached a totals of 1350 miles with GIPR extending to 875 miles, Madras Railway 680 miles, Sind and Punjab 400 miles, BBCI 300 miles, East Bengal 115 miles, and the Great Southern 170 miles. Between 1874 and 1880, there was great activity in the laying of railway lines – which was due to a famine in certain parts of India – helping to get relief to those areas affected. In 1874, Lord Salisbury, Secretary of State for India, stipulated the use of broad gauge to settle the gauge debate, and so work began on relaying many one-meter-gauge lines to broad gauge. At the same time the F class 0-6-0 metre gauge locomotives were introduced – soon to be among the most widely-

1855, was when the Fairy Queen rolled out for the erstwhile East Indian Railway. It rolled again on February 1 1997 from Delhi to Alwar and is the oldest working engine in the world.

An Indian one-meter-gauge class D 0-4-0 locomotive, which became a standard design. There were ten engines built at the Sharp, Stewart Great Bridgewater street foundry in Manchester, England in 1873.

The Darjeeling Himalayan Railway is a narrow-gauge railway from Siliguri to Darjeeling. It was built between 1879 and 1881 and is about 54 mi long . Shown is a Darjeeling goods train below Sonada c1910.

used in India for just about all kinds of duties; Dubs & Co. of Glasgow built the first few. In 1879, despite the broad-gauge policy instituted under Lord Salisbury, the Rajputana-Malwa Railway was authorized to build its lines to meter-gauge. By 1880, India had about 9,000 miles of lineage, of which 2175 was state owned. A further 5,000 miles was commissioned and private construction was resumed. It was also this same year that the durable L class 4-6-0 tender locomotives made their appearance. On January 1, 1882, and still under construction, the Victoria Terminus was opened to the general public and later this year the first A class tank engine was built for the DHR – Darjeeling Himalayan Railway. In 1887 the Dufferin Bridge was constructed over the Ganga at Varanasi, allowing EIR trains to go from Mughalsarai to Varanasi. Later this year the Victoria Terminus was named after Queen Victoria on Jubilee Day, and in 1889 the first B class locomotives of the DHR were built. 1895 saw the first locomotive built in India, at the Ajmer works, an F class 0-6-0 MG locomotive for the Rajputana Malwa Railway (F-734). This is now preserved at the National Rail Museum. Two foot, six inches was the narrow-gauge standard for all the imperial colonies, and so strategic considerations from the War Department now forced all new narrow-gauge lines to be laid to two foot, six inches instead of the two foot gauge, from 1897 onwards. In 1899, the Jamalpur Workshops officially began producing steam locomotives – earlier they had only been assembling locomotives with parts from other locomotives; the first engine to be produced was CA 764, Lady Curzon. In 1901 the Sir Thomas Robertson Committee submitted recommendations on administration and working of the railways. An early version of the railway board was constituted, with three members serving on it initially. The railway mileage had by now reached about 24,750 miles in India, of which 14,000 miles were BG, and most of the rest MG – with only a few hundred miles of two foot and two foot, six inch gauge lines. The railways had also started making some modest profits – for the past 40 years they had been making large losses. In 1904 the Moghulpura workshops, near Lahore, build six 0-6-2T ST class locomotives by using parts from other locomotives and therefore making them the only works other than Ajmer to build locomotives in British India. The F class 0-6-0 MG locomotives were introduced in 1905, soon to

Without doubt looking more than a little like Thomas the tank engine, this Indian Railway run locomotive is used for specific lifting duties.

be among the most widely used in India, for all kinds of duties; Dubs & Co. of Glasgow built the first few. In 1907 the government purchased all major lines and re-lease them to private operators, with the exception of Rohilkhund & Kumaon Railway and the Bengal & North-Western Railway. 1908 saw India's first internal combustion locomotive, a petrol-driven MG loco, delivered to the Assam Oil Co. by McEwan Pratt & Co. of Wickford, Essex. In 1909 India's first electric locos – two of them – were delivered to the Mysore Gold Fields by Bagnalls of Stafford, England, with overhead electrical equipment by Siemens. Also among the earliest electric vehicles, were electrically operated rail trolleys – White's patented rail motor trolleys – which were brought into use. At this same time a petrol-driven 0-4-9 loco was supplied to Morvi Railway and Tramways by Nasmyth Wilson. A couple of Thornycroft gasoline-driven parcel

Three Indian workers transporting their load of wood to the local factory. Not a lot of need for the man with the red flag, traffic is slow here.

This one is packed to the gunnels. One of the many vintage locomotives running on the two-foot guage system in northern India's sugar plantations.

This is an XC class Pacific 4-6-2 run buy Indian Railways. Very much resembling Gresley's Pacifics, both locomotives were introduced during the 1920s. The XC was a heavy-duty passenger 4-6-2 BG.

delivery vehicles were also in use by the EIR. The First World War placed a heavy burden on the railways, with railway production being diverted to meet the needs of British forces outside India. At the end of the war, Indian railways were in a total state of dilapidation and disrepair. 1915 saw the first ever diesel locomotive in India, a two foot, six inch gauge unit from Avonside, Bristol, England, which was supplied to the India Office for use on a tea plantation. By 1920, total trackage was at 37,000 miles about 15 percent was in private hands. The East India Railway Committee – chaired by Sir William Acworth, hence also known as the Ackworth Committee – pointed out the need for unified management of the entire railway system. On the recommendations of this committee, the government took over the actual management of all railways, and also separated railway finances from the general governmental finances. In 1922 an electric locomotive with overhead power collection was delivered to the Naysmyth Patent Press Co. at Calcutta, by British Electric Vehicles. On February 3, 1925, the first electric railway operated on the Harbour branch of the GIPR from the Victoria Terminus to Kurla using 1500 volts DC, overhead traction. The section was designated as a suburban section. EMUs from Cammell Laird and Uerdingenwagonfabrik were used. In the same year electrification of VT-Bandra was also completed and EMU services began there as well, with an elevated platform at Sandhurst Road. The GIPR suburban line was later electrified up to Kalyan. On January 1 of this year, the East Indian Railway Company was taken over by the state. In 1927, eight-coach EMU rakes were introduced on the main line in Mumbai and four-coach rakes on the Harbour line, and in 1928 the first batch of electric EMUs for Bombay arrived – made by British Thompson Houston/ Cammell Laird. In 1930 *The Times*, London, nominated the Frontier Mail the most famous express train in the British empire and on June 1, the Deccan Queen began running. This was hauled by a WCP-1 (No. 20024, old number EA/1 4006) and with seven coaches, on the GIPR's newly electrified route to Poona (Pune). Two BG diesel shunters from William Beardmore were now in use on the North Western Railway, who also procured two, 420 hp, diesel-electric shunters from the same company. In 1935, NWR purchased two 1200 hp, diesel-electric locomotives from Armstrong-Whitworth, with the intention of using them for a new Bombay-Karachi route. They were deployed

1909 saw India's first electric locos, two of them, were delivered to the Mysore Gold Fields by Bagnalls of Stafford, England. These had overhead electrical equipment which was supplied by the German company Siemens.

Many older locomotives are still serving well on the Indian continent even though they have seen better days.

on the Karachi-Lahore mail route, but then were withdrawn soon afterwards. After enduring several problems, it was decided they were not designed for Indian conditions. 1937 saw the infamous Bihta accident, in which the excessive oscillations of an XB class locomotive caused the derailment of the Punjab-Howrah mail, killing 154 people. The Flying Queen – predecessor of Flying Ranee – was introduced between Bombay and Surat, hauled by an H class 4-6-0 and making her run in four hours on May 1 this same year. With World War II, railways again came under great strain. Locomotives, wagons, and track materials were all taken from India to the Middle East – 28 branch lines were completely cannibalized for this. Railway workshops were used to manufacture shells and other military equipment and the entire railway system was left in poor shape by the end of the war. During the 1940s a large number of American and Canadian locomotives were imported into India – AWD, CWD, along with AWC, AWE, and MAWD classes.

Steamin heavily, this XD (Dominion) loco, which was widely used for freight duties. Nearly 200 were built in all with a second batch being built in the 1940s.

These engines seem to look their best at night, which is when they are hardest at work. This tank engine has just been fired up.

The XE (Eagle) locomotive was used for heavy freight. These locomotives were huge, as can be seen.. The boiler was 7 feet in diameter and it had an axle load of 22.5 tons. This one is run by Indian Railways.

Returning from having delivered its load, this steam engine has seen better days. Often these locos will have been modified to suit the work they carry out.

In its heyday the Darjeeling narrow gauge line ran 50 steam locomotives on the line and the journey took 6 hours from Siliguri. Sadly only about a dozen of these locos remain in working order today.

By 1942 most of the remaining large railway companies were taken over by the state. After the war, 15 diesel locomotives from GE, supplied by USATC and deployed on WR, were among the first diesel locomotives to be successfully used in many locations in India. Most of these were classified as WDS-1. In 1945 the Tata Engineering and Locomotive Co. (TELCO) was officially formed as a company. 1947 saw the independence and partitioning of India. Now the two big systems, Bengal Assam Railway and North Western Railway were no longer in India – these included the workshops of Saidpur and Mogulpura, respectively. Some 1,872 route-miles of NWR became the East Punjab Railway in India, leaving 5,043 miles in what was then West Pakistan. Part of the Jodhpur Railway also went to West Pakistan. Much of the Bengal Assam Railway went to the then East Pakistan – now Bangladesh. Exchanging assets and staff dislocated all normal work, as did the large-scale movement of people between India and Pakistan. One hundred WG class 2-8-2 locomotives were ordered

WP locomotives were standard express-passenger engines across India in the last 30 years of the steam engine. Many were endowed with ornamentation and decoration.

Indian Railways would hold a beauty competition for their locomotives and each railway was invited to submit an ornately embellished WP. This WP is on its way to Delhi to take part.

from North British in 1948, which saw the start of this very successful class in India. On January 26, 1950, the Chittaranjan Locomotive Works was established in West Bengal, for the manufacture of 120 steam locos annually. The first of the extremely successful WG class – number 8401, Deshbandhu – from the works was commissioned on November 1 this year. In 1954 the EM/1, later WCM-1, class of 3000 volt DC locomotives were introduced and a year later Fiat started supplying a dozen MG railcars – YRD1, coupled in pairs. At the same time the YDM-1, ZDM-1, and NDM-1 diesel locos were brought into use. By 1956 the EM/2, later WCM-2, class of 3000 volts DC locomotives were introduced. In 1957 following a decision to adopt 25 ks volt AC traction, SNCF were chosen as technical consultants for the electrification projects. An organization called the Main Line Electrification Project – which later became the Railway Electrification Project and still later the Central Organization for Railway Electrification – was established. Burdwan-Mughalsarai, via the Grand Chord, was electrified. Tatanagar-Rourkela, on the Howrah-Bombay route, was chosen as the next route to be electrified at 25 kv AC. 1958 saw 100 of the WDM-1 class BG diesel locomotives imported from Alco in the US, and nearly all were stationed at Chakradharpur, for use around Tatanagar, Rourkela, Burnpur. WAM-1 locomotives from Kraus-Maffei, Alsthom, Krupp, Brugeoise et Nivelles, and SFAC were brought into service in 1959. This same year saw the first steam locomotive

Indian Railways operated 30 of these giant 2-8-4 tank locomotives, which were designed in India for heavy suburban transportation use. This one is taking on water at Rajahmundry.

A local stands watching as a goods locomotive, belching out its black smoke, crosses over the river. A wonderful sight, but unfortunately one that will without doubt soon disappear.

Locomotives in India were built to a range of standard designs, that was known as the BESA – British Engineering standard Association. This BESA 2-8-0 was more suited to freight work but was also used for passengers.

Diesel locomotives have been the main player in the Indian Railways motive power scenario for over 30 years. In particular is the WDM-2 class of diesel-electric locomotive, a 2,600 hp, 1676 mm gauge Co-Co model.

to be designed and built entirely by CLW, introduced – the first being the WT class Chittaranjan. Then in 1961 CLW started producing 1500 volts DC electric locomotives, of which the first one was Lokmanya WCM-5, commissioned on October 14. An initial order of WDM-2 locomotives, supplied by Alco, reached India in 1962, along with the first MG diesels from DLW and the first diesel-hydraulic shunters from TELCO. Later this year, the Jamalpur workshops started their production of "Jamalpur jacks." For 1963, CLW started producing 25 kv AC

Narrow gauge classification in India was peculiar. The suffix Z was initially used for standard locomotives. Seen here is locomotive ZP 2.

electric locomotives, and on November 16 the first one, Bidhan, became the first entirely India-built electric locomotive. In January of the following year, Diesel Locomotive Works started production of the WDM-2 locomotives – about 40 every year at first. The initial 12 were assembled from kits supplied by Alco, and thereafter production consisted mostly of indigenous components. The first one from DLW was Lal Bahadur Shastri. This same year, CLW started manufacturing traction motors – the MG-1580 model. In 1965 the Taj Express ran at 66 mph, hauled by a steam locomotive, and the Asansol-Bareilly passenger train became the first long-distance train on ER, hauled by an AC locomotive. A fast freight service – Super Express – was introduced on several routes, especially those linking the four major metropolitan centres, and other important cities such as Ahmedabad and Bangalore. During 1967 the first diesel locomotive, with Indian equipment, rolled out of DLW, and WDS-5 shunters from Alco were also introduced. CLW began work on production of diesel locomotives, starting with the WDS-4 class shunters and CR ran its first superfast goods train – Freight Chief – from Wadi Bunder to Itarsi. In November of 1968 DLW produced their first indigenous MG diesel loco – YDM-4 Hubli. On March 1 1969, the Howrah – New Delhi Rajdhani Express started running, covering the 900 miles distance in 17 hrs 20 min – this was previously a 24 hour run. The maximum speed was 75 mph, with technical halts being made at Kanpur, Mughalsarai, and Gomoh. For 1970, CLW produced its first WAM-

One of many express trains that travel between Mumbai and Pune and back again, is the Deccan Express depicted here

4 locomotives and a year later in 1971, CLW started production of the TAO-659 traction motors. Something of a setback happened in May of 1974 when a total strike by railway workers, including the All India Railwayme's Federation – led by its president at the time, George Fernandes, later to become Union Minister for Railways – paralysed IR completely. Tens of thousands were jailed and it was these events that led to the imposition of a state of emergency in India, by the then Prime Minister Indira Gandhi, in June 1975. On February 10, 1983, the Great Indian Rover, a tourist train for Buddhist sites with a specially built rake, was launched. June

This is a passenger train near Gaziabad, on the Delhi to Mughalsarai section of track. It is a WAM-4 25 kv AC mixed traffic CO-Co locomotive.

of 1987 saw the introduction of the rarely seen WDM-7 locomotives, whilst on the NG, NDM-5 locomotives were introduced. In 1988 WAG5HB locos from BHEL, WAG6A from ABB, and WAG6B, WAG6C from Hitachi were brought into service, mostly for the heavy freight routes of SER. The first Shatabdi Express was also introduced during this time. This ran between New Delhi and Jhansi – later to be extended to Bhopal – and became the fastest train in the country. During 1994 the Royal Orient train was introduced by WR and Gujarat, and on August 27, CLW's first WAP-4 locomotive, Ashok was commissioned. January 16, 1995, saw the first

Seen here making a scheduled stop is an Indian Railways class WAP-1, 25 kv AC, Co-Co, electric passenger locomotive.

regularly scheduled services run on trains hauled by locos using the 2 x 25kV 'dual' system of traction. They ran between Bina and Katni on CR. Eleven WAP-5 locos were also imported at this time, from ABB (AdTranz), the first locos with three-phase AC technology in India. In 1996, six WAG-9 locomotives and 16 more in kit-form were imported from ABB. The second batch of three-phase AC locomotives were imported for 1997. On October 18, the Fairy Queen was put back into regular revenue service. November 14 1998 saw CLW begin production of indigenous versions of the WAG-9, the first of which was named Navyug. On April 29, CLW manufactured its 2500th electric locomotive, a WAG-7 which went under the name of Swarna Abha and in October the first WDP-2, number 15501, was commissioned. The Buddha Parikrama locomotive, a tourist train for Buddhist sites, was also launched during this time. On December 2, 1999, Darjeeling Himalayan Railway became the second railway site in the world to be designated a World Heritage site.

Passengers wait in the doorways of the carriages that about to be pulled by this 1200 EMU locomotive, owned by Northern Railway.

The photograph shows a diesel engine type WDG4. Siemens AG has been contracted to supply propulsion technology for diesel-electric locomotives by the Diesel Locomotive Works in Varanasi.

On May 10 2000, the first WAP-7 locomotive, under the name of Navkiran, was produced by CLW. Later this year, successful trials were carried out with the high-speed, 63 mph, BOXN wagon rakes, on the Gomoh-Mughalsarai section.The following year, and after successful trials of the new Alstom LHB coaches at 100 mph, IR announced that they would be using them on the Delhi-Lucknow route, but with a maximum speed restriction of 88 mph. This same year, on April 9, the first locally built WDG-4 locomotive, GM EMD GT46MAC, was commissioned. In 2003, the Golden Rock's new oil-fired B class locomotives, for the Darjeeling Himalayan Railway, were built and ready for trials. On July 1 2004, the Chennai area MG EMU services were discontinued – the last MG EMU ran from Egmore to Tambaram, marking the end of 73 years of these stalwart trains. This was also the day of the last YAM-1 run. In July of this year, SCR started using new aerodynamically designed DEMU rakes from ICF. In July, the Golden Rock workshops manufactured the second oil-fired steam locomotive, Himanand, for the DHR and trial runs were carried out with a diesel loco running on bio-diesel blended fuel on the Trichy-Tanjor passenger line. On September 15, the first public trial took place of KR's Skybus project in Madgaon. This demonstration showed the vehicle moving at 25 mph, for a distance of about one mile. A day few will forget was December 26 2004, when the Indian Ocean tsunami washed away tracks on the Nagore-Nagapattinam section. Today, travelling on the Indian Railway is a pleasure. The trains are modern, they generally run on time and although one has to appreciate different cultural habits and situations they provide good value for money.

A brand new WAG 6C, Co-Co, 25 kv AC electric locomotive, resplendent in it's blue and white livery awaits delivery to it's owners in India.

High-Speed Trains

The definition of a high-speed train relates mainly to the combination of elements that it is required to have, for example the track it runs on, the aerodynamics of the engine and the behaviour of all its elements. To actually be a high-speed train in the true sense of the term, it must be able to travel anywhere between 100 to 188 mph – although many today are able to reach considerably higher speeds than these.

The West JR 500 Series Nozomi shinkansen - bullet train. One of the fastest trains in the world, hitting speeds up to 188 mph on its Tokyo-Kyushu route.

The locomotive was the first practical form of mass transportion for people and goods. Its heyday came at the end of the nineteenth and beginning of the twentieth century. It was the development of the automobile and the progress of the airplane that stole the popularity of the railways, although it has to be said that lack of investment played a big part too. Japan has been a great developer of the high-speed train as has France, followed by the UK. Today many more countries around the world are seeing the benefits of these fast, comfortable and convenient machines. Although slow to get on the bandwagon, the United States is also looking at high-speed trains as a mode of mass transportation for the future.
The country with among the highest car ownership and some of the busiest roads in the world realised, perhaps late, that alternative forms of transport would be needed to cope with the continued demand for fast, efficient long- and short-distance journeys. California decided in 1993 to establish an Intercity High-Speed Rail Commission to develop a framework for the implementation of a high-speed rail network in the state. The group focused on potential for inter-city travel, i.e. journeys of between 100 and 500 miles, at speeds of over 200 mph. Discussions continue but America's Northeast Corridor, which links Boston, New York and Washington, is one of the most densely populated and fastest-growing areas of the country. With approximately 45 percent of the market in traffic between these cities, Amtrak has a strong presence, but is looking to consolidate its position in the face of growing competition from road transport, along the improved Interstate 95 free-

Front end view of the American Acela. This train runs between America's capitol city of Washington DC, up the coast through New York to Boston.

The Acela locomotive has a tilting facility. This allows higher speeds and better stability when running through the many curves of the Northeast Corridor.

way, and airlines. The first high-speed trains ran in December 2000, a year behind schedule. Amtrak decided the competition should be met through a complete rebranding of its train services and the introduction of a new fleet of trains, incorporating some of the latest technology available. When conceived in 1995, the project was first known as the American Flyer, but Acela – derived from the words "excellence" and "acceleration" – took over as the project took further shape, as a new brand, to reflect the main benefits which its promoters aimed to offer. An order for new trains, worth $35 million was placed in July 1998 by Amtrak with a consortium comprising Alstom and Bombardier. The first service train left Washington Union Station on December 12, 2000, with fleet service following on rapidly.

Generally, and mostly in highly populated areas, the high-speed train is more economical and cleaner than automobiles or aeroplanes. They are mostly powered by diesel or electricity, although many are now run on nuclear fission. The development of these trains moves as rapidly as they do, and travelling on them does now have its advantages over the airplane and automobile. Ticketing is easy, there is no waiting at the airport or having to be transported from the airport to the city center – most of the high-speed trains travel from city center to city center – crossing from one European country to another with ease. With the kind of traffic jams one can experience in pretty-much any major city today, the train really can take the strain.

The world's first high-speed train was developed by the Japanese and was called the Shinkansen, which was presented in 1964. Even then it could reach 125 mph.

One of the first high speed trains was the French TGV – Train du Grand Vitesse – whose design many of the other HS trains take after.

France probably has the largest high-speed train network in Europe, which covers many of the major cities of France and connections through to several other European countries. They do have their problems though when crossing borders, as different power supplies can be encountered and often signalling systems can differ too. As more trains from more countries travel across borders, these problems will be remedied, and as the network spreads so will their compatability. With border controls now non-existant in many European countries, these trains can whisk their passengers from one major city to another in a matter of hours, in comfort and with the greatest convenience.

The first French line to open was between Paris and Lyon, back in 1981 which saw the introduction of the TGV (Train du Grande Vitesse). Faster trains were soon developed and the lines spread to Bordeaux, Marseilles and Lille. Today sees even greater speeds and shorter travel times as a new gen-

The TGV is very distinctive, especially with the SNCF – French Railway logo – plastered on its nose. This one was about to depart for Lyon.

eration of trains are introduced – the AGV (Automotrice a Grande Vitesse), which has an incredible running speed of 219 mph.

Germany was some way behind its main European counterparts when it came to developing a network of high-speed railway lines, but its InterCity Express (ICE) concept allowed it to quickly make up for lost time,. The country's first high-speed railway lines, between Hanover and Wurzburg and Mannheim and Stüttgart, were unveiled in 1992 when services were introduced between Hamburg, Hanover, Fulda, Frankfurt, Mannheim, Stüttgart and Munich. Regular timetables offer 155 mph speeds, but the trains can run up to 175 mph should they need to make up for lost time. Developed and built by Siemens of Germany, the ICE1 design has been subsequently updated, while the network of lines on the ICE network has also grown, with services into the former East Germany having started in 1997. Since then ICE2, ICE3 and ICE-T tilting trains have expanded the network to include destinations in Holland, Belgium, Switzerland and Austria.

The route between Köln, Bonn and Frankfurt received a two million Euro grant towards its construction costs in 1997, as part of an EC initiative to improve rail links between member countries. This latest line opened fully in December 2002 after months of pre-service testing and trial services. A fleet of ICE3 and multi-voltage Siemens/Adtranz ICE3M trains was purchased for this route. The Köln-Frankfurt line brought DB to the top of the high-speed league, with trains capable of running at 206 mph, reducing journey times from two hours, fifteen minutes, to just over one hour. ICE2 began service from September 1996, offering more flexibility with its “half-train” format, able to serve two destinations after running as a full train over high-speed lines. DB introduced its first ICE-T tilting trains in 1998. Developed with the involvement of Siemens Transportation Systems, the trains have a top speed of 145 mph, even over rough terrain. Diesel and electric versions of the tilting ICE have reduced journey

The AGV is an experimental successor to France's TGV high speed trains. The name stands for automotrice à grande vitesse – high-speed self-propelled carriage.

Double-deck trains have been introduced on the Paris Sud Est (PSE) route to meet rising passenger numbers, although even this is now proving insufficient.

Although the aluminium bodied ICE3 is single voltage, the ICE3M version can operate on any of the four main power supply systems on the European mainland.

times and drastically improved passenger comfort on several "classic" routes, including those between Stuttgart and Switzerland, Saarbrücken-Frankfurt-Leipzig-Dresden and Munich-Berlin via Leipzig. ICE3, developed by Siemens/Adtranz, will reach well beyond Germany's borders, with Netherlands Railways (NS) also purchasing four ICE3M versions to improve the Amsterdam to Germany services in preparation for the opening of the Köln-Frankfurt Neubaustrecke line in 2003. To introduce ICE comfort and speed to non-electrified routes, DB has acquired a small number of four-car tilting DMUs, known as ICE-TD. The trains are very similar in appearance to the electric ICE-T and are used on the Nürnberg-Dresden and Munich-Lindau-Zürich routes. Germany is also testing and developing a magnetic levitation train system called Transrapid – a 19.6 mile track is in operation at Emsland.

The Italian "Direttissima" was the earliest high-speed train developed in Europe, which ran on the

Aerodynamic improvements to ICE3 trainsets over their earlier counterparts include bogie skirts and fairings to screen brake discs and axleboxes.

The design of ICE3 has been influenced by developments in Japanese Shinkansen high-speed trains, with a bullet-shaped nose emphasising its credentials.

How far can high speed travel go? It seems limitless but there has to be a ceiling. As shapes become leaner and more snake-like, designers will face stiffer challenges.

Rome to Florence line back in 1978. Today, Italy makes great use of its Pendolino trains – first developed in the 1970s by Fiat Ferriviaria – which use tilting technology. Meanwhile a new Treno Alta velocita – high-speed train – is having a new network built around it. This new network is expected to reach 625 miles by the year 2008. The new ETR500 trains were developed to allow Italy's rail network to integrate with its other European partners, its new lines being relaunched as Eurostar Italia. The project will endeavour to upgrade the old Direttissima line, allowing a higher 185 mph speed to be undertaken. Archaeological problems were causing some concern on the 127 mile, Naples-Rome line, but by 1999 work was completed on the first 12 mile stretch. The alignment of the new Florence-Bologna line was agreed on in 1995, and work should be completed in 2007 – the majority of the journey will be in tunnels through the Apennine Mountains – with the final journey time being cut by half. One of the most congested journeys is between Bologna and Milan. This line will have a considerable amount of money dedicated to it to improve route capacity and reduce the journey time. The Turin-Milan line reconstruction hit problems due to the route chosen, but work continues to double the line's capacity – it should reach Malpensa Airport by 2006, ready for the Winter Olympics. The Milan-Venice route is now chosen but has not yet been ratified by the government. Looking to the future, in 2010 a new line is planned between Milan and Genoa, which will include a

After Britain abandoned the tilting Advanced Passenger Train, the technology was sold to Italy, who in 1987 introduced the Pendolini ETR 450 HST.

Italy's own high speed train with a large smile on it's front – the TGV is a non-tilting train but speeds are comparable to other high speed trainsets.

Italy has done well with its series ETR 500, bringing the speed up to 300kph. It is a conventional high speed train in the fashion of the TGV and ICE.

mile-long tunnel to connect the port of Genoa with the existing rail system.

The first ETR450 tilting trains entered service in May 1988; they have two power cars with four first class and five second class trailers, offering 386 seats. The later ETR460/480 trains were the first to offer restaurant facilities in a tilting train; each is able to seat 480 passengers and can reach speeds up to 155mph.

The ETR500 is a 13 vehicle unit, seating 590 passengers and was introduced in 1996. It is capable of 185mph. These trains offer at-seat meals, business and family coaches, full air-conditioning and a fully depressurised cabin. The ETR500 is a non-tilting variant of the original Pendolino, which is designed and built by Gruppo Ferroviario Breda at their factory in Pistoia. Although the ETR500 trains are fitted with automatic train control protection systems, the ETR460 and 480 are only fitted with the conventional absolute block signalling, with in-cab warning system. The Italian high-speed network is relatively self-contained but for the future, the Italian and French governments are keen to integrate with the Trans-European Network System (TENS), which will extend lines beyond borders of these countries.

A new Dutch HSL-Zuid line is being built to connect the Netherlands with Belgium and France. It will carry the now familiar TGV-derived Thalys trains, along with domestic high-speed trains. By 2007 the Netherlands should be connected to the other European high-speed train networks, allowing its own trains to benefit from the extra speed and accessibility to other cities around Europe – initially Amsterdam, Schiphol, Rotterdam, Antwerp, Brussels and Paris. The new HSL track is 78 miles

The Thalys trains can fulfil their potential on the new Dutch lines. The sleek Grande Vitesse Trains, already a familiar sight throughout mainland Europe.

The new Dutch line will be the first to incorporate what is expected to become the international-standard ERTMS signalling. Eurostar trains also travel along this line.

long of which 53 miles is newly laid high-speed track, which will allow the trains to reach their maximum speed of 185 mph. At the present time an estimated 14 million people per year are expected to use the service. HSA, the train operator, now expects some 16 to 17 million domestic passengers and about 7 million international passengers per year, to use the service by 2010.

The United Kingdom already runs the Eurostar high-speed trains, which travel between the UK to France and Belgium via the Channel Tunnel. These trains are multiple voltage – with pantograph and third-rail possibilities – and can cope with seven different signalling modes. These trains are articulated with bogies between the carriages. A typical operating train will have 18 carriages and fully loaded can carry 794 passengers. At present the high-speed line runs from the Channel Tunnel to London Waterloo but a new Channel Tunnel Rail Link is due to open in 2007 and will terminate at the refurbished London St Pancras Station.

British Rail attempted to introduce its Advance Passenger Train, with tilting technology, back in the 1970s and 1980s. Unfortunately some real problems were encountered and the project was terminated. The technology was taken up by others though and it was developed successfully, for example by the Italians for their Pendolino trains. These trains were also initially introduced on the West Coast line, but more recently Virgin Trains run them on their London-Birmingham, Manchester, Liverpool and Glasgow services.

Japan had already started its plans to build a high-speed train service between Tokyo and Shimonseki in 1940, but due to the war in the Pacific, things were brought abruptly to a halt. Construction of tunnels and land purchase had already begun in 1941 and the line was to be completed in 1954. At that time only steam locomotives were running and their

Home of the British Eurostar trains, Waterloo station in London. This is a restricted platform and can only be accessed with your passport and travel document.

One in and one out. Eurostar has been servicing the London to Paris route for several years now, which varies by going either via Calais or Lille.

top speed was around 60 mph. The new train, Dangan Ressha – Bullet Train – would reach 93 mph initially and 124 mph at a later date. It took time for the Japanese economy to recover after World War Two but it wasn't long before the main line between Tokyo and Osaka was at full capacity. In the mid 1950s, the President of Japanese National Railways (JNR) presented a proposal for a new high-speed rail system and after much discussion the government agreed to support the project. Construction of the new high-speed line, named Shinkansen (New Main Line), was started in 1959 and over 300 miles were completed by 1964. There was a good reason for finishing the line at this date the Tokyo Olympic Games were due to be opened then also. In fact the line opened on October 1 1964, just ten days prior to the opening ceremony for the

Looking a little like a duck in distress, this is the front of Eurostar and the drivers area. New lines will make the journey from Folkestone to London even quicker.

Eurostar now connects with the rest of Europe and a traveller from the UK can, for example, be in Avignon in just over 6 hours, with just one change.

The original Eurostar departure station in London is Waterloo. New lines are currently being made so that the train will soon terminate at London St. Pancras.

Olympics. By 1956 the Tokyo to Osaka line was electrified and by 1958 trains were running on the line. The new electric multiple unit (EMU) type 20 trains, reduced the journey by an hour and were comfortable and convenient, having been fitted with air-conditioning – an advanced feature for the period. As more trains came on stream, the service became more popular and the success of the EMU train became the basis of the Shinkansen. Following the removal of speed restrictions, speeds increased and journey times lowered. The new train had an aircraft style nose and travelled at over 125 mph, with a twelve car set later to be increased to sixteen. The Shinkansen train had a different gauge to the normal trains and the carriages were also larger. There were no signals or speed restrictions either, just a display in the driver's cab. The speed and efficiency of the train attracted both business and general use of the trains and passenger numbers increased rapidly. Further expansion of the line was carried out during the 1970s but not as much as had been expected, partly due to money and partly due to unforeseen lack of passenger numbers. Progress was made later in the 1970s and with that industry and tourism benefited and established itself along the routes. Shinkansen wasn't without problems though and there were complaints, and even a lawsuit, regarding noise through urban areas. This directly led to measures dealing with these problems but at the same time restricted the trains from going faster. By the 1970s, aeroplane travel was also taking a hold and more people were deciding to fly, especially as prices were now being reduced. By the late 1970s and early 1980s, Shinkansen found itself with huge debts. There was little investment and ticket prices seemed to be hiked up every year, which resulted in fewer people taking the train.

A grand array of the Shinkansen trains that serve the Japanese high speed traveller. These are split into districts and vary in both coach size and top speed.

These 16 car 300 series trains were introduced by JR Central and JR West, to raise the speed of the Tokaido and Sanyo services to 170 mph.

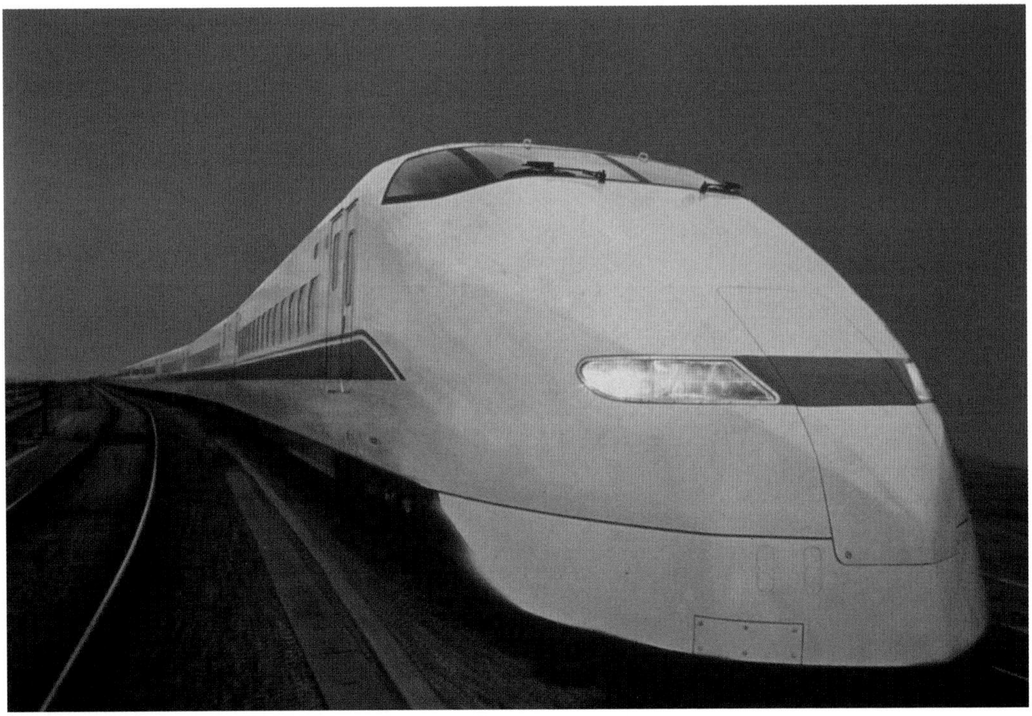

The 500 Series Shinkansen are the fastest, most powerful and most expensive trains yet to run on Japan's Shinkansen high-speed rail network

The 300 Series Shinkansen trains are designed with a top speed of 200 mph although they currently operate at a maximum of 185 mph in service.

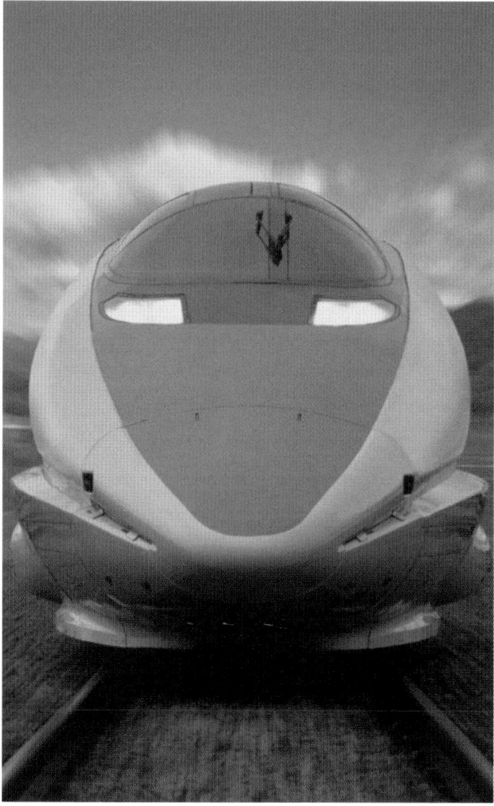

The top speed of the 700 series is 177 mph, but as higher speeds are only permitted on a few stretches of line, the journey is only a little longer than the 500 series.

The 700 Series Shinkansen trainsets for Japan's Shinkansen dedicated high-speed rail lines were built between 1997 and 2004, entering service in 1999.

Even the train's speed was barely faster than when it started back in the 1960s.

Lines between Omiya-Morioka and Omiya-Niigata were opened in 1982, which saw the trains having to negotiate the winter snows. Thanks to the new type 200 train, fitted with specialist equipment to cope with the exceptionally bad weather, the lines prospered and reliability was improved. A new 100 type train was introduced in 1986, to the Tokaido and Sanyo Shinkansen, which had two double-decked carriages in a sixteen car set. Times between Tokyo and Shin Osaka were reduced and the train had a top speed of 137 mph. Then in 1997 the faster 500 type train was launched which was capable of 185 mph. Along with the French TGV this was the fastest in the world – the trip between Hiroshima and Kokura marked the fastest average speed of any train in the world at 162,7 mph. In 1999 the 700 type train was unveiled, which wasn't faster than the 500 but was a more advanced design, giving more comfort. It had a better shape, which gave more interior room and was designed around high speed, but at the same

The 283 Series was introduced on the Kinokuni line in July 1996 as the "Super Kuroshiro" - Ocean Arrow - to give reduced travel times and improved service.

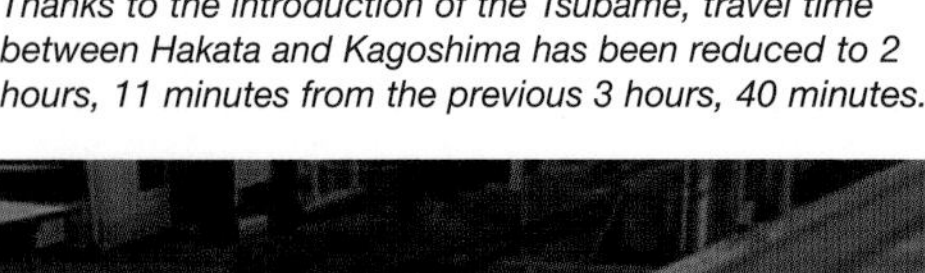

Thanks to the introduction of the Tsubame, travel time between Hakata and Kagoshima has been reduced to 2 hours, 11 minutes from the previous 3 hours, 40 minutes.

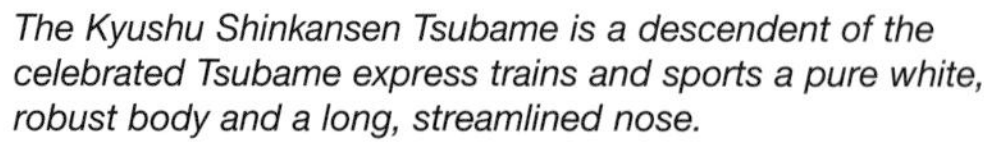

The Kyushu Shinkansen Tsubame is a descendent of the celebrated Tsubame express trains and sports a pure white, robust body and a long, streamlined nose.

Passenger cabins of the Tsubame are awash in white and marked by their brightness.They feature beautifully arranged wooden seating that offers a warm welcome.

Although these Shainkansen trains have all the latest electronic aids, the driver has to be totally focused on his work. An accident in one of these is unimaginable!

The E4 series 'Max' 8-ca,r bi-level shinkansen trains are broadly based on the earlier E1 series design, and are fitted with automatic retractable couplers at both ends.

time keeping cost and efficiency in mind. With this and a freeze on fares, passengers started to return to the Shinkansen and passenger numbers started to rise again. Although there was a slow-down when airlines were deregulated, a more comfortable version of the 700, with fewer carriages, was introduced in 2000. This also had better seating arrangement and special business seats, which allowed passengers to use laptop computers.

A mini Shinkansen was developed in 1992, which served the lines where the larger train was not viable. The type 400 was adaptable to the standard rail system and transported people between the less populated areas, therefore keeping costs down. As passengers started taking the train again, congested lines started using the type E1, all double-deck, twelve car train set, and from 1997 the type E4, all double-deck, eight car train set was introduced. By putting two together and having a sixteen car set, the E4 has a 1634 seating capability – the largest in the world.

The Shinkansen is due to get faster with the introduction of new trains such as the 700X, due to be in service in 2007. The struggle is always with the airlines but the train is starting to make its mark again. A new free-gauge train is in development, which can change gauge sizes, which will allow it to go from the high-speed rails to the conventional rails. Probably the most exciting development is the linear motor car, which will reach speeds of 310 mph, but due to cost and no great increase in passenger traffic on the busiest lines, there is no hurry to implement this system.

Spain has its high-speed rail system too. The Alta Velocidad Española (AVE) is based on the

Although not strictly a high speed train, the Super Raicho Thunderbird is a limited express locomotive of the 681type and is run by JR West.

The former Japanese National Railways was convinced that superconducting magnet technology held great potential for very fast rail travel, and began maglev R&D in 1970.

Experiments began in earnest on the Miyazaki Test Track in southern Japan. MLU002 and MLU002N were used for a wide range of experiments on the Test Track.

Shinkansen and TGV trains and powered by electricity. The inauguration was on April 20, 1992 and the first service was run between Madrid and Seville, corresponding nicely with the Universal Exhibition of Seville. New lines are being worked on, or are planned, and by 2010, Spain should have about 4,350 miles of high-speed track. This will not only link the main Spanish cities but will also connect to France, where it will join with the rest of the European network. It is foreseen that by the end of this ambitious plan in 2015 – which includes a tunnel some 17 miles long through the Guadarrama mountains – the whole Iberian peninsula, including Portugal, will be interconnected. Three companies are involved in the supply and build of these trains – Talgo, Alstom and Siemens AG.

China, a country whose economy is growing with alarming speed, has opted for a Maglev system. The

The Spanish AVE - Alta Velocidad Española – Spanish high speed train, is basically a converted TGV Atlantique built with a few Spanish components.

The AVE operates on the Madrid-Cordoba-Seville route and can whisk you to and from Madrid and Seville in just 2.5 hours - one of Europe's finest rail services.

Launched in 1992 during the World Expo in Seville, the AVE has been providing excellent service ever since. Its punctuality has been one of its successes.

These Chinese high-speed trains, named CRH3, will travel at a speed of 185 mph, have 600 seats and extend 200 meters in length. They will operate on the Beijing-Tianjin route starting in 2008.

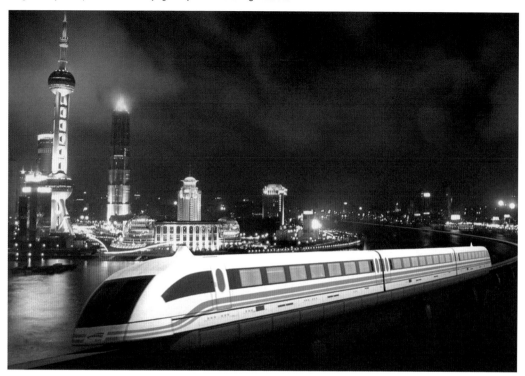

Siemens of Germany will work with its Chinese partner company, Tangshan Locomotive & Rolling Stock Works, for future construction of 60 high-speed trains for China.

Shanghai Maglev Train is capable of a speed in the region of 270 mph, although it can do 310 mph. This connects Shanghai to Pu Dong International Airport, and has done so since March 2004. Although this sytem is very high speed it is also costly, and to plan a future system for a country the size of China would be an enormous undertaking. This Maglev system was designed in conjunction with German companies and a second connection between Shanghai and Hangzhou is already being discussed – if constructed it would be the first inter-city Maglev rail line in commercial use in the world. China is also building a conventional high-speed line which is based on the German InterCity Express trains, which will run between Beijing and Tianjin and which is due to be operational in 2007.

The Korean KTX high-speed rail became operational in April 2004. It takes its technological background from the French TGV system and has a top speed of 185 mph. From December of 2005 the Korean government has made a "negotiation priority" for a new South Korean, high-speed technology named G-7. This will run faster than the current TGV system they have, reaching a speed of 216 mph. This train is a product of some ten years of research and development between the Korean Rotem and the National Rail Technology Institute. If the G-7 system goes ahead, Korea will join the likes of Japan, France and Germany as the fourth country to develop and use its own high-speed train system. Switzerland has had a train with tilting technology since May 2000, when the InterCity Tilting Train (ICN) came into being. It first ran from Geneva through Biel/Bienne, Grenchen South, Zurich, Winterthur through to St. Gallen. The ICN is now used on several routes and speeds of 124 mph can be reached. As Switzerland has tracks that are full of curves, it is the fastest Swiss train on Swiss tracks.

Turkey has recently started building high-speed rail lines. The first line, between Istanbul and Ankara is under construction and is due to open in 2007. The commercial high-speed trains are expected to reach a top speed of 155 mph, reducing the travelling time

Korea Train Express (KTX) is South Korea's high speed train system. The train's technology is largely based on the French TGV system, and has a top speed of 185 mph plus.

After twelve years of construction, the first sections of the Korean system connecting the Gyeongbu Line, and the Honam Line, opened on March 31, 2004.

Using high-speed track for only a part of the distance (Seoul-Daegu), the new line cuts travel time between Seoul and Busan from 260 minutes to 160 minutes.

of six or seven hours to three hours ten minutes. Several other lines between major cities are also being planned.

Taiwan has a high-speed rail system – Taiwan High Speed Rail – under construction which is due for completion in October 2006. It uses the Shinkan system technology as a base and the 700T series Shinkansen trains have been chosen to run on the system. When up and running, the journey between Taipei and Kaohsiung will take about 90 minutes – currently this takes four to six hours!

A track between Saint Petersburg and Moscow, Russia, is being updated to allow the German ICE type trains to run at 155 mph on it by 2008.

Many other countries around the world are also either looking at or have decided on new high-speed rail systems.

The track between Saint Petersburg and Moscow in Russia, is being updated to allow German ICE trains, bought by Russia, to reach 250 kph by 2008.

Glossary

Banking locomotives – This describes a locomotive temporarily attached to the rear of a train to augment the power of the train's locomotive when travelling over steeply graded lines.

BB – The shortened form of Bo-Bo. This means that the diesel or electric locomotive has two powered axles and that all axles on a bogie or wheel frame unit are individually powered.

Bogies – An engine using non-powered wheels as a part of the locomotive's wheel arrangement. In America, this would be a truck.

CC – The shortened form of Co-Co. This means that the diesel or electric locomotive has three powered axles and that all axles are powered.

Compound locomotive – A locomotive that uses steam in high pressure then in low pressure cylinders.

Garratt locomotives – These are articulated steam locomotives with the boiler mounted on a frame under which two units with driving wheels are pivoted.

Livery – The color scheme in which the locomotive is painted.

Push-Pull – This refers to the practice of having a locomotive at one end of the train that pulls the train on, say, the outward journey and pushes the train back on the return journey using specially fitted equipment. This avoids the locomotive having to run round its train before embarking on its return journey.

Rack Railway – A system that provides a toothed center track that engages with a toothed cog wheel or wheels on the locomotive to improve adhesion on very steep gradients.

Shunting Locomotive – This would be a switching locomotive in the USA.

TALGO Trains – These trains were developed in Spain and are articulated passenger coaches that automatically adjust to changes between standard and broad gauge.

Tank Locomotive – This describes a non-tender locomotive that carries its water in tanks on the side of the locomotive or in tanks that straddle the boiler.

Tilting Trains – These are trains that have the capacity to tilt as they go round curves to maintain a higher speed than would otherwise apply.

Wheel Arrangements - The description of steam locomotive wheel arrangements in this book follows the American and British practice in which each wheel on an axle is counted. A steam locomotive with four leading non-driving bogie wheels, six driving wheels and two rear non-powered bogie wheels would be a 4-6-2 under this system. The continental system counts the number of powered and non-powered axles. A 4-6-2 would be a 2-3-1 under that system. A refinement of that system allocates a letter for the driving wheels under which one set of driving wheels is letter A, two sets is B and so on. Under this system, the 4-6-2 would be a 2-C-1. This notation is also another means of describing the wheel arrangement of diesel locomotives.

Index

A

B

C

61264

D

FRY'S
BREAKFAST
COCOA
MAKERS TO
H.M. THE KING. H.M. THE QUEEN
DIEU ET MON DROIT
BY APPOINTMENT
H.M. QUEEN ALEXANDRA.
FRY'S
PURE
BREAKFAST
COCOA
J.S.FRY&SONS.LD.
BRISTOL & LONDON
4½D. PER ¼ lb TIN 4½D.

E

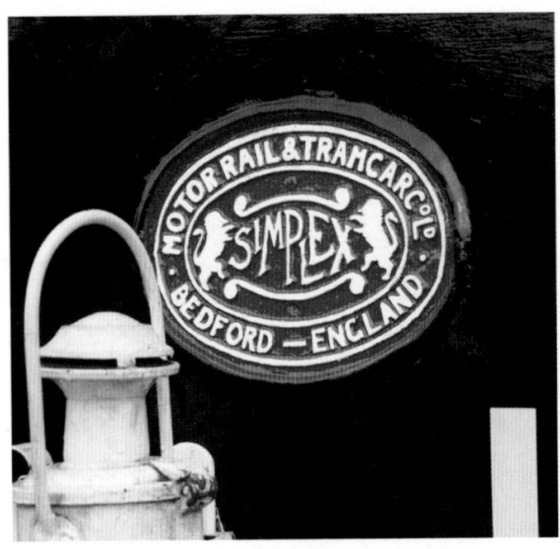
MOTOR RAIL & TRAMCAR Co LTD
SIMPLEX
BEDFORD — ENGLAND

F

1re Classe
151
151
VITESSE
NORD
TRAINS de

G

H

I

K

L

M

N

O

P

Q

R

S

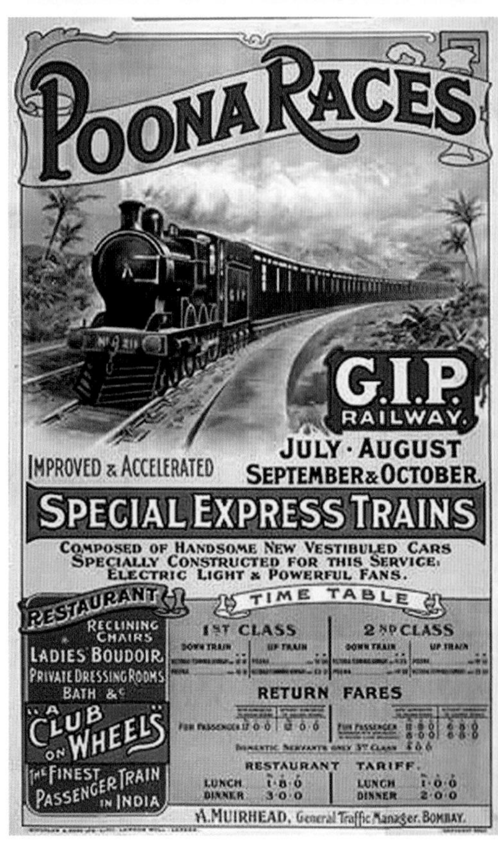
POONA RACES
G.I.P. RAILWAY.
IMPROVED & ACCELERATED
JULY · AUGUST
SEPTEMBER & OCTOBER.
SPECIAL EXPRESS TRAINS
COMPOSED OF HANDSOME NEW VESTIBULED CARS SPECIALLY CONSTRUCTED FOR THIS SERVICE. ELECTRIC LIGHT & POWERFUL FANS.
RESTAURANT
RECLINING CHAIRS
LADIES BOUDOIR
PRIVATE DRESSING ROOMS
BATH &c
"A CLUB ON WHEELS"
THE FINEST PASSENGER TRAIN IN INDIA
TIME TABLE
1ST CLASS
2ND CLASS
RETURN FARES
RESTAURANT TARIFF.
LUNCH 1·8·0
DINNER 3·0·0
LUNCH 1·0·0
DINNER 2·0·0
A. MUIRHEAD, General Traffic Manager, BOMBAY.

T

U

V

W

Y

Z

The authors would like to thank the following people and organizations for their enthusiastic support and help in supplying materials for this book:

Museum of Science and Industry, Manchester, England.
Museo Ferroviario, Bussoleno, Italy.
Musee Francais du Chemin de fer, Mulhouse, France.
Museo Ferroviario di Pietrarsa, Italy.
Italian Railways (FS) - TrenItalia.
Belgian Railways NMBS - P 152.
Swiss rail SBB - P185.
Andrew Morland Photographic Library, Butleigh, Glastonbury, England.
Courtesy of Amtrak - Page 37 top left; 53 top left; 54 bottom right; 55 bottom.
Michael McFadden via Amtrak - Page 54 top right.
Scott A Hartley via Amtrak - Page 55 top right.
Copyright Allen Zagel collection - Page 54 bottom left.
Courtesy of the Baltimore & Ohio Railroad Museum, Baltimore, Maryland, USA - Page 38 bottom; 39 bottom.
US Department of the Interior, National Park Services, Golden Spike National Historic Site - Page 42 top right; bottom; 43.
Copyright 2005 Mark Llanuza - Page 48; 49; 50 top.
US Library of Congress, Washington DC, USA.
Denver Public Library, Denver, Colorado, USA.
US National Archives, College Park, Washington DC, USA.
Dutch Railways (NS) - Page 56 top left; bottom left.
Deutsche Bahn AG - Page 74.
Siemens Transportation, Germany.
Rail Photo Library (railphotolibrary.com).
Alstom UK.
Department of Transportation, Federal Highway Administration (FHWA), USA.
Japan Rail (JR).
Austrian Railways (OBB)
ViaRail Canada.
Dmitriy Zinoviev (parovoz.com) - Special thanks for access to an incredible source of Railway pictures.
Russian Railways.
Mirco De Cet Archive, Edgmond, Newport, Shropshire, England.
Alan Kent Photographic Collection, Medomsley, Co. Durham, England.

Both Authors would also like to thank family and friends for their support and patience.